ALSO BY LEW FREEDMAN
AND FROM MCFARLAND

---

*DiMaggio's Yankees: A History
of the 1936–1944 Dynasty* (2011)

*The Day All the Stars Came Out: Major League
Baseball's First All-Star Game, 1933* (2010)

*Early Wynn, the Go-Go White Sox
and the 1959 World Series* (2009)

*Hard-Luck Harvey Haddix and the
Greatest Game Ever Lost* (2009)

Joe Louis

The Life of a Heavyweight

LEW FREEDMAN

McFarland & Company, Inc., Publishers
Jefferson, North Carolina, and London

ISBN 978-0-7864-5907-0
softcover : acid free paper ∞

LIBRARY OF CONGRESS CATALOGUING DATA ARE AVAILABLE

BRITISH LIBRARY CATALOGUING DATA ARE AVAILABLE

On the cover: Joe Louis (courtesy of the Burton
Historical Collection, Detroit Public Library)

Manufactured in the United States of America

*McFarland & Company, Inc., Publishers
Box 611, Jefferson, North Carolina 28640
www.mcfarlandpub.com*

Table of Contents

Introduction 1

1. The Brain Trust 5
2. Alabama 13
3. Detroit 22
4. Joe Who? 29
5. Laying Out the Big Plan 36
6. Jack Johnson 42
7. Going Pro 50
8. The Brown Bomber 57
9. The Brown Bomber Versus the Italian Man Mountain 67
10. Showdown with "Killer" Baer 78
11. An Eye for the Ladies 86
12. Working His Way to the Top 96
13. Max Schmeling 103
14. Schmeling, Hitler and the Nazis 111
15. Louis-Schmeling I 117
16. Joe Bounces Back 127
17. And the New Heavyweight Champion of the World 135
18. Being the Champ 143
19. Louis-Schmeling II 150
20. Bigger Than Ever 160

21. Two-Ton Tony and Tons of Others 168
22. The Tough Guy from Pittsburgh 178
23. You're in the Army Now 187
24. A Young Man Named Robinson 197
25. After the War 203
26. End Days of a Brilliant Career 211
27. Real Life Tougher Than Boxing 219

Chapter Notes 231
Bibliography 237
Index 239

Introduction

The man sitting in the wheelchair wearing a cowboy hat in the makeshift Caesars Palace gym had more eyes on him than the champion skipping rope as part of his workout. There were mostly strangers in the airy room because he had out-lived many of his contemporaries and these were younger fight fans and younger fight writers.

But he was in his element in the midst of the hubbub of fight preparations, the most honored spectator soaking up the air conditioning as the intense sun burnt a hole in the sidewalk outdoors on an early autumn day in Las Vegas.

Joe Louis' health was failing in late 1980. But being part of the boxing world he once ruled, even if only briefly, brought a smile to his face. Decades earlier the man who many believe is the greatest heavyweight champion of all, and perhaps pugilism's greatest fighter at any weight, attracted thousands of fans to his own workout sessions just like this.

They came from near and far to watch Joe Louis spar, to hit the heavy bag with his rock-hard fists, to snap the speed bag with his agile punches. In the late 1930s and in the 1940s, Louis packed them in to the big arenas for his bouts, commanding the highest prices at the gate. But those who were merely curious, who had only small change in their pockets, came up with two bits or a dollar to catch a glimpse of his greatness up close in training camp instead of Madison Square Garden or Yankee Stadium. The tickets were cheaper and up close, instead of from a balcony or bleacher view, and the champ looked bigger than life.

Louis wasn't signing autographs in Las Vegas at this late stage of his life, but his presence energized the hall, provoked whispers. We were in the presence of a legend and we all knew it. Some of us were lucky enough to exchange a word or two with him as he watched a younger generation of fighters do their thing. That was the only time I met Joe Louis, only to say hello, a soft "Hi Joe." He nodded back.

1

At the time I was the boxing beat writer for the *Philadelphia Inquirer*, on assignment in Las Vegas regularly to cover Larry Holmes, the reigning heavyweight champ, or Sugar Ray Leonard, the most charismatic fighter in the world at the time, or Marvelous Marvin Hagler, who was a more marvelous boxer than anyone else when he was at his best.

Sometimes men like Louis from bygone eras of the sport materialized in Las Vegas training camps when the modern warriors were fine-tuning their muscle for their title bouts. Sugar Ray Robinson, who had been friends with Louis since he was a teenager, showed up to add his aura to the scene. They were living embodiments of history, whose presence and graciousness, whose skills and determination enobled a hard game.

All around us those who hung back took notice. "There's Joe Louis," was the undercurrent of their talk. It was the old-age Joe Louis with us that day, not the vintage, sculpted, toughest-man-in-the-world Joe Louis of his prime. Still, it was noteworthy to be in the presence of such fame, greatness, a man whose accomplishments and distinguished life made America proud.

Louis' achievements in sport shone so brightly that for a time he was almost certainly the most famous person in the United States other than the president. For a time (along with the arrival of Olympic star Jesse Owens), Louis was surely the most famous black American in history.

The professional boxing career of Joe Louis spanned from 1934 to his retirement in 1951. He was the heavyweight champion for an astounding 12 years, from 1937 to 1949, and he made a record 25 title defenses. Overall, his record was 69–3 in 72 bouts. He stood 6-foot-2 and mostly fought at around 200 pounds.

Joe Louis' life was a Hollywood movie in the flesh. It was so rich with unlikely developments, so saturated with mighty accomplishments, and so remarkable in so many ways. He was a poverty-stricken African American youth in the South, yet was able to rise to such a pinnacle of respect with his unerring actions that he was impossible not to admire. In instances when the country needed him most, counted on him as a singular representative, Louis was grandly capable of seizing the stage, grasping the occasion, and wringing from it the maximum value and joy for the most number of Americans.

America's greatest sin against its own people was slavery. The Civil War that was supposed to settle the matter through bloodshed cured one aspect of the disease, but left enough minds poisoned that discrimination and hatred remained.

The Alabama where Louis took his first breaths and where he lived into his early teens was one of those places in the United States that had yet to receive the message that all men were created equal. A young black man growing up in the Deep South could expect a life limited by caps on his education and a belief that he would be nothing more than a laborer who picked cotton. To cross the white man still meant a black man might be lynched, as the local form of rough justice still prevailed with little threat of the legal system riding herd on the perpetrators.

Louis' family fled north as part of the Great Migration. Southern blacks relocated to the large industrial cities of Detroit, Chicago and elsewhere, re-establishing their lives. Louis' family chose Detroit, where jobs working for Henry Ford and his factories that turned out fresh automobiles were available.

It was in Detroit where Louis metamorphosed into a fighter. He was fortunate to have good handlers and good teachers, men who recognized his potential and looked out for his best interests. Despite the tenor of the times and the lingering bitterness in the boxing world against showman Jack Johnson, the only black heavyweight champion into the 1930s, they were able to guide him to the heavyweight title.

Those who only know the sport from its most recent decades cannot fathom the depth of discrimination faced by any black heavyweight contender in the 1920s and 1930s. There was a sport-wide conspiracy backed by public belief that no black man should be allowed the privilege of fighting for the most prestigious individual title in sport. Johnson's bravado, insouciance, and flamboyant style made him a hated man. Even more than attitude, whites despised his proclivity for dating and marrying white women. That was the great taboo and Johnson irritated and enraged the prejudiced white masses with his brazen actions.

The Johnson legacy was that even the finest African American big men of the following generation were never permitted to fight for the heavyweight crown. When Louis finally got his chance he was the first black to be offered a shot at the title in 29 years.

For most white fight fans, Louis was the anti–Johnson. He was friendly, polite, married to an attractive black woman, and unlike Johnson, never taunted his vanquished white opponents. Joe Louis changed minds with his demeanor. He gained fans with his boxing skills. And by the time world circumstances powered by forces much larger than any individual overran the societal landscape, he was an ingrained, popular figure in American society.

When he was most needed to uphold America's honor he did so in the ring, in his sport, and in uniform representing his country. Joe Louis was victorious, generous, and above all a man who was always seemingly in the right and one whose public actions always seemed perfect for the moment.

Louis was the idol of millions, but still very much a man, with foibles and flaws, who suffered setbacks and tragedies. For a time he was invincible in the ring, but he was ever-so-human outside of it. Anyone who expects perfection is foolish, but Joe Louis gave more to his country than many had the right to expect. He was not always rewarded for it, either, but never wavered in his convictions.

If he had only been great in his sport, that would have been enough. If he had been great in his sport and uplifted the hopes and dreams of everyday blacks in America that would have been sufficient. But Joe Louis the man, the fighter, the symbol, went way beyond that.

He was a man for his times and he shaped his times. In so doing Joe Louis led an extraordinary life that touched millions of people in so many ways. He should long be remembered beyond the walls of boxing halls of fame as a great American.

My contact with Louis was oh-so-fleeting, but the picture of him that day remains clear in my mind. He died not long after, on April 12, 1981. Although being in the same place at the same time as he appeared was coincidental, it is a memory to be cherished.

1

The Brain Trust

The trio of men that adopted Joe Louis the fighter treated him like a son as they nurtured him from neophyte in the ring into the world's heavyweight champion. They were hard men, trainer Jack Blackburn, and co-managers John Roxborough and Julian Black, but they were fair to him. By genteel societal standards they were pretty much considered to be rogues, but they were black men like Louis, understood that he was a young man of special promise, and whatever they hoped to gain from association with him — and they did gain wealth and fame in boxing circles — they were honest in their dealings in every matter that pertained to Louis' career.

All three of them, at one time or another, did jail time or were suspected of illegal activities. In their daily lives, away from Louis, they communicated to those they did business with in much harsher street talk than how they spoke to him. They trafficked in a netherworld of sorts, not quite the underworld, but not the aboveboard world of day-to-day store transactions, either.

Blackburn had been a great fighter, but relied heavily on the bottle. He had killed a man and done time for it. Roxborough was the numbers king of Detroit. Black operated in the same realm in Chicago and ran a speakeasy during Prohibition.

They were not on the list of those that matrons invited to tea, but they were guardians of a young man with potential, custodians of a great and dominating talent that they were determined to protect at any cost. Whatever else they were, however else they would be judged, by law enforcement officials sniffing around their activities, by their maker when they passed, what they did for Joe Louis was unimpeachable.

Combined, they possessed the wisdom, the savvy, the determination, the political know-how, and the special talents needed to guide Louis from a raw but skilled athlete into a polished champion while bucking the racism of the 1930s. Louis took care of business in the ring and listened to their sound advice out of the ring, and they maneuvered him past the many great obstacles that could have derailed him as he transformed from Joe Louis Barrow, the son of an Alabama sharecropper, into "The Brown Bomber," the feared and loved heavyweight champion of the world.

At the same time they made him king of the world of fisticuffs, they opened the world to him. Roxborough, Black, and Blackburn helped Louis bridge the distance between amateur fighter and professional, between professional and champion. They also gave him words — rules — to live by and assisted him in the transition from a somewhat cloistered 19-year-old with limited education to a mature man capable of contending with the world around him and all of its pressures.

Louis was already a fighter, though an amateur, when he was first spotted by Roxborough, who made the initial contact about representation. His course seemed to be set, though without the aid of his team it is an open question just how Louis' life would have played out. It has always been critical in the fight game for a boxer to have handlers he could trust. Without such aid a fighter can be lost in the shuffle of contenders, be taken advantage of by promoters, and see his chances to achieve his potential spoiled.

In the 1930s, not even a superb management team guaranteed success to an up-and-coming black fighter, especially a heavyweight. The myth of the heavyweight championship is that the holder of the title is the toughest man in the world. Boxing interest ranked higher in the hierarchy of American sport at the time, too, behind baseball, for sure, but next to horse racing and college football in the next tier of popularity. As always, being the heavyweight champ meant you were the face of the sport.

Those who ran boxing in the smoke-filled rooms where deals were hammered out and who made the matches that drew the biggest crowds believed that the public would not stand for a black heavyweight champion because the reign of Jack Johnson turned off so many in white America. No matter how formidable or skilled, a top African American fighter could be avoided by the match-makers and the best boxers. It was not easy for any black fighter to get ahead in the rankings, especially when there was a general understanding that no black man would be permitted to challenge for the heavyweight crown.

Such blanket prejudice would be denounced as unconscionable in 21st century America, but there was no governing authority, no groundswell of public demand, no one strong enough to break down the wall keeping black fighters on the outside looking in. That was the way it was in the land of the free and the home of the brave at that time.

These barriers loomed in front of any black heavyweight with aspirations and talent. As a young amateur Louis was ignorant of the shenanigans that

At various points in his life, Joe Louis, who adopted flashy dress once he could afford it from his boxing paydays, favored a mix of wide-brim hats (courtesy Charles H. Wright Museum of African-American History).

went on behind the scenes in the professional ranks, the forces that might be arrayed against him if he devoted his career to the sport.

It was Roxborough, a somewhat round-faced man of medium height who favored a thin black mustache and who was mostly bald, who first recognized Louis' potential. Louis had found his own way to the gym through friends to start boxing. He found out quickly he was pretty good at it and liked it. His earliest trainers turned him into a smooth enough amateur, but there is a Grand Canyon–sized gulf between a fighter doing well in amateur boxing and doing well as a professional. Amateurs fight just three rounds at a time and the scoring system differs, with an emphasis on boxing rather than power. Professionals fight longer. At the time the championship distance was 15 rounds. Harder punching was rewarded more in professional scoring, too.

Roxborough, like so many Detroit African Americans, was from the Deep South. He was born in New Orleans in 1892 and his family background included Spanish, Creole, and Jamaican heritage. He spoke more French and Spanish than English when he was a youngster. Detroit remedied that. The men in Roxborough's family were intelligent and ambitious. His father was an attorney. So was his brother Charles, who became the first black representative elected to the Michigan state legislature.

John Roxborough intended to follow the same path. He even spent a year in law school. However, too much of what he witnessed in daily life irritated him and demoralized him. He envisioned completing law school and not being able to get a job. African Americans with college degrees were being offered janitorial jobs or the like and he didn't want to waste his time on formal education if it was not going to pay off.

"To hell with education," Roxborough decided. "What good would it do me? I made up my mind that when I got a chance to make money, no matter how, I'd take it. I would avoid embarrassing situations. I also promised myself I'd help myself first and then I'd help my black brothers."[1]

For starters, Roxborough became a bail bondsman. Then he worked his way into the numbers racket, becoming the main man in Detroit black neighborhoods for those who wished to gamble for as little as a penny a try in attempts to win a bigger payoff by guessing the right numbers selected in this game of chance.

This was how Roxborough made his living. But he wasn't selfish or greedy. He lived up to his pledge of trying to help his black brothers. He did so in many ways, most of them financial. He made donations to organizations such as the Urban League and the Young Negroes Progressive Association. Those were his formal contributions. More informally, on a one-to-one basis, Roxborough was viewed as a kind of Santa Claus.

True to his pledge, Roxborough passed out money to black individuals in need, frequently giving aid to those who needed a few bucks to be able to make the rent, or even to eat. It was later estimated that over the years Roxborough dispensed money to put 30 or more young black people through college. Apparently, he did not retain his once-held view that going to college for African Americans was a complete waste of time, even if he declared that path not the right one for him.

So if some were high and mighty in their outlook of Roxborough being a shady character working the edge of the law, many others supported him because of his generosity. When Roxborough first noticed Joe Louis the amateur boxer and offered to get involved in the fighter's life, it may not have been completely altruistic (certainly there was a belief that money could be made). But it was far from a sure thing and Roxborough might well have viewed this effort as just one of the many ways he tried to open doors for young blacks. This was a matter of furthering Louis' education, too, just not in a classroom.

A more parallel consistency can be seen in Roxborough's support of local African American sports teams. One account has Thurston McKinney, the friend of Louis who first steered him to boxing at the Brewster Recreation Center, approaching Roxborough for money. "How come you're always laying out money for basketball and softball teams and you never help us boxers?" McKinney asked. "We need help, too."[2] Right then and there Roxborough reached into his pocket, peeled off some bills, and handed the cash over to McKinney.

McKinney was Louis' connection to boxing and probably his connection to Roxborough, though historical tellings differ. Some say that McKinney told Roxborough about Louis, seeking some money just for his pal with the tale, "He could sure use some help. He doesn't even own a pair of trunks. But he can punch."[3] Interest piqued, Roxborough said that he wanted to watch Louis fight. Other accounts have Roxborough discovering Louis' prowess on his own on a visit to the rec center.

If so, that was just a scouting mission, assessing if Louis was the genuine goods. Roxborough soon took in a Louis amateur fight against a more experienced fighter named Stanley Evans. He could tell that Louis possessed talent, but especially since the teenager lost the bout he could also see that he needed tutoring. After the fight, Detroit trainer George Slayton introduced Roxborough to Louis. He had just lost the fight, so Louis was feeling low and was surprised that anyone wanted to talk to him or that anyone seemed to believe in him. That is one aspect of boxing that many underestimate. To succeed at the sport a fighter must think of himself as practically invulnerable when he steps between the ropes. So if he loses he is not only vanquished physically, but also psychologically. In essence it has been proven that he is not as tough as he thought.

Roxborough made a good impression on the sweaty and downcast Louis. "This man had real class," Louis wrote years later in his autobiography. "He was a very light-skinned black man about six feet tall and he weighed about 190 pounds. He didn't seem flashy, but stylish and rich looking. He had a gray silk suit, the kind you don't buy off the rack. It made me look twice. His attitude was gentle, like a gentleman should be. Mr. Roxborough told me he liked the way I fought and he was interested in me. I couldn't understand why — hell, I'd just lost the fight. He told me to drop by his real estate office within the next couple of days."[4]

Soon Roxborough was financing Louis' living needs. He brought him into stores and told him to pick out anything he wanted, from boxing supplies to clothing. He invited Louis to his home for dinners and for Louis this was a revelation. For a son of poverty in a rural southern environment and of inner-city, big-city living where cash was dear, just seeing a well-to-do black family living in a plush house and eating regularly scheduled multiple-course meals provided fresh role models. Louis hadn't even thought about whether such black families existed. This kind of living was for white people.

While Roxborough was the point man in the Joe Louis team, with the official title of manager, he did not have key connections in the boxing world. A business partner from various ventures, and someone who had once bailed him out with a loan, Julian Black had promoted fights in Chicago. Roxborough invited Black into the partnership as a co-manager. Black had a pot belly, walked with a limp, had darker skin and more hair than Roxborough. He greased it back and parted it on the left side. Like Roxborough he also liked to invest in good suits. It was acknowledged that despite his prosperous veneer Black was all tough guy underneath and not someone to cross or have mad at you for cause.

Throughout their association Black was the lower-key participant, though always present for fights and always involved in major decisions. The first major decision was agreeing on the right man to train Louis. Roxborough and Black were convinced that Louis' punching power and innate skill could carry him to the heavyweight championship. That was the goal from the beginning. At the time Louis had not quite reached his full height, but was about an inch shorter than 6-foot-2, and he had not filled out through the shoulders and chest completely, so he weighed around 175 pounds, the light-heavyweight limit.

Roxborough thought that Louis should spend another year fighting amateur competition, but Louis had other ideas. His family was poor, he made little money, and he wanted to make a move right away. When he asked Roxborough if he could turn pro, his reasoning was simple and straightforward. "Mr. Roxborough," Louis said, "I want the money."[5]

Louis seemed malleable enough to accept criticism and instruction without his ego getting in the way. Roxborough and Black wanted to be careful in their selection of teacher, however. As it was, they knew a minefield of scheduling and bouts lay ahead, and it was going to be their considerable challenge to negotiate it, so they wanted a trainer they could place absolute trust in.

They did their homework and agreed on the best man for the job. The only problem was they weren't sure if the best man had the slightest interest in working with them, and if all of their personalities would mesh. This was a reasonable question because although he was a renowned trainer, Jack Blackburn toted more baggage with him than a 747 flight across the United States. He could be ornery and sarcastic and while it is not clear if Roxborough and Black knew from the beginning, Blackburn also was an alcoholic. Blackburn had once been an exceptional fighter, falling shy of a world championship, it was assumed because of the color of his skin and never getting the chance he deserved. He had also done time in prison for murder. He was never going to be nominated for father of the year, but he might well be trainer of the year. Roxborough and Black laid the foundation of a support system for Louis. It was up to Blackburn to see that he absorbed every nuance of what it took to become a professional winner inside the ring.

Born Charles Henry Blackburn on New Year's Day 1883 in Versailles, Kentucky, the trainer had been an accomplished fighter with a record of 99-26-19. His documented fights ranged from his debut in 1901 to 1923, though there are indications he fought many more times, probably in exhibitions. Although Blackburn was mostly a lightweight, he made frequent forays into classes well beyond the 135-pound level. Over time Blackburn lost his birth name and was always referred to as Jack.

Admired for his boxing skill, especially his left jab, Blackburn also mixed in a powerful left hook. Among the fighters he battled were Joe Gans, Harry Greb, Sam Langford, "Gunboat Smith" and "Philadelphia" Jack O'Brien. Those were the most prominent names on Blackburn's roster of opponents, and he fought some of them many times. He also fought many men whose records were not quite as distinguished and whose careers were not as memorable. No one scared Blackburn, regardless of the weight differential, and he fought often for the payday. He was lean, black and bald, but to some only the fact that he was black mattered and he never got the break he needed to fight for the title.

A pivotal moment in Blackburn's life came in 1909. He and another man became embroiled in a fight over Blackburn's common-law wife. Blackburn was left with a long scar on the left side of his face. The other man died and Blackburn was sentenced to 15 years in prison. He was released after five for good behavior. He went back to fighting because that was what he knew. Blackburn could be mercurial and standoffish, and he didn't let many people get close to him. However, if he liked you he called you "Chappie" as a term of endearment, and some took to calling him that as a nickname right back.

After he retired from boxing Blackburn transferred his own skills into work as a trainer. Based in Chicago, Blackburn set up shop at Trafton's Gym on Randolph Street. George Trafton was a rugged lineman for the Chicago Bears who briefly turned to boxing as a sidelight and compiled a 4–1 record. He got out of the ring quickly enough, but stayed in the sport by opening his gym.

It was at this stuffy, liniment and sweat aromatically tinged site that Roxborough and Black appeared one day in the summer of 1934 in an effort to sweet-talk Jack Blackburn into taking care of their promising fighter. Blackburn did not need the work. He was busy enough handling other fighters. His coaching was renowned and people were forever showing up at the door seeking his services. He could pick and choose his pupils depending on his mood, the value of a payday, or how much he believed in that week's touted prospect.

One thing was important to Roxborough and Black: they wanted a black trainer. They did not want any white faces in Louis' corner. The boxing world was white enough and they knew they would contend with enough difficulties from white promoters if Louis amounted to much.

Blackburn was a cynical man. Being black had prevented him from fighting for the title even in a lower weight class, never mind the heavyweight division. Everyone knew that a black heavyweight was doomed, could only go so far. When Roxborough and Black approached and informed him they had a young heavyweight they wanted him to look over, Blackburn presumed the boxer was white. The story has been told many times and there is no disputing it.

"Bring around this white boy and I'll look him over," Blackburn said.[6] Blackburn was astonished and skeptical when the duo told him that the fighter they were promoting was black. Blackburn's initial reaction was that he wanted nothing to do with this boxer. He didn't want to waste his time building up a black heavyweight that was going nowhere. "I won't have no truck with a colored boy," Blackburn said. "Colored boys ain't got much chance fighting nowadays — unless they just happen to be world beaters."[7]

Roxborough and Black laughed, as if they were in on a private joke. A world-beater. That's exactly what they believed they had, someone that could beat everyone in the world. Yet Blackburn remained unconvinced. He was not going to take these strangers' word for it. The only way he agreed to take a look-see at Louis to see if he was worth his trouble was if the managers put him on salary. Nothing doing on spec; he wanted guaranteed payment for working with Louis. Four weeks' worth. That was the deal, take it or leave it. No problem, Roxborough and Black agreed.

So Blackburn accepted the assignment of evaluating Joe Louis' prospects for $35 a week with a fresh confab scheduled in a month. From the moment Louis fell under Blackburn's sway it was if he had acquired a new daddy. From the moment Louis, Roxborough, Black and Blackburn formed an official partnership, the demarcation line in Louis' life was drawn. Behind him were the days of his youth in Alabama, in Detroit, the days of poverty and struggle. Ahead of him lay riches and fame and an everlasting place in the hearts of his countrymen.

2

Alabama

Cotton. That's all the family could see in its future. Back-breaking cotton picking was a way of life in the brutal frying summer heat accompanied by sapping humidity. The work was hard, the pay was small, and the dignity was limited.

There was no American dream within reach in small-town Alabama for African Americans during the early years of the 20th century and that was true for most whites, too. But for blacks, the reach was longer, the odds more daunting, the opportunities slender for anyone to out-run the past and the present and grab for a brighter future.

Joseph Louis Barrow was born on May 13, 1914, and while the record is firm on the date, the location is open to some interpretation. His birthplace was recorded as Lafayette, Alabama, but he was delivered with a midwife named Susan Radford helping his mother, Lillie, on a farm in the Buckalew Mountains in Chambers County. The distance from Lafayette was approximately 10 miles and the farmhouse was on County Road 50. He was named after his father's brother-in-law, Joe Louis Nichols.

Record-keeping in that backwoods area was sketchy and not even Louis was 100 percent sure of his heritage and some other particulars. It is said that he was a big baby, the seventh child of eight produced by Munroe and Lillie Barrow, weighing about 11 pounds. His mother was part–Cherokee Indian and Louis was a light-skinned black man with a pug nose and a winner's smile. One of his mother's ancestors was Charles Hunkerfoot, a Cherokee chieftain.

There may have been shades of skin, but there were no shades of grey in discrimination. It was even written into the law in some states that if a person had a tiny percentage of African American blood then he was African American. Lighter skinned or not, Indian blood mixing in his veins or not, Louis never for a second pretended to be anything but black. "My family looked black and was black," he said. "A lot of people tried to pass themselves off as white or even Indian because they had some of that in their blood, but I was always proud to be black, a Negro."[1]

On the other side, the family traced its lineage back to slaves owned by James Barrow, but it was not clear if Munroe Barrow was actually James' son or if he simply took the last name of the family he was reared with, as commonly occurred. Munroe's parents were slaves on the Barrow plantation.

Louis had a slew of brothers and sisters — Susie, Lonnie, Eulalia, Emmarell, DeLeon, Alvanius and Vunice — and legend has it that all in the family who were old enough and able were working in the fields on the day Louis was born except his mother, who was otherwise occupied.

Photographs of Louis as a young man when he was just breaking into the fight game (and as he matured) all flatter him. He was indisputably a handsome man with dark curly hair, and as he filled out his broad chest rippled with muscle. As he often appeared half-naked in public in the ring and at weigh-ins, there was little doubt his muscularity worked to his advantage with the large number of women attracted to him through the years. While Jack Johnson, the only previous African American heavyweight champion, flaunted his sexuality and his escorts, Louis was discreet. But he was hardly a monk; women of all ages and skin tones propositioned him and threw themselves at him.

That was later. Louis as a boy was basically shy. He was not chatty and there are mixed reports from various relatives about whether he engaged others of his age group in fisticuffs, or if there was little in the way of background to indicate he might one day become a star in the boxing world.

It might be said that much of Alabama was itching for a fight in the first quarter of the 20th century if a black man took a wrong step. Discrimination was a humiliating and omnipresent fact of life in cities where there were white and colored drinking fountains, where schools and pools were segregated, where whites and blacks did not share the same restaurants and hotels, or even the same playing fields. The Deep South may have nudged the calendar into the 20th century, but many minds and outlooks were locked into the 19th century.

Blacks felt the sting of hatred at every turn and feared for their lives from those who might attack them or even lynch them and go unpunished. The country as a whole was gradually becoming preoccupied with the outbreak of World War I in the year of Louis' birth (although the United States would not enter the war until 1917).

For all of the negative policies in place, daily life in rural areas played out somewhat differently in the mingling of the races, particularly among children. The sons and daughters of whites and blacks played together, even if they did not attend the same schools. At least early in life Louis said he did not encounter much prejudice against black people.

"I guess we got along with the whites because we kept in our place," Louis said, "but there wasn't bad feelings between whites and blacks in the country like in the city. I didn't know about bad feelings until I got to the city. We didn't know the difference between blacks and whites in the country because most everyone farmed and worked hard and was poor in the country. We didn't know the difference between rich and poor because no one had nothing."[2]

Perhaps in the cities the discrimination was more overt because the whites believed blacks might compete, or take, what they had. In the country there was nothing to take. The Barrow family lived in a shaky wooden home that to some appeared to be on the verge of collapse. The outside was not painted and seemed as gloomy as the long-term family financial prospects. It was crowded inside, with bedrooms shared among the siblings, but there was a roof over their heads.

Munroe Barrow cut a deal to sharecrop on a 120-acre farm and picking that cotton was a family operation. The family also grew vegetables and wheat on the property, working the hard red clay for whatever could be gleaned from it. Everyone had responsibilities year-round. Lillie picked cotton, too, although she also took care of the household and cooked the meals. Louis and his siblings had a home and they ate, but the family was living on the edge. There was no money for luxuries, by any definition, and there was no end in sight. Prospects were forever bleak for advancement.

There was no doubt that Louis' mother, the former Lillie Reese, held the family together heroically. A large and strong woman, she worked the fields and worked the kitchen. She was a full-time parent, as well, especially when her husband cracked from the strain of trying to support the clan. A big man at 6 foot 3 and 200 pounds, whom Joe resembled in size, Munroe Barrow suffered a mental breakdown when Louis was just two years old.

Louis' father was confined to the Searcy Hospital for the Negro Insane in Mount Vernon, Alabama, another small community not far away. Once in a while Munroe Barrow ran away from the institution and returned to the family, sometimes staying for a few months before being re-committed. After the initial breakdown he was never the same. Louis was a toddler during this tumultuous family time and had little memory of his father. He hardly knew him at all.

As a religious woman and adopting the optimistic attitude "trust in God, work hard, and hope for the best"[3] Lillie hustled to keep the family going, wheeling and dealing with other local farms for their produce and meat. Pork chops were the main course quite often and so was chicken. Louis loved his mother's chicken and it was probably his favorite menu item for the rest of her life, even after he was well into adulthood and was able to eat anywhere in the country or the world.

Louis was more devoted to his mother for her affection than for her culinary talents. He recognized that she endured a lot to raise the kids. He also recognized that she put up with a lot from him when he got lazy about doing his assigned chores. Everybody in the family had to work and pull their weight, but the young Louis preferred playing sports over living up to his end of the bargain. Lillie Barrow let him know that attitude was unacceptable, and most of the time he wanted to please her anyway.

"Mamas was special," Louis said, summing up a broader view of all the hard-working mothers of the era. "They worked harder than anyone. Mine did. Mine was special. I knew it. At least I knew I'd do almost anything for a smile from her. She always said I was the worst crybaby of the bunch. She always said I howled the loudest when she took a stick to me for running out on my chores. But sometimes when I'd scrub the floors and she'd pick me up and give me a big kiss I was in heaven."[4]

Louis was a mama's boy, for sure, in his Alabama days, but it is ironic that Lillie considered him to be a crybaby. One of the most impressive characteristics Louis displayed later in a life that had its disappointments was never making excuses, never complaining, and always stoically accepting the bad with the good. He was most certainly not a crybaby in his profession, but always exhibited the traits of a stand-up guy.

As a little boy, Louis was slow to develop. He did not walk on his own well until he was about a year old and he didn't talk much until he was about six. Louis said his mother felt he possessed abnormal strength, though. His klutzy walking ways resulted in many stumbles and she was surprised when he knocked over a full butter churn. In later years, the first sports writers who got to know Louis failed to respond warmly when he did not offer up witty quotes. It was not in his nature to be voluble. They could have just asked his mother. It was nothing personal with them really, Louis was just sparing with his words from the time he was small.

By the time Louis was three years old his father, Munroe Barrow, was out of his life, sequestered in the insane asylum except for his brief freedom runs. Then those ceased and Lillie Barrow was told that her husband had died. She was a widower with eight children to guide. Not long afterwards she was attracted to an area man named Pat Brooks, the father of eight children.

A merger was effected. Lillie Barrow married Pat Brooks and the kids all moved under the same roof—Brooks' house—in Mount Sinai. There were not enough beds to go around. From the other brood, Louis became closest to Pat Jr., who was his age. It was as if every night the children all went camping, sharing tents, only instead they crammed three to a bed. Brooks turned out to be a loving substitute father and in Louis' mind as he grew up, Brooks was his dad. "He was a good stepfather," Louis said. "He was the only father I ever knew."[5]

Besides sleeping arrangements, the next biggest challenge was loading all of the kids into Brooks' car, a Model T with a snap-on top, come Sunday when, as Lillie insisted, they attend the Baptist church six miles away.

The nature of their home and the neighbors' growing production meant the Barrow-Brooks family was able to obtain sufficient food, even if warm clothing for periodically chilly December and January months was lacking. Everyone worked those long hours picking cotton, so free time was at a premium, even for the kids. Play might involve a mule ride or taking advantage of being out in nature in the immediate vicinity. Fishing was a major pastime and it also provided food for the family. Louis liked to catch snakes. Games of hide and seek involved climbing trees and hiding above ground behind the leaves on the limbs.

"If the fellow was 'It' found you, he had to tag you by climbing the tree," Louis said. "If he got near you, you'd get a good hold on that sapling and bend it down 'til you dropped to the ground. Sometimes we'd just swing in the trees like little Tarzans. It sure was good for the development of shoulders and arms."[6] Louis also learned to ride a horse and he loved doing it. Later in life, when he could afford it, he bought horses and rekindled his passion.

For the most part it was hardly sophisticated play. A century later American kids type on computers, play video games, talk on cell phones. It seems nearly everything they touch is electronic. The era of Louis' youth was barely electronic, particularly outside of big cities. The family did not own a telephone, and neither did any of their neighbors. The Wright Brothers lifted off in the first airplane in 1903 and there was no passenger service in Alabama going. Automobiles were around in limited numbers. In 1914, the same year Louis was born, and relying on the assembly line, Henry Ford led the way in the mass production of cars for the average American. A car rolled off Ford's manufacturing line every 15 minutes. While there is no particular evidence supporting the notion that Ford followed Louis' career developments, Ford's achievement did have a major bearing on Louis' life.

There is not a large body of anecdotal material suggesting that Louis was much of a backyard brawler or engaged in fights when he was growing up.

He was larger than his schoolmates so it would seem most would not wish to arouse his anger. Lillie said that Louis did not get into scraps in his youth. Louis never spoke of doing so. After he became famous as the heavyweight champion, a reporter headed to the Alabama hills to get to the bottom of the matter. An uncle claimed that Louis "used to knock four boys at a time."[7] It is a fitting image to portray Louis going around bashing everyone into submission, but it's probably not true. At least once Louis did get into a fight with another student, and a teacher caught them and punished him. But there is no real suggestion this was an everyday occurrence. Louis' immersion in the sweet science lay in the future.

Louis skipped school when he could. He hated going to the school that housed only a dozen or so students and being singled out to give oral reports, or even to answer questions. Not only was he shy, but he admitted, "I stammered and stuttered, and I guess I was so plain nervous that the other kids laughed at me."[8]

Neither a natural troublemaker nor a choirboy in his behavior, Louis said he did get into fights sometimes protecting the honor of his sisters. "Another time I'd fight was when I played marbles with the other kids, but only if they bothered me," he said. And once half-brother Pat Brooks hit him with a brick, leaving a scar. "There was another fighting game we played called 'Knocking.' I'd put a chip on my shoulder and dare bigger guys than me to knock it off. If they did, we would fight. Most times it was more noise and running and throwing a few stones than anything. I usually didn't fight because I didn't get into a situation where it was necessary."[9] Perhaps this 'knocking' game is what Louis' uncle referred to when he recalled the boy clobbering a quartet of fellows at once.

Contradictorily, Louis' mother, Lillie, said he never had any fights and she felt he was one of the quietest kids she ever saw. Could be that each relative remembered what they believed to be appropriate. The uncle may have wanted to boast of the early prowess of his famous nephew. The mother may have wanted to show she had not given birth to a natural-born killer. At least once Louis said he never had the slightest bit of interest in boxing until he was 14.

Louis figured out early on how to use his size to his advantage if challenged, but he was not a bully. He also was not much of a student. He did not enjoy school, he did not benefit from much schooling, and he did not apply himself, all of which he regretted as an adult. When Louis first burst upon the scene gaining attention as a fighter, sports writers peppered him with questions about his background and expected long-winded, story-telling answers in response. Usually, they only coaxed a few words at a time, or at best a sentence out of Louis.

In a cruel rebuttal, the reporters who didn't get what they were after began referring to Louis as illiterate. The reality was he lacked self-confidence in his ability to banter with them, was shy, and didn't trust the mostly white reporters. The relationship between Louis and the writers gradually warmed, but his lack of in-depth, formal education, dating back to blowing off school in Alabama, was a factor in early national perceptions of him.

There was not a lot of pressure on Louis to succeed in school, anyway, and certainly not from truant officers or local authorities. Seemingly what educational opportunities there were for young African Americans were provided in underfunded schools, and only under duress. And in a house where there were many young mouths to feed and where a sense of defeatism about how the black man would be held back, it was paramount to bring in as much money from labor as possible. Louis' mother may have wanted him to make something of himself, but she didn't envision the route for this child to pass through Harvard or some such institution of higher learning.

When he was much older, Louis had gained intelligent perspective on what his school days were like in Alabama, his own fault for lack of initiative, and the school system's fault for not providing much incentive to do well. "I'm mighty glad to be champion," Louis said during his long reign as heavyweight champion, "and I've been powerful lucky to get where I am. But I sure wish I'd started in a good school like the kids up North do, and gone regularly. I'd sure like to be a smart man — more'n anything else, I guess."[10]

Many of Louis' most memorable lessons were learned not in the tiny schoolhouse, but from his mother directly. She stressed that "a good name is better than riches" and urged him to always "do the right thing."[11] There was definitely some irony involved in the first phrase. Louis did always maintain a good name before the American public, even when the riches he had earned were lost.

Lillie Barrow and Pat Brooks married in 1920. About five years later an incident occurred that stirred up Brooks' wanderlust and left him fearful for his own well being and his family's. He had an encounter with Ku Klux Klan members and the white-sheeted racists of the region, known for burning crosses on blacks' lawns. Their taunts and their deeply rooted animosity to blacks scared him. One night he and Lillie were driving home from visiting relatives of a deceased friend when white-sheeted men on horseback surrounded their car and menaced them. Brooks felt he was on the verge of being yanked from his car and tormented in some unknown way when a voice cut through the air saying, "That's Pat Brooks. He's a good nigger."[12] And the group let Brooks and his wife go.

Brooks was shaken by the experience. At the same time, Brooks was hearing good reports from Detroit. There were jobs to be had. A man could earn an honest wage in a factory. He didn't have to be chained to back-breaking cotton picking for the remainder of his days.

It was easy to sell African Americans on the big cities of the North in 1925. They were prospective internal immigrants, hearing the kind of stories that had spread overseas about America's streets being paved with gold. Just as Europeans flocked to the United States to start anew, the early 1920s — the Roaring Twenties — seemed to offer possibilities to a man with a strong back and a willingness to work.

Blacks by the thousands abandoned the Deep South, packing their belongings in cars, loading their families onto trains. Life had to be better in Detroit or Chicago, Pittsburgh or Cleveland, even in St. Louis. The Great Migration, as this period was called, was fundamentally about economic betterment. But it was also about hope and dignity. Not only did the black man who was the head of a household believe he could take home a superior wage at a job in the North, he also believed there was a far better chance that he would be treated fairly and that he would not automatically be looked down upon because of the color of his skin. For some the experience would be hit-and-miss, but there was no doubt change held appeal.

There were constant reminders of just how despised African Americans were in their home state of Alabama. Mobile actually had a curfew in effect that required all black people to be off the street by 10 P.M. Birmingham, the state's largest city, had a building ordinance that required all of its functional public structures (as well as outdoor sites) used for sporting events, entertainment such as concerts, stage theaters, movie houses, and convention halls to have separate entrances for whites and blacks located at least 25 feet apart. The laws were so draconian that in a later age it seems they could not possibly have been real, yet they were.

During the period in the South from right around Louis' birth into the 1920s, there seemed to be a fresh wave of vigilante violence against African Americans. After years of lying dormant, the Ku Klux Klan was on the rise again throughout the region, rearming and resurging. The Klan no doubt played as instigator in some of the violence.

Even William C. Oates — who had been a general on the side of the Confederacy during the Civil War and governor of Alabama in the 1890s, and someone who might be viewed as holding less than sympathetic views towards blacks — announced that he was appalled by the horrors of the violence taking place. People, he said, seemed determined "to kill [the Negro] and wipe him from the face of the earth."[13]

Given such a hostile climate, it was no wonder that African Americans looked for better options in other states. Pat Brooks decided to take a chance. He went exploring in Detroit, and although he did not find a job immediately, he was convinced that the lifestyle and the opportunity to find a good job in the near future far outweighed the dead-end prospects as a sharecropper in Alabama.

Pat, Lillie and some of the older boys left for Detroit first, seeking work. They all found some type of employment and they were hoping to get on at the Ford plant, which did hire blacks. After several months of members of the family living apart, Louis and the younger children, who had been cared for by relatives, were also on their way north to reunite.

By 1926, Brooks and his entire family, including Joe Louis Barrow, were residents of Detroit, Michigan. Louis was 12 years old.

3

Detroit

By 1925, the black population of Detroit was 80,000. Thousands and thousands of people moved north from their desperate southern circumstances looking for better jobs. The lower east side of the city, eventually called the Black Bottom, was the area that attracted the most settlement in a segregated city, as those migrants discovered it was.

A working man's town, Detroit was a noisy, bustling city, huge compared to the rural, more peaceful setting of small-town Alabama. The Barrow family embraced the change, though, because it represented hope and improved status. In addition, the home they shared with relatives on McCombs Street, and then in their own house on Catherine Street, had all the comforts of modern living that were absent in Alabama. There was running water, electricity rather than kerosene lamps, and indoor plumbing instead of an outhouse.

For Joe Louis Barrow, the countryside lifestyle was gone. If there were horses around, they were hitched to wagons doing a day's work. The days of catching snakes in the woods were over. It was easy to be overwhelmed by the teeming city after a lifetime spent on a farm.

"You can't imagine the impact that city had," Louis wrote in his autobiography. "I never saw so many people in one place, so many cars at one time. I had never even seen a trolley car before. There were other things that I had never heard of—parks, libraries, brick schoolhouses, movie theaters. People dressed different. But one thing I knew, Detroit looked awfully good to me."[1]

His job was to attend school and once again he wasn't all that enthusiastic about the role. Playing hooky in Alabama had not done him any good. When it came time to assign him to a class at the Duffield Elementary School, Louis' skills trailed the field in his age group. Already large for his age, he stuck out even more when placed with younger children. Shy, still coping with a stutter when he talked, Louis was not outgoing, did not really mix with the other kids. He was behind in book learning and he did not really attack his deficiencies. For him school was a pain in the neck.

"It was too much for me," Louis said. "They had all kinds of routines I didn't know a thing about — assemblies, fire drills, and stuff like that. So I kept myself quiet. It bored me. Most times I'd just look out the window. All I can be sure about was that I'd rather have been anyplace else than in that classroom trying to listen to something I didn't understand."[2]

It was probably equal parts failure on Louis' side for not working at school and on the teacher's side for not taking the time to care more. The first good friend Louis made at school was Freddie Guinyard, who became a life-long pal. An incident involving Guinyard at Duffield was the first time in his life he thought about racial issues, Louis said. The way Louis recalled it, a teacher spoke only to the black students and said that if they got good grades they would get the chance to shine shoes at the Hudson department store on weekends. Guinyard immediately sensed the racism in the deal. He leapt to his feet and challenged the teacher by saying, "Why would you need to have good grades to shine shoes?" The act of insubordination got Guinyard sent home and made Louis think.[3]

Guinyard and Louis became running mates and one way they whiled away time on Saturdays was to attend triple-feature cowboy movies. Louis loved westerns and was particularly partial to Tom Mix, but also liked Buck Jones and Ken Maynard pictures. These cowpokes churned out the films by the dozens, first the silent variety in the 1920s, and then some talkies.

For decades, white teachers pigeon-holed black students falling behind in their class work, frequently dismissing them as useless students, unable to learn and stigmatizing them as stupid. The easiest way to deal with them, instead of offering special instruction to help them catch up, was to farm them out, get rid of them. The catch-all dismissal was that they were too dumb to learn so there was no point in them following the regular curriculum or a college path. Louis ran across a teacher who disposed of him in this manner.

In the case of this teacher, Vada Schwader, an instructor whom Louis liked and said was nice, was responding as much to Louis' own intransigence in attempting to adapt to book learning. He did not help his own case and was being held back in sixth grade; in fact his younger sister Vunice caught up to his class. Schwader may have thought she was truly doing Louis a favor when she said, "He's going to have to make a living with his hands. He'd better start now."[4] By that Schwader undoubtedly meant that Louis would have to become a laborer, a woodworker, or metal worker as a career. Surely, she had no conception of the irony of her phrasing and that the boy she helped transfer to Bronson Trade School would employ his meaty fists to become heavyweight champion of the world. Working with his hands indeed.

At vocational school, which more aptly fit his personality, Louis made cabinets and tables. He didn't mind that so much, but he did want more out of life. The idea of becoming a boxer had not yet crossed his mind, but it was coming. He was engaged by baseball, however, and played often on the local sandlots. Louis also became a fan of the Detroit Tigers.

By his mid-teens, Louis had become interested in the opposite sex. By the time he was 14, he had begun a secret relationship with Bennie Franklin, one which lasted for years. His first girlfriend, who had also moved north from Alabama, was the step-daughter of one of Louis' sisters. Although they were not blood relations, Louis said he knew family members would object, so they kept things quiet.

"I always loved beautiful girls," he said, something which would become more apparent when he was a little bit older.[5]

The Roaring Twenties followed the grim Teens after World War I ended. It was a time of prosperity in America, of living high. Blacks could make the move north with assurance, feeling confident they could carve out a better living. In baseball, the lively ball had been introduced to the sport. Babe Ruth had conquered the home run and shown how it could be an exciting and devastating weapon. The demand for tickets to watch the Yankees was so great in New York that the team built a new palace of a stadium and it was termed "The House That Ruth Built."

There seemed to be outsized personalities in every sport. Red Grange energized football fans. Big Bill Tilden was the king of the tennis circuit. Bobby Jones ruled the links. And in the fight game Jack Dempsey was the heavyweight champ, at least until stunningly, Gene Tunney dethroned him. Their first fight in 1926 in Philadelphia attracted 120,000 fans.

Also in 1926, an African American dentist in Detroit sought to move his family into an all-white neighborhood with a home purchase. Dr. Ossian Sweet became a trail-blazer, but suffered intense discrimination because of his boldness. He was charged with murder for fighting back and defending his home against a white mob. The famed attorney Clarence Darrow handled the case and won an acquittal for Sweet.

The Dempsey-Tunney boxing rematch, in which Dempsey sought to regain the crown, took place in Chicago in 1927 and was one of the most famous bouts in history. It came to be called the "Long Count" fight. The 105,000 fans in attendance were shocked when Dempsey put Tunney down on the canvas. However, he did not adjourn to a neutral corner, so the count could not proceed. If Dempsey had retreated to the corner Tunney would have been counted out. Instead, he rose before the official count of 10 to continue, and then won the fight.

After he became heavyweight champ and reporters asked such questions, Louis said that when he was a teen in the 1920s he rooted for Dempsey. He even called Dempsey his first sporting hero. Dempsey was one of the ubiquitous figures of the Twenties, until Tunney succeeded him. "We listened to his fights on the radio," Louis said. "It was always Dempsey does this, Dempsey does that."[6]

The second loss to Tunney was a dark day for Dempsey, but one of the darkest days for the nation lay ahead. On October 29, 1929, Black Tuesday, the stock market crashed, marking the beginning of what would soon be the Great Depression, the most devastating economic collapse in U.S. history. By the end of the decade many of those optimistic black migrants were out of work in Detroit and other big cities, victims of the last-hired, first-fired doctrine in some cases, or perhaps because less sympathetic employers felt it easier to let African Americans go on the unemployment rolls.

Life became a greater challenge for those who lost jobs at the Barrow family. DeLeon Barrow, one of Joe's brothers, was hired at the Ford automobile manufacturing operation in 1928 and escaped the layoffs. He made a career out of working at the Rouge plant, staying on for 45 years.

When times got hard Louis took on odd jobs, including delivering groceries and ice and shoveling coal. The Catherine Street abode was not in the fanciest of neighborhoods. Indeed, there was a popular whorehouse down the block. Louis began running with a local gang and Lillie was disturbed. She was certain he would get hurt or be arrested. Although there did not seem to be much logic behind the move, her way of getting her youngest son involved in a respectable activity was to scrape up 50 cents a shot for violin lessons.

Not even teacher Schwader likely ever considered that one of the professions Louis might tackle with his hands was training to become another Jascha Heifetz. Louis never really professed an early-life commitment to any type of music, but if he was drawn to anything in the early 1930s it was probably jazz, not classical. Nonetheless, what Lillie Barrow wanted, she made happen. Louis began taking violin lessons and toting the instrument through the neighborhood. Mostly, that earned him ridicule from the other guys in the streets.

Nat Fleischer, the esteemed boxing writer who founded *The Ring* magazine, the self-described bible of the sport, once wrote of Louis' flirtation with the violin: "There was music in his soul, but no great yearning to become a musician."[7] That sounded like a pretty fair analysis.

As much as he loved his mother and appreciated her good wishes for him, Louis knew he was no musician. An alternative soon presented itself to him. One friend, Thurston McKinney, was a regular at the Brewster Recreation Center. One day he urged Louis to skip his violin lessons and accompany him to the gym. That proved to be a capital idea, indeed a life-changing one.

Louis put the gloves on for the first time in late 1932 when he was 18 years old, though he had done some backyard sparring with another friend, Amsey Rinson, in a very informal setting. McKinney had already won a Detroit Golden Gloves championship, and when he talked about Louis joining him at the gym, it was not a lark. Rinson had previously planted the idea of hitting the gym when they hit each other, but he and Louis never made the trip.

When Louis ditched his violin lesson for the gym, the violin came with him. That must have been a conversation piece at the Brewster Rec Center. "It was my first time in a professional gym," Louis said. "I looked at the ring, the punching bag, the pulleys, exercise mat, and it was love at first sight."[8]

Louis was finished with the violin, even if his mother was not yet aware of that development in her son's life. He took the money she gave him and rented a locker at the gym and to pay the basic fees, and he began working out. For a time that's all he did, getting accustomed to the equipment.

One day McKinney insisted that Louis spar with him. McKinney was far more polished, although he was a smaller man, and he used his experience to box circles around his friend at first. Even Louis admitted that McKinney got the best of him and hit him with one shot to the jaw that nearly toppled him. It also made Louis mad and "I let go my right. It caught him on the chin. His eyes got glassy and his knees buckled, and if I hadn't moved fast to hold him, I would have knocked him out." McKinney held no grudge, but he did make an astute observation. "Man," he said, "throw that violin away."[9]

It was one thing to make an impression on McKinney, particularly with him holding that Golden Gloves title, but quite another for Louis to make his mother see that this was where he belonged, not prepping for a symphony orchestra. For a short while Louis just made a quiet detour to the gym when he was supposed to be sitting for his violin lesson. He was too nervous to talk about the situation with his mother.

Soon enough that option was taken out of his hands. The violin teacher showed up in the Catherine Street home to inquire what had become of his pupil. Lillie had the same question for Joe. Where have you been going? was the gist of what she asked. Quite edgy about what she would think, Louis explained that he was more focused on becoming a boxer than a violinist and

It's time to put the gloves on. Heavyweight champion Joe Louis slips his hands into the tools of his trade before a workout (courtesy Charles H. Wright Museum of African-American History).

that he had been visiting a gym regularly. To his surprise, she didn't give him any grief. Instead, Lillie supported him and said he should just be the best that he could be as a boxer if he was going to pursue it.

Louis obtained a $25 a week job moving truck bodies mounted on dollies into the spray paint assembly line at the Briggs factory. Those were good wages at the time and more than financed his needs to continue his boxing education, even while sharing some of his income with the family.

Joe Louis Barrow, a son of Alabama, was now launching what would become one of the greatest boxing careers of all from his new home in Detroit, Michigan. There was so much to learn, but this was a subject the young man cared deeply about. He wasn't going to be staring out the window daydreaming when class was in session at the Brewster Recreation Center.

There were hard times outside the door, where grown men without jobs pleaded for work at every store or factory in the area and some were reduced to peddling fruit to make a few cents. There would be hard times inside the musty gym where other men tried to make their own opportunities with their fists. Now Louis was one of them and it was on his own broad shoulders to see how far he could go.

4

Joe Who?

He was born Joe Louis Barrow, but became Joe Louis. The how and why of it, however, have been obscured. Just about everyone who has written about the one-time heavyweight champ seems to offer a different theory about how it came to pass that the boxer's name was shortened.

Sometime after Louis obtained his own locker at the Brewster Recreation Center it was determined that he have his first amateur fight. It was time for a test to see how much he had learned in workouts and whether he was really going to be a fighter. Up until the first match of a boxer's career he is exercising. After he has faced competition, he is a real fighter.

One early report on Louis' career portrays his name-shortening as a sudden, spur-of-the-moment development. The way the scene was described by early biographer Margery Miller, Louis was standing in the ring when the notion came to him that "Joe Louis Barrow" sounded too long for the announcer to handle. In her account Louis decided then and there to become Joe Louis. "Joe was struck by the fact that the name was long for a boxer and told him to omit Barrow," she wrote.[1] This scenario is possible, but unlikely. Louis was a person who usually thought things out and, besides, "Joe Louis Barrow" was not a particularly long name.

Still, that story is echoed in another early book about Louis, presented in this way: "The announcer crossed the canvas and spoke. 'Your name Joe Louis Barrow?' In that instant, Joe made a decision that was to influence his whole future life. 'Just Joe Louis,' he told the announcer, for it occurred to him that his full name was too long for people to remember easily."[2]

Recalling the origins of Louis' first visits to the gym — in lieu of violin lessons — the case has been made by others that Louis changed his name from Joe Louis Barrow to simply Joe Louis as a way to stay under radar when he began competing in bouts so his name would be reported in the newspaper in a way that would not attract suspicion to his real identity. "He adopted the ring name Joe Louis so his mother wouldn't find out he was boxing," author Chris Mead reported.[3]

That seems unlikely, as well, because Louis came clean and admitted he had spurned the violin in favor of the violence pretty early on in his boxing career, certainly well before he turned pro, and at the latest very soon after he had his first fight. If he preferred, at that early stage, it would have been easy enough to go back to Joe Louis Barrow.

Richard Bak, the veteran Detroit author, tried to get to the bottom of the mystery and heard many variations. One intriguing story was a report that one of Louis' sisters made him a gift of a satin jacket to wear into the ring with the name "Joe Louis" stitched on it. A more-often told story was that when filling out the application form for his first fight Louis wrote in very large letters and just ran out of room on the line that was supposed to include his name. This transformation from Joe Louis Barrow to Joe Louis was apparently accomplished by Joe's first amateur fight against John Miler in 1932. After all of these questions and after all of the debate about Louis' name change, Bak discovered most of the early newspaper mentions of the fighter's names in his first amateur bouts referred to him as "Joe Lewis."[4] That was one spelling Joe Louis Barrow never chose.

When he participated in his long-awaited biography in the late 1970s, Louis did address the issue and said he was still trying to hide his boxing from his mother when he changed the name leading up to the match against Miler. "I didn't want my family to know anything about it yet," Louis said, "so before I boxed Miler I decided I'd drop the name Barrow and just be plain Joe Louis. That way, if it got into the papers Momma wouldn't know the difference."[5]

Of course if Momma had come across a boxer called Joe Louis he would have been hard-pressed to convince her that the name was mere coincidence and that it was somebody else. The precise timing of Lillie Barrow's awareness of her son's boxing ambitions and how it compares to his name change and his amateur debut are unclear. Later in life, when the boxer sired a son, he named him Joe Louis Barrow, Jr. That was probably the most visible way that the champion ever used his birth name again.

The birth of Joe Louis the fighter took place in Detroit, inside the Brewster Recreation Center, his first fighting home, whether it was striking the heavy bag, trading punches with Thurston McKinney, or taking the first steps to becoming the polished fighter who later made millions of dollars in the ring.

Any boxing man who glimpsed the 17-year-old Joe when he showed up at the gym would be impressed by his energy and enthusiasm, his size (though he was still a light-heavyweight at under 175 pounds, he was filling out) and his punching power. Although unschooled, Louis was able to push McKinney around the ring. Only a few years later Louis would be able to turn opponents' hearts to stone with merely a scowl. For now, he was learning his trade.

When Louis' mom found out he was investing in his fists, not his fingers with the violin, he was sure she was going to lecture him and forbid him to continue. She did not. Sensing his passion for the sport, Lillie said she would support him and wanted him to do the best he could. She may have hoped that a few bloody noses would cure Joe from his desire to become a pugilist, but if she harbored any such quiet ambitions things did not play out that way. As tough a game as it was, Louis was in it for good.

Louis' first trainer at the rec center was Holman Williams, who began by teaching him the fundamentals of the game. It was apparent he was not going to be a stick-and-move specialist because he was not a speedster. Yet Louis possessed a hard-hitting, stinging jab, so that flicking left could be a great weapon setting up the dynamite right hand he owned.

The jab can be the greatest weapon in a fighter's arsenal and Louis' was very effective. His power was very impressive, but he had to work hard to develop the necessary footwork to stay out of the reach of foes and to put them in harm's way. Boxing is an ego sport and the best fighters must have inflated egos, a solid core belief that opponents can't beat them, that no one in their weight class can beat them.

"Holman Williams encouraged me a lot," Louis said. "I respected him. He was a beautiful boxer. He told me I had the stuff to be a champion and I knew he was serious."[6]

Williams had a lengthy career as a pro welterweight and middleweight, putting up a record of 145-30-11 before he turned to training. He only trained Louis for about a year and died in a fire in his sleep when he was 55.

No athlete is born great. He may be stamped with greatness that can be tapped, drawn out, but to achieve the pinnacle of a sport takes hard work and the donation of sweat by the bucket-load. Louis did his part, but it still took time to adapt. Once the first punch lands on your chin in the ring there is a tendency to forget every word your trainer told you. The contact tends to scramble clear thinking.

The first amateur fight of Louis' career was staged at the Naval Armory in Detroit in 1932. It was not wise scheduling. Louis was matched with Johnny Miler, a member of the 1932 United States boxing team in the light-heavyweight division at the Olympics in Los Angeles. While some old reports spell his name as Miller, most of the reports of his fight with Louis call him

Miler. The fighter was born John Miletich, and he adjusted his name for the sport. In retrospect, Miler, no matter his official name, had far too much experience for the novice Louis, no matter his potential.

The result was disastrous for Louis and could have ruined his desire to fight. Amateur fights are scheduled to go just three rounds, but Louis didn't last that long. The smoother Miler knocked him down seven times in two rounds and the fight was stopped. It was an inauspicious showing for Louis, the beating so thorough that it would have been easy to become discouraged and quit the sport. Then as now, amateurs did not earn paychecks for their efforts, but Louis was presented a check exchangeable for $7 worth of merchandise.

"Next day I went back to the gym," Louis said. "I tell you I was sore and aching, but my pride hurt more. When I got home my step-father sat and had a long talk with me. He told me he was getting to be an old man and except for marrying my momma and getting out of Alabama, he hadn't accomplished much. I was young, he said, and maybe I should just try to get a regular job, settle down and marry some nice girl."[7]

Certainly Pat Brooks, Louis' step-father, would have been happier if he quit the ring outright. Brooks did not really want Louis to fight. He wanted him to work and provide money for the family. Brooks felt the defeat was an ominous sign for Louis that he had chosen the wrong way to make a living. He lobbied Louis to quit boxing and find a better job. For the time being Louis heeded his step-dad's advice. That's when he got a job at the Ford Rouge plant. Louis backed away from training and did not fight again for months, spilling into 1933.

The physical labor Louis took on at the plant tired him and left his muscles as achy as boxing had. He was making a steady $25 a week, but knew if he was a successful boxer he could make much more. Eventually, he decided that if his body was going to be his bread and butter and his physical attributes were going to be his vehicle of support, he might as well do something he liked. In January of 1933, Louis asked his boss at the plant for a six-month leave of absence. Many felt Louis was being foolish by surrendering steady work during the depths of the Depression, but he went with his heart.

Louis plunged back into training and after a respectable interval Williams fine-tuned him for more amateur bouts. Louis scored a knockout in his second amateur fight over a foe named Otis Thomas. "It was my first official knockout," Louis said. "I was on top of the world."[8]

The whipping Miler gave Louis was not repeated. As he matured, grew into his body, developed excellent training habits and as his instincts sharpened, Louis found the best ways to apply his lessons when under fire. One of those lessons was not to rely so devotedly on his right hand. He would need strength and power and confidence in both hands to get very far in this business. One day at the gym, Williams, and Atler Ellis, another handler who had sway over Joe's career at that time, tried to make a point. During a workout they tied Louis' right hand to his corner so he couldn't use it. He had to fight one-handed, all with the left, or weaker hand, against Thurston McKinney. It was frustrating, but Louis knew he needed to bring his left up to par.

After KO'ing Thomas, Louis knocked out 13 men in a row. He entered tournaments and traveled to Chicago, Boston and Toronto. For the first time, as he turned 18 in 1933, and 19 in 1934, he was not living at his parents' home and liked the freedom of being on his own. In body he was already a man. In mind, he was becoming one.

By the end of 1933 Louis was competing for a national Golden Gloves championship in Boston, still fighting as a light-heavyweight. By then he had acquired a glowing reputation among those who had seen him box, and although he lost the title match to Max Marek, one influential viewer never forgot the promise he spied during Louis' defeat in Boston.

Boxing writer Nat Fleischer was the witness in question and he promptly wrote that if either Marek or Louis turned professional he would be worth watching. Marek, the recipient of a football scholarship to Notre Dame, did try the professional ranks and was very active, if not nearly as successful as Louis. During a pro career that ended in 1939, Marek went 33-20-11. One thing Marek could always say was that he had beaten Joe Louis — and he said it often. He billed himself as "The Man Who Beat Joe Louis." And it was for a national amateur championship, too.

While that may have been the height of Marek's boxing career, it was only the stepping-off point for Louis'. Later the same year Louis won an amateur boxing national title in Chicago. Fleischer saw him again and was even more impressed. "I had the pleasure of watching one of the most finished amateur boxers it has been my fortune to see in 30 years," he wrote. "The name of the Negro boy is Joe Louis, a name that will soon be headlining the sports pages of America if he decides to turn professional. Although a novice in experience, he handles himself in all departments of the sport like a tried veteran. He bears watching."[9]

Nat Fleischer was right about Joe Louis and Pat Brooks was wrong.

Fleischer had an eye for talent in the fight game, and he saw that Louis was the genuine article. He laid it on quite thick for his readers, employing animalistic synonyms that were later disparaged as chosen only because Louis was black. Although there was plenty of that to come in sportswriters' lingo about Louis, Fleischer's word choice seems more indicative of the flowery, hyperbolic style of writing of the time period than racist.

"Who is this Joe Louis?" Fleischer wrote. "He is a pugilistic symphony with a tempo geared to bring him across the ring with all the grace of a gazelle and the cold fury of an enraged mountain lion. He is a new type fighter who shows a style combining exquisite harmony of movement with crushing power stored in each hand."[10]

As Louis grew in stature his merchandise prizes expanded, as well, though only to the $25 per fight range. While Williams did tutor Louis expertly during the limited time he supervised him, he was succeeded by trainer George Moody. With Moody's guidance, Louis became a more complete boxer. He avenged an early loss to Stanley Evans and won a second national amateur title.

By the time Louis reached the apex of his amateur career he had posted a 50–4 record with 43 of his victories coming by knockout. This was the power Fleischer saw in those clenched fists.

During his amateur days in Detroit, when Louis fell in love with boxing and appreciated coming into his own as a fighter and harnessing his power, he made some important friends. One was Eddie Futch. In the 1930s, Futch, like Louis, was an amateur fighter representing Detroit. Unlike Louis, Futch was a man of the lesser weight classes. He was also a southerner by birth, born in Hillsboro, Mississippi, in 1911. In his later years Futch, who died at 90 in 2001, became one of the greatest trainers in boxing history, renowned for his work with heavyweight champ Joe Frazier and others.

Futch was a slick amateur and won Detroit Golden Gloves championships, but a heart murmur was discovered when he considered going pro, so he retired from inside the ring to teach outside the ring. However, he was still active, and he frequently sparred with Louis. The idea was to give practice to Louis catching up to faster men.

Futch used to joke that he had to be fast to stay away from Louis' artillery because at 135 pounds or so, Louis might have killed him if he connected flush. "In the ring, I couldn't force Joe anywhere," Futch said. "But I could lead him if he was following me. I would go to the corner, then I would come out and make a circle quickly before he knew what I was doing. I would feint the left hand into the body, watching him drop his right hand to parry the punch. The minute I saw him drop his right hand I'd throw a quick left hook to the head because he had nothing up there. His right hand was down."[11]

That was a telling observation, because a few years later making that very same mistake proved very costly to Louis in a big fight. Futch pulled off the stunt often enough that Louis became wary. He studied Futch and stopped falling for the move. Louis said, "I want to see how you do it because if you can hit me with a left hook somebody who can hurt me with a left hook can hit me."[12]

At various times during his training career, Futch reminisced about his days going toe-to-toe with Louis — sort of. Sort of, in the sense that he was alone in the ring with him, but never stayed still long enough to do battle because he didn't want to get clobbered by the much bigger man. Why would Louis want to spar with a lightweight? "He said, 'If I can hit you with anything, I know I'm alright,'" Futch said once. "I said, 'Joe, I don't intend to allow you to hit me with anything.'"[13]

Also in those Detroit days Louis made the acquaintance of another gym rat named Walker Smith, Jr. The lad was seven years younger than Louis and looked up to him. At the time the boy was called "Junior" around the neighborhood and every day when Louis walked past his home there he would be waiting outside. Junior insisted on carrying Louis' equipment bag to the gym.

Louis did not know what to make of the young teenager, but he kind of liked him so he put up with the bag carrying even though the gesture embarrassed him and made him the butt of a few jokes when people referred to Junior as his valet. This association only lasted for a chunk of 1932 then, but eventually evolved into a life-long friendship when the youngster grew up.

The boy born Smith also took a ring name a little bit later and became known to the world as Sugar Ray Robinson, one of the few, if not the only, boxer in history regarded as Louis' superior.

Back then, when Louis was first getting started, Junior bragged to his friends about knowing him. It didn't make much of an impact at first because Louis wasn't known for doing very much yet. But the link was established and within a decade they had become true pals. By then Robinson had compiled his own 85–0 amateur record and Louis was long established as the world's heavyweight champion.

After capturing a couple of national amateur titles, Louis was pleased with his progress and proud of his accomplishments. But he couldn't eat those merchandise certificates. They were not redeemable at the best restaurants. He aspired to more, though when he spoke of financial goals his mind did not wrap around the concept of becoming rich. All he wanted to do, he said, was make $60 a week. That was riches enough for him at the time.

Little did he know he was dreaming way too small. It was Louis' trainer Moody who introduced him to John Roxborough when the businessman showed up at the gym.

5

Laying Out the Big Plan

Jack Blackburn was the talent evaluator. John Roxborough and Julian Black were pretty sure about what they had, but they needed a specialist to make the final call on Louis' skill and potential.

The trio of black men understood the odds against their black fighter getting his due, even if he was good enough to challenge for the heavyweight championship. Roxborough and Black were believers and soon enough Blackburn was.

Blackburn had endured the heartbreaks of being a black fighter with skill but no connections. Roxborough and Black understood how harsh the boxing world could be, too. They all agreed that justice was a difficult commodity to grasp, that the world was unfair to African Americans, and that they were going to be heading down a hard road that might dead-end. But they were bold enough and determined enough to give it a shot. They had seen the spark of greatness in Joe Louis and they wanted to bring it out, nurture it, and get him a shot at the biggest individual prize in sport.

They wanted to do it for Louis and they wanted to do it for themselves. But they also (and Roxborough perhaps was more conscious of this than the others) wanted to do it for the black race. Lord knows their brethren were downtrodden enough in the United States, punished for the sin of being born with black skin, taken advantage of by the white power structure at every turn. These were not naïve men committed to guiding Joe Louis to the top.

They comprehended that if Louis won in the ring they all won in the financial game and that everyone, all of the country's black people (including all of those that didn't even know they existed) could become big winners too, by proxy. They may never have crystallized the image in their minds of what they would all live to see and experience in the coming years, but in their souls they knew that a Louis success would be every black man's success.

He also had to do it the right way. That was critical. Jack Johnson should have been one of the greatest heroes in the black community, but he was so hated by white people that even those who liked and admired him among African Americans understood that he had not been able to uplift the entire race. The backlash against Johnson was so powerful in white America that he was a pariah. Johnson's success, which might have led to more opportunities for black Americans in the sport, had the reverse effect.

Just being black and the best was enough to make Johnson enemies among whites. But being black, the best, boastful, smug, often arrogant, and freewheeling on the edges of society earned him undying resentment. Was that right? No. Was that fair? No. But that was the reality of the moment in the 1930s when Louis turned professional and set his eyes on the prize of the heavyweight title.

To enable Louis to obtain the chance that they believed his skills warranted, Roxborough and Black played the public relations game. They wove Blackburn into the web, as well, though his responsibilities were mainly focused on the physical development of Louis. With a singular goal in mind they laid the predicate for Louis' behavior and lifestyle from the moment he joined forces with them. The idea was to have no skeletons in the closet that could be found out later to Louis' detriment. The plan was to position him as the anti–Johnson.

If Jack Johnson was threatening to whites, Louis would present a friendly image to whites. If Johnson's personality grated, Louis' accommodated. If Johnson could lick any man in the house, as John L. Sullivan had so aggrandized, Louis could do so, too, but he would not gloat about it. If there was such a way to do so, it was planned that Louis would kick all contenders' butts in a polite manner.

The code of conduct for Louis was a strict and prudent one to follow if he wished to make a run at the heavyweight title. In a society that feared any black man of physical stature, that distrusted any black man big or small, and that held the notion that any black man was inferior, it was going to be some trick to guide Louis to the top of the heavyweight rankings.

There had been many first-rate black boxers of other eras, and since Johnson, who never were allowed to climb between the ropes against the leading white heavyweights and champions. John L. Sullivan, the last bare-knuckle champ, who was still alive, said white men should not fight black men. Nor was there any cooperation with contenders shown by Jack Dempsey when he held the title. Nor was there a willingness of anyone else for the last three decades to meet a black man if the title was at stake.

Harry Wills, nicknamed "The Black Panther," was a tremendous fighter who was an active campaigner between 1911 and 1932. He compiled a record

Wherever he trained, indoors or out, at a favored training camp in New Jersey, or when he was on the road prepping for bouts at other locales, Joe Louis gave the speed bag a workout (courtesy Charles H. Wright Museum of African-American History).

of 79-10-4 and although he was ranked, he was ignored when it came time to make a match with the heavyweight champs of his era. Finally, in 1926, Dempsey agreed to fight him, but pulled out when he did not receive the $100,000 he had been guaranteed.

Sam Langford, a Canadian black man born in Nova Scotia, was a Wills contemporary and in later years was called "the greatest fighter nobody knows." His record was 178-32-40. Both Wills and Langford held the "World Colored Heavyweight Championship" over the years, but the phrase alone explained their plight of being locked out of the contests that determined the true heavyweight championship.

So that was the backdrop of history for Louis and his handlers as they sought to find a way around public opinion and fight officialdom's obstinate ways. From the start the goal was clear. But Louis had to perform, had to mature from the 50–4 amateur champ into a more sophisticated professional contender. Roxborough and Black knew he also had to be on his best behavior so that he could be above criticism.

The rules of Louis' behavior included how to act in public in general and how to act in the ring. Among the things Louis was not supposed to do was hang out in nightclubs alone, not under any circumstances be seen alone with a white woman, and not pose for photographs with white women. As a fighter he was not to badmouth an opponent during the period leading up to a bout, and he was not to smile in victory or talk badly about a vanquished opponent. Virtually every one of these things had been habits of Johnson's and won him enmity.

Although the rules were authored by the managers, Blackburn was on board for enforcement and believed the correctness of Louis' actions in public would be as important to his future as his power in the ring. That was why Blackburn had originally scoffed at the suggestion that he train an African American pursuing the heavyweight title. He was convinced that the establishment would never allow Louis to get close.

"You're colored, Joe," Blackburn once said. "And a colored fighter's got to be lots better than the other man if he's gonna go places. "But you gotta have more than just two good hands. You gotta do the right thing. And never leave yourself open so people can talk about you."[1]

These three older men tag teamed Louis with advice. They listed the rules of engagement for him to hear and absorb. "To be a champion you've got to be a gentleman first," Roxborough said. "Your toughest fight might not be in the ring, but out in public."[2]

Blackburn had been the big doubter when Roxborough and Black took him on. He reveled in his four-week deal with the payday commitment. Being on salary seemed like being on easy street for him rather than worrying about a percentage of purses. "This will be the best job I ever had," Blackburn said. "Usually, I've got to whip my man to collect my pay. I got to tell you, you'll never make a success of this kid, but I need the job. He ain't gonna make no money worth shaking your finger at. Remember, he's a colored boy."[3] There was only one thing Blackburn said that he was right about. Training Joe Louis was the best job he ever had.

Roxborough made the decision to move Louis to Chicago to live and train. Louis was initially reluctant and made Roxborough play the middle man in informing his mother. Roxborough paid all of Louis' expenses. He bought Louis new clothes, fed him, took care of his training and workout fees, and made Louis a full-time project. Louis left Detroit behind as his home and he left regular factory pay behind, too.

As part of Louis' new life in Chicago, he lived in an apartment picked out for him by Roxborough and Black. But there was an added twist. The place was owned by Bill Bottoms, an expert chef, who was to prepare Louis' meals and make sure he ate nutritionally. These days a 20-year-old left to his own devices might often get bogged down with frequent meals taken at McDonald's or by eating unhealthy late-night snacks. Roxborough and Black headed off any such potential habits, if Louis had wished to indulge in any 1930s-era equivalents.

When Louis first met Blackburn, the trainer called him "Chappie." That was a habit of Blackburn's. But in Louis' case it truly became a term of affection and Louis returned the favor. He called Blackburn "Chappie," as well. It was their personal way of expressing friendship. Still, Blackburn was a stern taskmaster from the beginning. He told Louis how it was going to be and Louis listened carefully and agreed to the conditions. Blackburn said, "You got to jump when I say jump and sleep when I say sleep. Other than that you're wasting my time."[4]

Blackburn set to work training Louis properly to become a real professional boxer, but he did not neglect his mind. In between making sure his pupil's work ethic was sound and that he did work hard — Louis did not have to be pushed — Blackburn told the younger man stories about what boxing was like when he fought and made him privy to some of the inner workings of the game. Sometimes the stories were exciting and sometimes the stories invited Louis to recognize that the fight world was not all about glory, but was sometimes seamy. Louis recalled Blackburn telling him that he wore a size 8½ shoe, but when he fought he wore size tens in order to stash his payday in his foot gear.

"Most importantly, he told me that sometime, someplace, somebody was going to try to get me to throw a fight," Louis said. "He told me about all the pitfalls. 'I've done a lot of things I haven't been proud of, but I never threw a fight,'" Blackburn said. "'And you won't 'cause I'll know, and then it's going to be you and me.'"[5]

One promise Roxborough and Black made to Louis was that he would never be put into such a position. The dark side of boxing could be unscrupulous where shady deals might be made. If you throw this fight we will give you a title shot — that might be a deal someone was after. The co-managers assured Louis they would never allow that to occur. They wanted everything to be on the up-and-up.

Roxborough was very much conscious of white discrimination and he had demonstrated his commitment to helping young blacks get an education. But he wanted more. If Louis was the African American athlete capable of what he thought he was, then Roxborough was going to help his people even more by ensuring that the young man remained unspoiled and untarnished.

One thing Roxborough insisted upon (and given the way the fight game worked he knew he might have to take a stand and fight back against vultures) was that Joe Louis' management team remain all black. He did not want any white men horning in on his discovery, and he hoped Louis was going to be good enough to become a symbol or an ambassador to black America. No white man could understand that goal and a white man on the management team might detract from that image.

Ambassador to black America? Such a thing was difficult to imagine in the beginning stages of the team's partnership, but Roxborough did an exemplary job of looking ahead to possible events that in 1934 were only on some distant private horizon in his head.

More relevant at the moment was how Louis and Blackburn would fare as teacher and pupil. Blackburn put more structure into Louis' daily life than he had known since he was an infant and demanded feeding at regular intervals. One notable aspect of training was the early-morning run. Some boxers thrive on the running necessary to build their wind and stamina. Some hate it. Louis, assigned to run six miles a day, enjoyed the exertions.

It only took about a week for Blackburn to decide that Louis was a keeper. He might have only signed on for four weeks' pay, but he sensed that in Louis he had a fighter who might be the rare jewel. The kid cooperated. He did everything that he was asked to do. He worked hard. He got up early in the morning for the road work. He ate well. He responded to criticism and learned from his mistakes.

Blackburn found it hard to believe, but he might be training the black fighter that would make Americans forget Jack Johnson.

6

Jack Johnson

They were very different types of men, but the public couldn't know that just by looking, so Joe Louis' handlers went to elaborate lengths to distance their protégé from the only previous African American to hold the heavyweight title.

A century after Jack Johnson's reign, it is unfathomable to most people how much the dark-skinned man with thunder in his fists was despised by the boxing world and American society at large. Johnson rankled white folks by his mere existence, and then he piled it on, as if he purposely dreamed up every mannerism and act he could to irk them, annoy them, and elevate blood pressures.

Over time Johnson seemed to become the American white world's public enemy No. 1, even though he was no criminal. It took some time, but that white world actually made him into a criminal in order to subdue him. All of this for a sporting figure.

The story of Joe Louis is inextricably tied to the story of Jack Johnson for two reasons — they were both heavyweight fighters and they were both black men. That is about all that they had in common, but it was enough.

For Louis this meant that the routine obstacles placed before a maturing, growing, improving fighter following the normal path to a heavyweight title fight opportunity represented just one part of his challenge. The list of rules of behavior that John Roxborough and Julian Black placed before him and that Jack Blackburn reinforced came about solely because of Jack Johnson's wild history. It was Blackburn who informed the other men, when they came to him asking for training assistance, that no colored fighter had a chance to succeed as a heavyweight. That was because of the Johnson precedent. What Blackburn was saying was that Johnson had spoiled things for everyone else by being who he was.

The climate of the times in the early 20th century during Johnson's rise reflected the deeply rooted prejudice of Americans. It was unthinkable for whites to acknowledge the superiority of a black man in so primal an endeavor as boxing. Too scary. The inner workings of the game were designed by conspiracy to prevent African Americans from even getting a shot at the crown, lest an accident happen and one of those men actually win the most coveted individual title in the sport.

Johnson maneuvered around every problem set in his way and triumphed anyway. Then he compounded this felony in the eyes of the white discriminators by gloating, celebrating, and flat-out enjoying the hell out of being heavyweight champ and by dating and marrying white women (probably the larger sin). Johnson made himself into the symbol of the weakest white men's nightmares. He was a big, strong, powerful, black man accomplished with his fists, and God Almighty he was bedding white women, too! Oh, how they hated him.

So the Johnson of the recent past presented the image of the heavyweight black fighter that Louis had to conquer to get where he wanted to go. The white world's cry after Johnson lost his title was "Never again!" Clearly, Johnson and Louis were two different people. Clearly, what Johnson did with his life had nothing to do with what Louis was trying to do with his. But nonetheless, they were inseparable in many minds.

Johnson's notoriety is part of his legend, but what he is notorious for is really only a part of his story. Given how Muhammad Ali was eventually accepted despite his braggadocio, and how comparatively forward-thinking America seems in the area of interracial marriage today, perhaps Johnson was simply born in the wrong century.

John Arthur Johnson was born on March 31, 1878, in Galveston, Texas. He boxed 114 times, winning 80 bouts, losing eight, recording 12 draws, and competing in 14 no-contests. He won the heavyweight championship in 1908 and held it until 1915. He was a worthy contender long before he was able to obtain a shot at the title. He had to chase champion Tommy Burns of Canada to Sydney, Australia, for his chance, and he polished him off in 14 rounds in front of 20,000 fans. Only the kangaroos seemed happy about it.

From the moment Johnson won the crown there was a huge outcry and campaigning began shamelessly to find a "great white hope" that could defeat him. The level of racism aimed at Johnson was almost surreal. This was not merely back-room whispering, but in newspapers, where he was routinely depicted in demeaning fashion in cartoons. Always caricatures of the real-life handsome Johnson exaggerated, showing him with thick lips, wide, popping eyes and often looking fearsome. And the words in the articles? Disgusting in their application and venom, the color of Johnson's skin was mentioned

and described in such fashion as to dehumanize and insult. He was referred
to in print as "the Texas Darky," or "big smoke," or "coon."[1]

Also, although Johnson's southern-tinted English was quite intelligible
to those who heard him speak, the words he uttered turned into barely com-
prehensible sounds when translated for white audiences, as if Johnson had
just arrived off a boat from the jungle.

It is doubtful that any minority public figure in American history was
more vilified and eviscerated than Johnson.

The man who struck such fear and loathing in white Americans once
said, "There ain't gonna be but one Jack Johnson." He was right, but not
for the reasons he surmised. Johnson was unique, for sure, because of who
he was, not what he symbolized. Johnson's personality would have stood out
at any time, though not necessarily for what was singled out during his lifetime.

There were two aspects to the Johnson phenomenon that defined his life
and also affected Joe Louis'. One was his boxing skill. The other was his personality. Of Johnson's fighting prowess there is no question. He was as good
as he thought he was and he could lick any man around, anywhere in the
round world. His personality was extra-large. He played in vaudeville, he
dressed so fine, he spent money lavishly on creature comforts such as slick
clothes often topped by a derby and accompanied by a cane and big cars, and
he had a gold tooth that he flaunted with pleasure when he smiled big and
broad. Of course there were the women.

If it was his personal taste to prefer white women for sexual companions
and marriageable ones, then that was his right, even if almost no one else during his prime thought so. He did not sneak around. He did not pretend. He
did not live a double life. He lived the only life he had the way he chose to
and didn't countenance interference, although just about everyone wanted to
interfere.

Dispensing with the emotion attached to Johnson, he was indeed a fabulous American character, the stuff of great story-telling. Not only did he
reach the pinnacle of his profession, he had to overcome childhood economic
deprivation. He was colorful and outspoken. He dared to be great. And
although reality was complex enough, as he aged Johnson wove a personal
history that was equal parts fact and fiction, as if he was standing behind a
bar making a mixed drink.

It wasn't as if Johnson was a homebody who kept returning to Galveston
after he hit it big, but he was one of nine children with strong roots in Texas.
But not even Texas-sized was big enough for his thinking, and once he realized
his fists could take him on a long journey he set out on it. He rode the rails

and engaged in battle royals in big cities to get noticed, somewhat ridiculously fighting four men at once.

The sport of boxing was described as "the Sweet Science" by writer A.J. Liebling years later, but long before that Johnson was a practitioner. As powerfully muscled as his arms were, and with his own capability of hitting foes so they felt as if bricks were descending on their heads, Johnson was a wise fighter stressing defense first. He worked harder at making opponents miss than he did at clobbering them — at least in the early rounds.

It was a strategy that let the other man's energy play out so that when he was ready Johnson could pick him apart. "It's not how hard you hit that other fella," Johnson said. "It's how tired he gets tryin' to hit you."[2]

Johnson's first recorded official bout was a second-round knockout of another gent named Charley Brooks on November 1, 1897, in Galveston. This victory gave him the somewhat limited Texas middleweight title. As the years passed, the miles mounted up, and Johnson gained weight, he campaigned all over the United States, with fights in Chicago, Memphis, Denver, Bakersfield in California, Oakland, Waterbury in Connecticut, Los Angeles, Victor in Colorado, San Francisco, Boston, Philadelphia, Colma in California, Chelsea in Massachusetts, Baltimore, New York, Topeka in Kansas, Wilkes-Barre in Pennsylvania, Gloucester in Massachusetts, Millinocket in Maine, Lancaster in Pennsylvania, and finally, on November 26, 1906 in Portland, Maine.

By then, Johnson, who could hardly be expected to recall which town he was in for which fight, had a record of 39-5-8 and held the title of "World Colored Heavyweight" champion, certainly an honor less than separate and equal. Still, there might as well have been a tall concrete wall with barbed wire on top between Johnson and the real heavyweight championship. He embarked to Australia to campaign in 1907 and introduced himself Down Under with two victories. On July 17, 1907, in Philadelphia, Johnson scored probably his most notable triumph to date.

Bob Fitzsimmons was from Cornwall, England, and he was the first boxer to win a world championship in three weight classes. Regarded as a heavy hitter, Fitzsimmons was instead punched out by Johnson in two rounds in Philadelphia. The win improved Johnson's reputation, but merely frightened off other opponents.

Johnson's tour continued with fights in Reading, Pennsylvania, Bridgeport, Connecticut, San Francisco again, and Plymouth, England. At last Burns agreed to meet him with the true heavyweight title at stake. Australia was no bastion of equality for a black man and Johnson was greeted by the typical spewing of racist commentary in the local papers when he arrived and as he prepared for the bout.

On fight day Burns, who was 5-foot-7, weighed in at 167 pounds, an unheard of low amount for a heavyweight, while Johnson distributed 192 pounds on his seven-inch taller body. Shades of Muhammad Ali and opponents much later, but also likely to be examples of true venom, Burns and Johnson insulted each other vigorously in the days leading up to the fight. That kind of give-and-take has always helped sell tickets to matches, though it seems likely the disdain was genuine this time.

Johnson's personal defensive style played a role from the first bell. He infuriated Burns when the head-strong champ came at him, prompting Burns to utter such phrases as "Come on and fight, nigger!" Also, "Fight like a white man!"[3] Johnson had the ability to ignore hateful words. It was a case of sticks and stones may break my bones, but words will never hurt me.

Johnson did his thing, wounding Burns with well-placed punches and in the 14th round, as he dominated, the police stepped in to perhaps save the outgoing champ a worse beating. Descriptions of the fateful end to the historic fight indicate that fans seemed to be in a kind of shock. They were quiet as Johnson was declared the new champion. That was the last time fight fans or fight figures were quiet about anything Jack Johnson did. Almost from the instant he won the title there was a groundswell of urgent emotion, of plotting, planning, pleas, all designed to find the proper white man who could whip Johnson and seize the title back for the white race, to rectify this mistake.

That was not so easy to arrange. Johnson was too good and genuine contenders too few. There was an immense lobbying effort to talk former champ James J. Jeffries out of retirement and restore white supremacy.

Jeffries became heavyweight champ in 1899 by defeating Fitzsimmons, and he held the title through 1904 when he retired. Jeffries was a very athletic man, a sprinter and high jumper of some skill, and he weighed 225 pounds in his 19-0-2 undefeated fighting years. He handled Fitzsimmons twice and Gentleman Jim Corbett twice during his reign. But he had been retired for six years when he allowed himself to be talked into the fool's errand of saving face for the white race and meeting Johnson. As an illustration of how hopeless his task was, Jeffries had ballooned into a gargantuan figure and had to lose 100 pounds to get back to fighting weight.

Pressure mounted and Jeffries got swept up in the fantasy. The hugely hyped fight with the fierceness of hatred fueling some of the emotion resulted in a tremendous letdown for Jeffries' backers. The fight took place in Reno, Nevada, in a specially constructed ring, and Johnson prevailed by technical knockout in 15 rounds. Johnson battered Jeffries bloody. Most tellingly, Jeffries admitted, "I could never have whipped Jack Johnson at my best."[4] It was an admission the racists did not want to hear, but a truth Jeffries felt compelled to utter.

It appeared that Jeffries was the only level-headed realist in the land after he was battered. In an astounding series of events and display of hatred that would be beyond unfathomable now in response to the result, riots broke out in numerous cities. Stunningly, in some places whites outraged by Jeffries' failure prowled looking to beat up or murder innocent black people on the streets. From Little Rock to Shreveport to New Orleans, from Washington, D.C., to Pueblo, Colorado, and elsewhere, there was violence in the streets. As insane as it sounds from the view of hindsight nearly 100 years later, there was a segment of the white community that simply could not abide the ascension of a black heavyweight champion.

After Jeffries, there really was no white contender in line for a title shot. A few non-descript boxers took their chances and Johnson took care of them. Johnson made sure he had fun as champ. He partied when he felt like it, drank too much, was seen in the company of white women, married and divorced some of them. Seemingly everything he did enraged popular opinion. The voices raised against him were unreasonable, unconscionable, racist, and intense.

Johnson was hounded where he traveled and ultimately forces ganged up on him sufficiently to have him prosecuted for violation of the Mann Act, the law prohibiting the transporting of women across state lines for illicit purposes. At one point while he was jailed, the white prisoners, estimated at 530 in number, chanted, "Hang Johnson!"[5] And those were criminals. Lord only knew how the so-called decent people felt.

Johnson fled the country, jumping bail, and when he finally lost the heavyweight title on April 5, 1915, to Jess Willard, it was in Havana, Cuba. He was not at his finest, having spent too much time on the run and imbibing and too little time training. When Johnson was counted out in the 26th round in the searing heat, he lay on the canvas, one arm seemingly shielding his eyes from the sun. There was speculation he could have gotten up and continued, but either gave up or was throwing the fight. But he may well have been worn out and worn down.

The pitfalls of Johnson's career, from his gaudy style to his superiority attitude, were what Louis' managers wished to avoid. After Louis turned professional and began winning and gaining attention, Johnson, who was still living but had lost his fortune, endeavored to meet him and even sought to convince Louis and his entourage that he should become his trainer. The last thing Roxborough and Black wanted was to embrace Johnson and have him in the inner circle. They rebuffed him. Louis' management feared that any misstep would draw comparisons to Johnson, though Louis was polite to the one-time champ and to that point the only African American heavyweight champ.

Later, in his autobiography, Louis recounted his first impression of the man of whom he had heard so much. "My biggest thrill up there [at training camp in Pompton Lakes, New Jersey] had been to meet the last black heavyweight champion, Jack Johnson," Louis said. "I liked him. He never mentioned the problems he was having and never asked for any money or anything. He was an impressive-looking guy and a good talker. He told me I was going to run into every kind of situation possible and he wanted me to keep my head at all times."[6]

The commentary on that encounter was reported decades later and long after Johnson died in a car crash in June of 1946, and maybe Louis was feeling mellow. But when Johnson was still alive there was some tension between the sides. Johnson sometimes predicted defeat for Louis in big fights when Louis prevailed, and that did not generate warmth.

Periodically, it seemed, a sports writer was hoping to goad Louis into badmouthing Johnson, but he did not choose to take that bait, usually opting for a live-and-let-live approach. "Every man's got a right to his own mistakes," Louis said. "Ain't no man that ain't made none. When I got to be champ, half the letters I got mentioned Jack Johnson, lot of them from old colored people. They thought he disgraced the Negro, but I figure he did what he wanted to do and that didn't affect me."[7]

Jack Johnson's life and career most closely paralleled Muhammad Ali's, among other heavyweight champions, but Ali did not come along until much later, when it was routine for a black man to be the star of the heavyweight division. Ali was vilified for changing his name from Cassius Clay, the name he called his "slave name," for changing his religion and joining the Black Muslims, and for opposing the Vietnam War and becoming a conscientious objector. There was more than enough on Ali's plate without being vilified for sexual escapades. But he was bold and brash, just like Johnson. He was the best heavyweight of his time, just like Johnson. And he was a magnet for criticism and hatred, just like Johnson.

With his showman ways, his love of the limelight and his disdain for convention, Johnson would have been more at home in 21st century America than he was in 20th century America.

What Joe Louis had in common with Jack Johnson was minimal. They were both heavyweights and they were both black men, though Johnson was dark-skinned and Louis was light-skinned. While Johnson's personality demanded that he be out front gathering attention like a heat-seeking missile,

Louis preferred to hang back. He tried to never say a controversial word. He was a man of apparently immense sexual appetites and with no shortage of women who wished to explore his firm muscles, but he was absolute in his discretion of affairs with white women.

By the 1930s, as Louis rose through the heavyweight ranks, Jack Johnson had been the only African American heavyweight champ. It was inevitable that the two men be compared. Roxborough, Black and Blackburn understood that when those comparisons were made that it was imperative that Louis be viewed as everything Johnson was not. If Louis was ever to earn his way to the top without promoters, matchmakers and boxing commissioners lining up to stop him, he had to be the anti–Johnson.

Louis had no choice. He was fortunate that his natural personality inclined him in the same direction his handlers demanded. Jack Johnson was still a vivid presence in boxing fans' minds. He was still very much a live presence in the boxing world. It was a tricky and difficult assignment to both pay Johnson deference for what he had achieved and put miles between him and Louis in terms of personal style.

For all of his greatness as a fighter, which was acknowledged first, it was Louis' gradually revealed character and demeanor, which became fully formed and fully appreciated with the passage of time, that distinguished him as much more than a sports hero. Not only did Louis have to relegate Johnson to the past to succeed, but the nation had to mentally distance itself from Johnson for Louis to succeed.

As for Johnson, the more time passed, the more his life was appreciated, and the more readily the injustice that he suffered was recognized. On Broadway, his achievements were assessed in the play *The Great White Hope* that opened in 1968 and also became a movie. He was elected to the International Boxing Hall of Fame. In 2004 a book titled *Unforgivable Blackness* appeared and became an in-depth documentary of Johnson's life filmed by the estimable Ken Burns.

Johnson had not been a conscious pioneer. He had been out for himself, No. 1, when he began his boxing career, and even as it progressed. Still, the racial overtones of the time, holding the average black man down, infected him and Johnson later said he "believed it was his duty to uplift the black race."[8]

Whether he did so or not is not easily answered. There were pluses and minuses in his accomplishments and actions, but in no way did Jack Johnson deserve the vilification he received.

7

Going Pro

Joe Louis was still an amateur when John Roxborough assessed his potential, and the young man's new manager hoped to guide Louis through a polishing process before he turned pro. He wanted to delay his protégé's advancement just a little longer, perhaps like a fourth grader being held back in school for a year to gain in confidence and size so that it would pay off later.

But that was just the issue with Louis. As cool as he thought it was winning merchandise prizes worth $25 at first, he wanted to be paid for his fisticuffs as soon as possible. His was a family in need in Depression Era Detroit and you couldn't eat trinkets like clocks. Hard cash, as always, was the principal currency of doing business, and in Louis' family there was hardly a surplus.

As generous as Roxborough was with Louis, feeding him, clothing him, and providing a roof over his head, Louis wanted more. He wanted to earn his way. He also spent enough time at the gym where he had to recognize that he was better than many of the pugilists acting as professionals.

Roxborough, Julian Black and Jack Blackburn had established the rules, almost like Joe Louis' personal Ten Commandments, of how they wanted the fighter to behave in public. Blackburn had been working with Louis on his form, his style, his punching, teaching him how to better employ his left hand to advantage, his rules of the ring. One day Louis just decided it was time to make the move and that 54 amateur fights for him were enough, especially with national championships in hand. In his mind, it was time to chase the bucks.

As the spring of 1934 approached, Louis informed Roxborough, his protector, where his head was at. "Mr. Roxborough," he said, "I want the money." Roxborough, someone who had been impatient about his own future when he was a young man, could relate. "That I could understand," Roxborough said. "That was why I was in the numbers racket — and I was never ashamed of it."[1]

One story about his training that followed Louis was told as both proof of his naivety and his devotion to Blackburn. Although Louis appeared to learn from the first and he and Blackburn hit it off immediately, Blackburn tested Louis to see if he really would listen to him when he invoked his authority. One day early in their relationship Blackburn told Louis he had to drink two quarts of hot beef blood to build his strength.

Louis returned to the gym sometime later, all apologetic. He said he just could not make himself do that and if that meant Blackburn wouldn't train him, then so be it. Blackburn smiled, and said, no, that was all right, he would manage without that booster. Although theirs would always technically be a business partnership, it is clear that there were elements of a father-son relationship between Blackburn and Louis.

Once Roxborough and Black committed to Blackburn as Louis' trainer, the entire operation was headquartered in Chicago. Louis was still only 19 and he was not really a full-fledged heavyweight yet. He was too big for the 175-pound light-heavyweight division, but he was no 200-pounder. That would come later.

As an amateur, Roxborough could take his time guiding Louis' career, waiting for his young fighter to mature. Once he turned pro, however, Louis was on the path that would either lead to the heavyweight championship or bust. He still didn't have to be rushed, but sometimes when a young heavyweight, especially an exciting one, moved into the public eye, pressures grew to speed along the arc of his career. Forces bigger than the four men could intervene and affect any carefully laid out game plans.

Joe Louis made his professional boxing debut on July 4, 1934, at Bacon's Arena in Chicago. His opponent, Jack Kracken, was more seasoned than many handlers would have bargained for in selecting a prized property's rookie fight opponent. While in retrospect Kracken was not much of a threat, at the time his experience made it seem so. Kracken was born in Lillehammer, Norway, and his birth name was Emil Ecklund. His entire boxing career was compressed into the years 1930 to 1934 and his lifetime record was 10–7.

Louis' amateur career had begun with the wrong choice of foe and he had been soundly whipped. There were hopes that fighting Kracken was not an instant-replay mistake. Before the scheduled six-round bout, Izzy Klein, a trainer of some top talent such as Barney Ross, remembered another manager making the comment, "Those guys [Louis' handlers] must be nuts. Kracken will kill that boy. Louis is in over his head."[2]

That would be one of the few times in his boxing career Louis would be underestimated. As was to be expected, Louis admitted later that he was very nervous for his first fight in the pros. "I was scared," he said. "This was my first fight for real money. The other guy was white and looked like he'd been around. He looked confident in the ring. But Chappie [Blackburn] told me not to worry. He told me to hit him in the belly until I brought his guard down, then go for the jaw. I did what he told me and it worked."[3] That was not the last time that Louis followed Blackburn's advice to perfection.

One of the gospel philosophies of boxing is that if you kill the body, the head will follow. The often underutilized strategy of employing body punches rather than penetrating to the head and face regularly pays off. For those who only saw Louis later in his career when he had become a contender or the champion, there would have been surprise expressed at his reaction to the victory. Louis jumped in the air in celebration after he stopped Kracken.

This was a no-no for his management team. One reason Jack Johnson had been so despised was his post-fight gloating over fallen white opponents. Later in his career sports writers took note of how Louis didn't even smile after demolishing an opponent in the ring. That trait led to Louis being described as a cold-blooded hitter. Actually, after the bout with Kracken, Blackburn ordered Louis to tone down his enthusiasm. "You're gonna knock out a lot of guys before you're done," Blackburn said. "You can't get carried away with it every time. You got to take it in stride. Don't show your emotions."[4]

Louis slugged Kracken into submission in the first round. The young man from Detroit was 1–0 as a professional and it took less than three minutes. Still, Louis' team wondered why he didn't appear sharper. Turns out Louis, unbeknownst to them and contrary to any known plan for nutrition, had ingested a dozen bananas before the fight. "After that, everybody watched me like a hawk before every fight," Louis said.[5] Just so he didn't eat himself out of a victory.

The entire purse for Louis' endeavors was $59. Rather than take the traditional manager and trainer cuts, Louis' management team didn't even bother, allowing him to keep the cash. They did this for a number of his early bouts, all of which were low paying. Losing to Louis was the most famous and best-remembered performance of Kracken's pro career.

At the time $59 seemed like a fine payday for Louis. "Well, when I got that first check I just couldn't believe it," Louis said. "Fifty-nine dollars. It looked pretty good to me for two minutes worth of work."[6] He sent most of the money home to his mother and used the remainder on incidentals like hot dogs and hamburgers. He called it eating junk food and saved a little to spend on a night of bowling. He also mused later that within a couple of years he passed out $50 bills as tips.

Once Louis was in the pro ranks his team wanted to keep him busy. Eight days after Louis finished off Kracken he won his second fight, a third-round technical knockout of Willie Davis, also in Chicago, 2–0. Before July was through Louis went to 3–0 with a second-round technical knockout of Larry Udell. In August he won twice more, for the first time by decision over eight rounds, against Jack Kranz, and again by knockout in the second round over Buck Everett. Louis' first five fights were held in Chicago, numbers three, four and five at the Marigold Gardens Outdoor Arena. By his fifth fight, the bouts were scheduled for eight rounds.

As is common with all fighters at the start of their careers, no matter who they are, there was limited coverage of Louis' first professional bouts. Once he turned pro, though, Louis' handlers kept him busy. There was limited time for training.

Although the amounts of Louis' early paydays (all turned over to him in full without Roxborough and the others deducting a share) seem puny by modern standards, in the 1930s, when the entire nation seemed to be struggling to make a buck, the fighter was quite pleased with his take. Besides that $59 check for beating Kracken, Louis took home such amounts as $62, $101 and $125 for his first fights.

When Louis stopped Alex Borchuk back in his hometown of Detroit on September 11, it was a four-round technical knockout, although the fight had been scheduled for 10 rounds. That meant by his sixth win Louis was fighting in main events. Of course, with his punching power, Louis also was rarely tested enough by opponents to go the full 10 rounds, particularly in the early stages of his career.

After his first handful of bouts Louis' price went up. If he was going to be a 10-round fighter, by golly, he was going to be paid like one, even in the small venues he was helping to sell out. He collected $250, $300 and even $450 for some of his next fights as his name spread and he developed a Chicago following.

As the good boy he had been raised to be, Louis did regularly send money home to his mother. But not all of it. He kept enough to increase the level of his own luxury beyond those hot dogs and hamburgers shared with his long-time friend Freddie Guinyard. Louis had been born poor and the early part of his life was spent in backwoods Alabama. Yet city life suited him, and when it came to suits his taste ran to the flashy. He invested in nice suits and then a new car, a Buick. A five-passenger Buick had a list price of $925 for the 1934 model and gas cost 10 cents a gallon, so Louis was making enough money to indulge his motoring habits.

Except for the victory at the Naval Armory in Detroit, Louis remained a Chicago-based fighter, reeling off four straight wins at Arcadia Gardens. He toppled Adolph Wiser, Art Sykes (a step up in class), Jack O'Dowd, and Stanley Poreda (another fighter with a good reputation) to improve his record to 10–0 by November of 1934.

Sykes was a tough fighter, but in the eighth round Louis leveled him with a powerful right to the head. Sykes went down, was unconscious and stayed that way for much longer than the count of 10 officially ending the bout. Sykes received in-ring assistance from medical personnel, and was taken to the hospital and admitted before he was revived.

The failure of Sykes to rise from the canvas bothered Louis and frightened him. "I was scared I'd killed him," said Louis. This is one of the hazards of the ring that fighters do not like to discuss. "I don't know if I coulda handled that. I think I might have quit."[7]

His one appearance in Detroit against Borchuk was a success, but Roxborough and the others did not bring him back there right away for a reason. When Roxborough went to the offices of the Michigan State Athletic Commission before the Naval Armory fight, he found himself the object of a strong-arm attempt to muscle in on Louis' career. Commissioner Bingo Brown and a group of white managers wanted to ease out the all-black management team and take control of Louis. There were witnesses of this try to gain a piece of Louis' hide as he worked his way up the ladder. Roxborough resisted.

The story was relayed to Louis, who said years later, "When Mr. Roxborough said, 'No way' Bingo Brown said I couldn't ever fight again in Michigan. Mr. Roxborough took the chance, said if that's the way they wanted it, then it would have to be that way. I think about it now and get even madder. Those white people couldn't stand to see a black on the rise, and if you were moving up, they wanted a piece of you for free. Mr. Roxborough held his ground and that gang backed down."[8]

Louis' hometown embraced him for that Detroit bout and he worked to defeat Borchuk, softening him up in the early rounds, then unleashing a knockout attack in the fourth. "That night I was the toast of Detroit and I earned it," Louis said.[9]

Louis's team kept him busy, and he was not pressed seriously by most opponents. There was some suggestion that Stanley Poreda, who was known as the Polish Giant, might offer some competition. Poreda stood 6-foot-2 and weighed 210 pounds in his prime, not measurements thought to be gigantic decades later, but with a 28–11 mark he had some success in the ring. Just not against Louis, who crushed Poreda in the first round with repeated knockdowns. Poreda took a nine count on the first one and another nine count on the second one. The third knockdown was the knock out. A Louis punch sent

Poreda through the ropes, and the referee actually counted to 21, never mind 10, before he climbed back in the ring. Three strikes and you're out.

The Louis entourage returned to Chicago and that was as fine a place as any town for a young fighter to be based. After the four straight triumphs at Arcadia Gardens, Louis took on Charley Massera in a scheduled 10-rounder at the coliseum on November 30. Massera was supposed to be a tougher challenge.

Massera, from Philadelphia, was regarded as a dangerous hitter at the time. *The Ring* magazine ranked him eighth among heavyweights in the calendar year ending 1933. Massera posted a 37-27-5 record during his years of boxing, but he never progressed much once Louis knocked him out in three rounds. That made Louis 11–0. Nat Fleischer, editor of *The Ring* magazine, described the end after a body punching exchange: "When the referee stepped between them, Massera foolishly dropped his hands to his sides and as he did so, Joe saw the opening, crashed over a short right to the body, another to the jaw, and Charley sank to the ground, his head hanging out of the ring. When he got back at the count of five, he remained on his knees in which position he was counted out."[10]

Much more potent was Louis' next opponent on December 14, 1934. Lee Ramage, a Californian who earned great respect in compiling a 49-14-9 career record, met Louis at the Chicago Stadium. Ramage was a deft puncher and it took eight rounds for Louis to solve his style and finish him off. While Ramage was slickly boxing in the early rounds and Louis could not get to him with hard shots, trainer Blackburn had a sage suggestion in the corner between rounds. If Louis couldn't deliver the big hits, he should keep pounding on Ramage's arms that he was using for defensive purposes. The plan worked. In the later rounds Ramage's arms were so weary he could no longer protect himself.

"He was considered just as tough as I was," Louis said of the pre-fight attention for the Ramage fight. "He'd never been knocked out and he was supposed to be very smart. They were right. He was smart. He knew all about boxing. I knew my only salvation was to back him in a corner. Finally, I got my chance."[11]

Louis' paycheck had grown to $2,750 with the adulation he gained from fans who watched him finish 1934 with a 12–0 mark.

Also during training for the Ramage bout, Louis made the acquaintance of Marva Trotter. She would become his wife. One day at the gym, Louis, who had as sharp an eye for a pretty lady as he did for the openings in his opponents' defense, spotted Marva in the crowd. Even in the midst of his workout, Louis was attracted.

"Out of the corner of my eye, I saw the most beautiful girl I'd ever seen," Louis reflected years later. "She was about five feet, six inches tall and well dressed. Pretty hair, pretty complexion, classy looking." Louis was told later a friend of Marva's brought her to the gym to meet the next heavyweight champion of the world, although they did not meet that day.[12]

Louis could not forget her, and when he decided to throw a party he did enough research on the young woman who was just 18 to find out her name and get her invited. They did meet at the party and Louis learned that Marva was originally from Oklahoma. She was five when her family moved to Chicago. Working as a stenographer, Marva took courses part-time at the University of Chicago, but wanted to attend design school. It was a pleasant meeting and Louis fully expected the relationship to blossom in the new year of 1935, just as his own career was doing.

First, however, Louis made a triumphant return to Detroit to spend the Christmas holiday with his family. His biggest expenditure was buying a new house for his mother, Lillie. "It's yours, ma," he said. "All yours."[13] He spent lavishly on other gifts for his mother and siblings, buying them new clothes and watches. A handsome man who wore his clothes well and was developing a sense of style and fashion, Louis also invested in his own wardrobe, buying wide-lapel suit jackets and wide brim hats. All of it combined to give him a dashing appearance.

At the start of 1934, Louis was an amateur boxer of some renown, but that was all. By the end of 1934, he was the ninth-ranked heavyweight contender in the world, according to *The Ring* magazine. The Roxborough-Black-Blackburn master plan was proceeding on a lickity-split schedule.

If the last six months of 1934 had been a whirlwind, with Louis living up to every expectation and conquering every challenge, then 1935 promised more of the same pace and bigger and bigger challenges. Yes, it seemed, as they all had predicted, Joe Louis was going places. But also, as Blackburn said when he realized that he was going to be training a "colored boy" for a shot at the world heavyweight title, no one was going to make it easy for them to fulfill Louis' and their goals.

8

The Brown Bomber

Joe Louis had his glorious Christmas homecoming as the Big Man On Campus in Detroit at the end of 1934, and he got to celebrate New Year's Eve, too, but within days after the start of the new calendar year he was back in the ring, back to the intense grind and pace of training and fighting every few weeks.

If there was a bit of a question-mark of how Louis would fare when he turned pro in mid–1934, there was no doubt about the accelerated pace of development he was now on for the team that had full faith in him and saw in him that potential to become the heavyweight champion of the world.

Louis began 1935 more or less how he ended 1934. On January 4 he faced Patsy Perroni and claimed victory number 13 in a row. It was via points, though, a full, 10-round decision instead of a knockout. That may have reflected the festive atmosphere Louis enjoyed in Detroit over the holidays, a little slackening off in training. But sometimes it's also up to the other guy, and the way he fights, in determining if he gets knocked cold or merely beaten.

The most notable thing about the Perroni fight was that Louis was back in Detroit for the bout. Clearly, the hometown boycott of the greedy local promoters had not held and he was not banned from Michigan. Louis was already getting too big. The fans wanted to see him, and when it comes to just about anything in boxing money talks. Sellouts govern common sense. This bout took place in the Olympia Stadium, home of the Detroit Red Wings National Hockey League team. Years later the stadium would be renamed for one of the city's most popular athletes ever: Joe Louis Arena.

Louis improved to 14–0 by stopping Hans Birkie in the 10th round in Pittsburgh on January 11 and then moved on to a rematch with Lee Ramage. To that point Ramage had clearly been Louis' best opponent and he still harbored his own hopes of moving up the heavyweight ladder. Also, this time the bout was scheduled for the West Coast, Ramage's home territory, instead of the Midwest.

Slated for 10 rounds at Wrigley Field, the minor-league ballpark with the same name as the Chicago Cubs' home stadium, and also owned by the Wrigley chewing gum family, Louis whipped Ramage inside of two rounds. The magnificent performance not only kept Louis unbeaten at 15–0, but established a trademark of his career. Throughout his boxing years any time Louis had difficulty with a foe and met him in a rematch, Louis turned in a superior performance. Either you got Joe Louis the first time around or you didn't get Joe Louis at all. Time and again Louis prevailed more easily, more dominatingly, and fought better the second time around against an opponent. At the very least it showed he was an ardent pupil, a man who learned from experience.

In Louis-Ramage I, Ramage was the smoother, sharper boxer in the early going, piling up a points lead. Louis' power prevailed and he clocked him in

Joe Louis during one of his indoor workouts, his movements followed by a crowd of onlookers (courtesy Charles H. Wright Museum of African-American History).

the late going. Still, some boxing experts believed that Louis was still too green for such a difficult West Coast road trip and that he would regret the rematch. Instead, Louis showed his maturity.

In Louis-Ramage II, the California boxer could not repeat his earlier showing. He managed some good shots in the second round and Louis' lips showed the wear, swelling slightly. But then Louis spied an opening, rushed in and delivered a short left followed by a right uppercut and Ramage went down. Ramage struggled to his knees after a five count, and stood upright at eight. However, he was still woozy and Louis moved in for the kill, pummeling Ramage with a left hook to the jaw, and when he went down the second time his cornermen threw a white towel into the ring before any mathematical progression from the ref. "Louis' second knockout victory over Ramage at Wrigley Field established him as one of the world's leading heavyweights because of the standing of his victim in world boxing," Nat Fleischer wrote.[1]

The fight ended with Ramage half-sitting with right knee bent and left leg extended on the canvas, his left arm resting on his thigh and his right, gloved, hand grasping for the ropes above his head. Ramage's head was tilted back and his mouth hung open. A spectacularly muscled Louis was herded into a neutral corner, but there was no reason for the ref to bother counting to 10.

As long as they were in California, the Louis team accepted an offer to fight Don "Red" Barry in San Francisco. Louis knocked him out in the third round for his 16th straight victory.

When a hot boxer comes along fans get excited, word of mouth spreads, and expectations increase. Pressure grows on the fighter, too. If he doesn't knock out every opponent people start to question his skill, to wonder if he is the real deal after all, or has simply been built up based on exaggerated reports. Louis found himself in this situation. He was now expected to KO every man who stepped into the ring against him.

With few exceptions at the start of Louis' career, his exploits received minimal newspaper coverage. But after he had dispatched his first dozen foes, sports writers in the cities where he fought began to take notice. Louis returned to Detroit and the Olympia for a bout against Natie Brown in the last couple of days of March 1935. In a long career, Brown recorded a 40-30-10 mark and was regarded as a difficult opponent because he was an excellent defensive fighter.

The Brown fight came at a crucial time in Louis' career. Roxborough, Black and Blackburn huddled and evaluated what their charge had accomplished in a short time and they liked what they saw. Louis was popular in Chicago, his home base. Louis was popular in Detroit, his hometown. And he had done well on the road. But they all agreed that just like theater and Broadway, a fighter made it to the big time when he was a hit in New York.

Roxborough and the others were protective of Louis, they were proud of Louis, and they were certain they had a future heavyweight champion on their hands. But the behind the scenes political world of boxing was a slippery and often evil one. As black men they faced difficult odds not only hanging onto Louis and managing his career, but in steering him clear of any promoters, gamblers or gangsters that might want him to fix a fight, to throw one for the betting odds. They had promised Louis in exchange for his early allegiance to them that they would never bow to that type of pressure and require him to lose on purpose. There had already been that one end run in Michigan where those in power sought to edge their way into control of Louis and had been rebuffed.

Madison Square Garden was the Valhalla of the sport. A fighter who made it to the Garden was at the pinnacle of boxing. Conversely, no matter how big you were in the hinterlands, if you didn't fight in the Garden you weren't going to be seen as the biggest and baddest.

The Madison Square Garden at 26th Street and Madison Avenue between 1890 and 1925 was the first building of that name to host big-time boxing events. Heavyweight champs Jess Willard and Jack Dempsey fought there. A new Garden opened in 1925 at Eighth Avenue between 49th and 50th Streets and was the center of the boxing world until it was replaced by the current Madison Square Garden in 1968.

Boxing promoter Tex Rickard was the power behind the creation of the Garden on Eighth Avenue, and given the era it is no surprise it came to be called "The House That Tex Built" since only a couple of years earlier the new Yankee Stadium being constructed was unofficially christened "The House That Babe Ruth Built."

Rickard was a colorful figure. Rickard made a small fortune in the Klondike gold fields, and as part of the late–19th century Alaska Gold Rush, ran a saloon in Nevada, built the Boston Garden, and also founded the New York Rangers hockey team. By virtue of his position as Madison Square Garden boxing promoter, he was the dominant figure in the sport. However, after supervising the construction of his palace, Rickard died in 1929 from complications following an appendectomy. That left a bit of a void in boxing affairs, though whoever could seize control of the Garden schedule would become the de facto biggest power broker in the sport.

Jimmy Johnston won the power struggle and emerged as head of the Garden's boxing program. A comparative newcomer on the scene, Mike Jacobs, made waves. Jacobs, a white promoter who had been hustling since he was in elementary school, earned the trust of Louis and his handlers and guided his career to its greatest success.

As a youngster, Jacobs, whose family needed any money he could bring in, sold newspapers and candy to the passengers who rode on Coney Island excursion boats. He was shrewd enough to recognize that disparate boat ticket prices sold by competitors caught buyers off-guard. He ended up scalping tickets for the rides and as he grew, his business grew. Jacobs became a guy who could find tickets to Broadway events and all types of entertainment activities even if they were sold out.

While Rickard ran Garden boxing, Jacobs worked in partnership on other matters. When Rickard died and Jacobs was frozen out of the Garden boxing operations by Johnston, he began promoting his own fight cards at the Hippodrome. The power resided with Johnston, though, until a fateful development gave Jacobs the opening he sought.

During this time period, William Randolph Hearst's New York papers were powerful players on the Manhattan scene. His wife Millicent's pet charity was the Milk Fund program that provided free milk for impoverished babies starting in 1921 and continuing for decades. A key element in its fund-raising was a cut of boxing match proceeds.

Working on the sly, and looking out for themselves, as well, three New York sports writers who worked for Hearst newspapers, Damon Runyon, Ed Frayne and Bill Farnsworth, made a deal with Jacobs to take over promotion of the Milk Fund fights, wresting them away from Madison Square Garden. Working together they founded the Twentieth Century Sporting Club as a direct competitor to the Garden.

Jacobs was the president and front man. The sports writers were supposed to be silent partners and particulars are not known about how much they may have benefited financially from the change. Jacobs provided a bigger cut of ticket sales to the Milk Fund. His newfound leverage also made him a formidable figure in boxing promotion and standing to dicker with Roxborough and Black about Joe Louis' future.

From the moment he laid eyes on Louis, hitched his own future to him, and signed Blackburn as a trainer, Roxborough knew that one day the all-black management team might run into a roadblock in guiding Louis to the heavyweight title. The overriding stigma of Jack Johnson's reign still hung over the atmosphere like smoke from a forest fire. Although about 15 years had passed since Johnson last held the title, no black man had been given a chance as a challenger to capture the crown. Prejudice still ruled.

Jacobs was white. The entire Louis entourage was black. But Jacobs mostly believed in green. And he now had the wherewithal to say that if Louis' career was entrusted to him he would make sure he got his shot at the title if he proved deserving. That meant if he kept winning. Both Louis and Jacobs held up their ends of the bargain in ensuing years.

An official deal was hammered out at the Frog Club, a night club predominantly for African Americans, in 1935. Although it was never completely clear, it is probable that Nat Fleischer (who also did publicity work for Jacobs) touted Louis to the boss and convinced him that it didn't matter if Louis was black, he was still going to be a drawing card and something special in the fight game.

After the linkage was made, both Louis' and Jacobs' careers ascended, although the unexpected nearly intervened the first time they worked together. Rather than bring Louis to New York immediately, Jacobs brought New York sports writers to him in Detroit for the Brown fight. It was like an off–Broadway opening for a stage show that might still be tweaked.

In a grand gesture, both to the Louis team and to his New York constituency, Jacobs rented a train car for 30 sports writers and with drinks and food on the house (or at least on the rolling wheels) and carted them to Michigan to unveil Louis. There was only one problem. Nobody told Brown that he was supposed to be mere cannon fodder for Louis. Brown was a tough customer with boxing skills and although he wasn't destined for greatness, he was destined to become a hard-nosed fighter that many of the best sought to avoid because he could make them look bad.

When it came to his showcase night, Louis could not rid himself of Brown. The man with such vaunted power in his fists could not KO Brown. He did enough to show off his own skills, though, to win a 10-round decision and impress the cynical New York crowd. Louis was disappointed he wasn't able to deck Brown, who ran most of the night, but the New York guys, who had seen it all and were difficult to please, wrote positive accounts about his work. Harry Markson, later the supervisor of Madison Square Garden boxing, but then a writer, spoke glowingly of Louis. "Even though he didn't KO Brown, Louis was exciting and impressive," Markson said. "You could see this kid had it, the way you could the first time you'd seen Ray Robinson or Willie Pep."[2]

Louis' assessment of the new agreement with Jacobs at the time of the Brown fight was summarized by the men surrounding him. Roxborough, he said, was sky high about the deal, Black remained calm, and Blackburn trained him even harder. On fight night, Louis said, "I wanted to make a good impression, but I was nervous and overanxious. Natie Brown was what you call a spoiler. He was trying to show me up and I could hardly get through his guard. I had him down in the first round, but he stuck it out for the limit.

He was clumsy and had an awkward style that would make anyone look bad. I decisioned him in 10 rounds, but I didn't feel happy about it."[3]

In his autobiography, Louis said he did not formally meet Jacobs until after the Brown fight at the Frog Club. At that session Jacobs told Louis, as well as his team, what they all probably really already knew, that there was a silent conspiracy among boxing officials to prevent another African American from winning the heavyweight title. He believed that he could break that cabal with Louis, but one of the first things Louis would have to do was fight the Italian Mountain Primo Carnera. Louis shrugged and said he would fight anybody his management team approved.

At the time Carnera was a big name, as well as a big man at 6-foot-6 and something on the order of 270 pounds. Jacobs figured that with a little bit more seasoning, a few more wins, and the right hype, it was time for Louis to take on a bigger name foe in a big arena. Let me take care of it, kid, was essentially what Jacobs pledged. Many have wondered how Jacobs ever gained the nickname "Uncle Mike" because he was not everyone's friendly uncle. But perhaps they were looking at it the wrong way. Mike Jacobs was more like the black sheep of the family uncle who could fix things for you. No one else ever confused Jacobs' first devotion as being to anything but money, but he always abided by his word and his early promises to Louis. He never once failed him when it came to making a fair match that showcased his abilities, and he guided his career through whatever barriers Louis would have faced to become the heavyweight champ, as if navigating between icebergs in the Arctic Ocean.

No one ever suggested this was due to altruism either because Jacobs benefited financially whenever Louis benefited. But when it came to his dealings on Louis' behalf, he followed through completely on the plan first discussed at the Frog Club. Some said that Jacobs never had more than a handshake deal with Roxborough, but as suspicious as Roxborough was about the threat of a white power broker taking control of Louis' career, that seems unlikely. Even those who suggest Roxborough never had any signed paperwork committing Jacobs to a promotional deal said that Black did.

And Louis years later said that when he met Jacobs at the Frog Club in the midst of a party celebrating his victory over Brown, it was so noisy that they adjourned to the men's room to haggle over final details and sign the contracts. Louis made it clear papers were signed, which was only logical when all of the men involved were dreaming about millions of dollars being at stake.

Even though Jacobs offered a cash advance as part of the deal, Louis said his side turned him down in favor of a bigger percentage of the gate of upcoming fights. There would be a couple of other tune-up fights before Jacobs could line up Carnera, and even Louis promptly grasped that was like an orchestra's vamp-till-ready, to keep him sharp. Jacobs impressed him, though, as a man who thought big, who "was going for the big casino."[4]

Uncle Mike was off to take care of the negotiations for the big match against the big man. On April 12, 1935, Louis fought Roy Lazer in Chicago and knocked him out in three rounds. On April 22, in Dayton, Ohio, Louis fought Biff Bennett and knocked him out in one round. At that point, less than a full year into his professional career, Louis was 19–0. He was ready for the big-time, ready to meet Primo Carnera over 15 rounds at Yankee Stadium.

By then the fighter who had been amateur and was known only by those who appreciated Golden Gloves competition was being touted as one of the great punchers of his time and as someone who possessed championship potential. However, because he was a black man living in a racist society, the coverage of Louis' rise through the ranks of heavyweight boxers often bordered on the bizarre. Reflecting the times, Louis was frequently described in animalist terms, as if he was not truly a human being because he had dark skin. He had learned his lessons well from Jack Blackburn and the others about not gloating, or even smiling, when he dispatched a white opponent, but instead he was viewed as a merciless, almost savage killer, a powerful punching machine rather than a man.

Whether the sports writers, almost all of whom were white — excepting those employed by the black press, such as the *Chicago Defender* or the *Pittsburgh Courier*— were consciously racist, or simply unconsciously applying terms they did not think much about, viewing their work in hindsight reveals a stunning array of nicknames thrust upon Louis as he went about his efficient business in the ring.

There is no official list of terms used by newspapers to describe Louis, but they almost always linked together some form of ferocity with a reference to the color of his skin. So over time and many bouts in various cities and publications, Louis was referred to as "The Dark Destroyer," "The Saffron Sphinx," "The Saffron Sandman," "The Mocha Mauler," "The Ebony Assassin," "The Sepia Slugger," and "The Dusky Dynamiter." On and on it went, including references to "The Dusky Destroyer," "Black Moses," "The Detroit Destroyer," "The Alabama Assassin," "The Mahogany Maimer," "The Ethiopian Explorer," "The Brown Cobra," "The Tawny Tiger Cat," "The Zooming Zulu," "The Tan Tarzan of Thump," "The Chocolate Chopper," "The African Avenger," and "The Coffee Colored Kayo King." Sometimes the efforts at alliteration were mind-boggling and certainly tongue-twisting. Almost all of the time referred to the color of Louis' skin to differentiate him from white fighters. There was no television at the time, and the unusual achievements of a black fighter were notable enough that they felt the readership had to know he was black.

The name that stuck over time was "The Brown Bomber." It apparently was first used in connection with Louis on his California sojourn to fight Lee Ramage the second time. Commenting on the knockout he saw in the ring when Ramage was finished off, promoter Scotty Montieth called Louis "the Brown Bomber" in conversation. The phrase began appearing in newspapers and was carried forth. In the end, all of the other names disappeared. Would any journalist, in newspaper, on the air, or in an Internet column in 2012 casually refer to an athlete as "The Brown Bomber"? That is doubtful if they wished to hang onto their job, or unless the athlete labeled himself, something which is not that difficult to imagine for a modern self-promoting sports figure.

Although he is little remembered for his work as a sports writer, Jack London, the giant of literature around the turn of the 20th century because of his famed works from Alaska and the Yukon describing the Gold Rush, did spend time penning non-fiction stories about sporting events. His coverage of Jack Johnson, the first African American heavyweight champion was so outrageously racist, it's a good thing for London's legacy that his sports reporting is rarely read compared to his novels like *Call of the Wild* and *White Fang*.

When Johnson won the heavyweight crown from Tommy Burns in December of 1908 in Australia, London was there and wrote, "Jim Jeffries must emerge from his alfalfa farm and remove the golden smile from Jack Johnson's face. Jeff, it's up to you. The White Man must be rescued."[5]

Expressing such outright racist sentiments in print in the 2000s would have run London out of the journalism profession. Instead, at the time, slightly more than 100 years ago, it reflected the broader sentiments of many Americans who couldn't abide the notion of a black man becoming heavyweight champion of the world. The residue of that sentiment still ran deeply through the veins of many in 1935 with Joe Louis on the rise as the first black man since Johnson threatening to regain the coveted title. The nickname "The Brown Bomber" was alliterative, like the others, addressed Louis' skin color like the others, and included a word calling to attention Louis' punching power, like the others.

Only this nickname was less inflammatory. For many it was written, and said, with admiration. And among those many were other blacks who came to identify with Louis' fists as powerful symbols of the black race. It is not too brazen to say that each time Louis lashed out and struck a white man in the face the punch connecting was about far more than a blow struck in a sporting contest. The Joe Louis phenomenon at the grassroots was young when Mike Jacobs took control of his career, but it began to mushroom and grow exponentially when Louis was matched with Primo Carnera.

This was probably the first time that "The Brown Bomber" was truly fighting on behalf of all those Americans with brown skin, black skin, dark skin. It was less Joe Louis' choice than his destiny.

9

The Brown Bomber
Versus the Italian
Man Mountain

The first time Joe Louis fought for his country was in his bout against Italian Primo Carnera.

In a bit of foreshadowing for what would follow when Louis battled Max Schmeling, he became a symbol of defiance against Italian leader Benito Mussolini. The bellicose dictator was poised to invade and conquer Ethiopia, which many American blacks considered an extension of their own allegiance.

Mussolini, the man later given the backhanded compliment of "At least he made the trains run on time" as something deserving of praise as his rule wrecked the nation, used Adolf Hitler as a role model in justifying his efforts to expand Italian territory. On the surface, it made little sense for Italy to attempt to conquer Ethiopia, but there was a background of history and grudges that helped propel Mussolini. In 1896, Ethiopia had defeated Italy in the decisive Battle of Adowa to save itself from falling under Italy's spell.

Mussolini, a Fascist who rose to power in 1922, was jealous of European powers which ruled colonies in Africa, and he felt by invading Ethiopia he would not only avenge the defeat of 40 years earlier, but he would raise Italy's stature among other countries on the continent. As a by-product of subduing Ethiopia, Italy would gain valuable mineral rights. Also, in December of 1934 an incident occurred on the border between Ethiopia and Somaliland that enraged Mussolini. In the skirmish, 200 Italians were killed. However, world opinion ran against Italy.

While heavyweight boxer Carnera had little to do with Mussolini's political and global ambitions, by sheer weight of his success, he was someone Italy could point to with pride. At least if the analysis did not cut too close to the quick. History has proven Carnera to be a pitiable character whose naïve nature was exploited by others who manipulated him, disregarded his welfare, and ultimately abandoned him.

Mike Jacobs felt it was time to bring Joe Louis to New York as the next stage of his development as a heavyweight contender. The deal was sealed for Louis to meet Carnera on June 25, 1935, at Yankee Stadium. This was a major step in Louis' career. He was 19–0 and had pretty much demolished everyone he faced. He needed to step up in class with a name opponent and at that time Carnera had a name.

Carnera stood 6-foot-6 and weighed about 275 pounds. During that era, more than 75 years ago, that basically qualified him for giant status. There are photographs of Carnera where he is surrounded by other men and they do not even come up to his shoulders. In those photos he also seems twice as wide as they do. One of Carnera's nicknames was "The Ambling Alp," probably since his shoulders seemed as wide as a mountain range.

Carnera hailed from Sequals, Italy, the son of a stone cutter, and he made his professional boxing debut in 1928 at age 21. After winning his first six bouts in his home country, Carnera's handlers transported him to the United States. Very carefully managed, Carnera won 17 fights in a row. Intimidation and size played a role. Later it was hinted that several of the bouts were fixed.

Building Carnera into a ranked contender without risking him losing at the wrong time was at the foundation of the plan. Eventually, Carnera would have to meet someone with skills, but he had also come along when the heavyweight division was weak. Twice defeated by Gene Tunney, Jack Dempsey had retired after dominating much of the 1920s. Then Tunney retired.

Ernie Schaaf was a respected fighter signed to meet Carnera in 1933. The big man pummeled his foe and Schaaf died from the blows a couple of days later. This enhanced Carnera's image as being invincible and put him in line for a shot at the heavyweight crown against the current belt holder Jack Sharkey. On June 29 of that year Carnera stopped Sharkey to capture the coveted title amid swirling rumors that the fight was fixed.

Nonetheless, the gargantuan mauler from overseas had possession of the heavyweight championship, the most prestigious individual title in sport. For Carnera it was a personal miracle. He had grown up in poverty and despite his size he was not known as an aggressive personality. For those who met Carnera and craned their necks upward, it was also a fact that the foghorn power of his voice could add to his intimidating countenance.

Growing up under the iron will of an uncle who he said worked him to the bone and fed him little, Carnera said he had an awful childhood. He eventually joined the circus and was shown off to the public as a strong man. Later he dabbled in wrestling. Carnera was definitely ripe for opportunity when discovered by handlers that moved him to France because they saw in his size great potential waiting to be harnessed.

Leon See, one of Carnera's newfound benefactors, made the link with American Jeff Dickson, who was based in France. When Dickson first saw Carnera he was stunned. "Jesus, he's two heavyweights rolled into one," he said. "If he can put up a halfway decent show in the ring, he could be a terrific attraction."[1]

There was considerable doubt about Carnera's boxing talents from the start. He could fight a little bit, but he was definitely not a natural, and he was definitely in the beginning, not a polished performer. But being extra large made him a curiosity and the men taking charge of his career hoped hard work would make up for what he had not yet learned.

After a handful of bouts, Carnera was matched against Young Stribling in London. Stribling was a deft boxer who fought at numerous weights from as low as the 118-pound bantamweight class to the heavyweight division. When he faced Carnera he was basically a blown-up middleweight, weighing 160-something. However, Stribling was faster than the big man and after more than 200 fights he had experience and speed on him.

The fight ended in a disqualification of Stribling and they met again. This time Carnera knocked him out by hitting the smaller man on the back of the head. While Stribling was pounded unconscious he was ruled the winner, as Carnera was disqualified. That was the end of Carnera's European apprenticeship.

He made his American debut on March 23, 1930, knocking out Frank Zaveta in Jacksonville, Florida, in the first round of a scheduled 10-round contest. Carnera toured the countryside after that, disposing of every virtually unknown heavyweight put in front of him. Whatever his true skill level, whatever was going on behind the scenes (and there were suspicions not all of Carnera's bouts were on the up-and-up), he kept on winning.

Kansas City, Denver, Los Angeles, Emeryville in California, Portland in Oregon, Detroit, Philadelphia, Omaha, Cleveland, Atlantic City, Newark, Chicago and Boston, Carnera covered the bases. In Boston, however, he lost a 10-round decision to Jim Maloney. Before that he had won 13 fights in a row on American soil. Most of the opponents were no-names, though one victory came over George Trafton, that old Chicago Bear football player-turned-fighter.

The loss to Maloney temporarily derailed the Carnera Express in the U.S. It was time to pause, anyway. Carnera hadn't even gotten out of 1930 yet and he was on a ridiculous pace. At the end of November, Carnera returned to Europe and took on Paulino Uzcudun, one of the period's legitimate contenders. Carnera faced the Spanish fighter in Barcelona just after Thanksgiving.

Just before that, when he returned to Italy, sailing by ship to Genoa, Carnera discovered he had become a Somebody, a sporting hero beloved by the masses. Although Mussolini did not himself indulge in the deification of his countryman, high officials delegated by him did play a role in receptions for Carnera. He was begged for autographs and mobbed by fans wherever he went. He was a peasant boy made good and he was one of them, from humble circumstances making his living the hard way during the Great Depression that was dragging everyone down.

Although he is best remembered for fighting and losing to most of the best boxers of his era, Uzcudun was a genuine threat to wipe the floor with Carnera. He was the European Champion and when Carnera out-lasted him over 10 rounds, it was a major triumph. Carnera then knocked out Reggie Meen in London to wrap up the calendar year. He was ranked by some as high as fourth in the world in the heavyweight division. Carnera's rise had been a swift one. His year of 1930 was a wonder.

The myth of Primo Carnera the great pugilist spread in 1931. He avenged his loss to Maloney with a 10-round decision and by the end of the year he was matched with Jack Sharkey. In less than two years Carnera had toured America blasting out opponents, most of whom few had heard, and positioned himself for a shot at the heavyweight title. It seemed too-good-to-be-true, though just how good and how true Carnera's rise, while suspected, was not unveiled.

The fight was important for both men. Sharkey had been the heavyweight champ and lost the fight for the vacant title on a disqualification for hitting Max Schmeling with a low blow. He needed to best Carnera to get another shot at the title and he did so. Sharkey knocked Carnera down in the fourth round of the 15-round bout in Queens, New York, and it set up his title bout against Schemling. Sharkey won the event by split decision to gain the title.

After the loss, Carnera went back to building his resume. It took until 1933 for Carnera to obtain a rematch against Sharkey. But when he did he seized the crown with a sixth-round knockout based on a right uppercut to the chin that demolished the champ. It was an astounding triumph, well worth celebrating. From a hardscrabble existence in a tiny community in Italy, Carnera had become the unlikely king of the world.

Unknown to him, Carnera's management had quietly sold him out somewhere along the line to a mobster named Owney Madden, who was proud of having killed a few foes as he gained control of some New York underworld rackets. It is Madden and associates who are blamed for aiding Carnera's wins through fixes on his way to the top. Madden was a visible New York figure since he owned the Cotton Club, the most famous nightclub in Harlem, and he was eventually reported to have bought off many fighters scheduled to fight Carnera.

After finishing off Sharkey and winning the title, Carnera did go home to Italy for a bit. This time Mussolini, no doubt employing the philosophy that it is always good to associate with a winner, greeted Carnera personally. He even gave him a gift of a black shirt that was the uniform of the Fascists.

Carnera also adjourned to California and to Hollywood, where he appeared in a couple of movies. It was reported that when a sports writer asked Carnera what he thought of Hollywood he responded, "I'll knock him out in the second round." Whether he was quizzed at a time when he did not know what Hollywood was or was joking was almost beside the point.[2]

After capturing the title Carnera fought some lucrative exhibitions and defended the crown against Uzcudun and Tommy Loughran by early 1934. Both of the fights went the 15-round distance, to the judges' scorecards, and Carnera won both. The March 1, 1934, victory over Loughran in Miami was probably one of the last great nights of Carnera's life.

A little more than three months later, Carnera incurred one of the most savage beatings in the history of heavyweight title fights. Max Baer mercilessly pummeled him, knocking Carnera down 11 times before stopping him by technical knockout in the 11th round. If Carnera had been protected by onerous management and secret deals at any time, the protection had been lifted. Rarely has one man absorbed so much punishment in a fight. Carnera was shorn of his dignity punch by vicious punch, but the one thing he displayed was great courage in rising to his feet each time Baer blasted him to the canvas.

It was impossible for Carnera to remain ignorant of the rumors that hissed about his career, but it was also felt that he believed all of his fights were the real thing and that he was not directly involved with any of the gangsters operating behind the scenes who won money betting on him. By the time he was matched with Louis, Carnera, one of the unlikeliest of heavyweight champions, had won four additional fights. Carnera may have been massacred in the Baer fight, but he still was a name figure among many pretenders because he had once held the heavyweight title.

Facing Carnera made sense for Louis. He had to beat anyone with a name to advance into a position to one day get his championship shot. In fact, Carnera's side was guaranteed 35 percent of the gate at Yankee Stadium to Louis' 18 percent. At the weigh-in, Louis supposedly took a gander at the taller (by five inches) and heavier (by 70 pounds) Carnera and said with regard to his heritage, "With those feet, Primo sure can cover a lot of grapes."[3]

Until now Louis was known within the sport, but by taking his act to New York and fighting an ex-champion, he was catapulted into the limelight on a broad stage for the first time. It has even been argued that from the moment Louis signed to fight Carnera he became the best-known black man in the nation. That was perhaps premature, but in any case, it was true soon enough.

It must be remembered at that time — pre–Jesse Owens' triumphs in the Olympics — there were no African American sports heroes. Baseball was a closed door. Black jockeys had long before passed from the scene in the Kentucky Derby. Segregation was rigid, an iron door barring entrance to participation in most professional sports. Blacks did not get anywhere in politics where they were disenfranchised from the vote in many states.

Bob Pastor, another heavyweight who later fought Louis, once was asked about his association with black people. He didn't know any, hadn't grown up with any, and hadn't seen any in most sports. "It was an all-white country at that time," said Pastor, speaking metaphorically, if not literally, though to many individuals it might have seemed so. "It was all white, everybody was white, there was no black people around at all."[4]

Satchel Paige was the best-known ballplayer in the Negro Leagues, but hadn't quite transcended into white society. Bill "Bojangles" Robinson was a well-known entertainer, and so was Steppin Fetchit. Amos and Andy may have been black on the radio air waves, but they were white men. Civil Rights leader W.E.B. Du Bois was, among other things, the first African American to earn a doctorate from Harvard, though he did not quite attain the mainstream fame of a Louis.

Fame was not an easy commodity to obtain for a black person in 1930s America where segregation prevailed in many areas and many forms of advancement were completely blocked. Feeling ran so high against any kind of integration, even in so-called comparatively liberal northern states, that when Louis for the first time established what became a second home to him for training in Pompton Lakes, New Jersey, the Ku Klux Klan reportedly made threats against his host. They were ignored, but the fact that the night riders of the South were confident enough to make noise in New Jersey certainly expressed the tenor of the times.

The international political climate intruded on the prelude to the Louis-Carnera fight. Blacks who barely knew of the existence of Ethiopia saw Carnera as an agent of the aggressor Italian government and expressed resentment towards him. Ethiopian Emperor Hailie Selassie was appealing to the world's conscience for help. Certainly Joe Louis did not ordinarily follow international political developments. Much was made of Louis' lack of schooling in his early years in Alabama and as a drop-out in Detroit, but later his handlers quietly engaged a tutor to work on his writing, spelling, and speaking skills. As his skills in the ring matured, so did Louis outside the ring.

Carnera was a known quantity to the knowledgeable fight fan, but Louis not so much yet. The proximity of his fight camp in New Jersey, roughly an hour away from New York City where the drumbeat for the fight built in the numerous daily papers, made it easy for the curious to descend and watch Louis spar. It was estimated that about 6,000 people turned up at his camp one weekend. Louis definitely was making a name for himself.

It was at this training camp that a famous incident involving black stereotyping occurred. Editorial cartoons portraying Louis were rife with racist images. He couldn't control what sports writers wrote and cartoonists doodled. But on one occasion a photographer sought to snap pictures of Louis devouring watermelon. He refused and staring back at the picture-taker said no, "Because I don't like watermelon."[5] It was a fib. Louis liked watermelon just fine. He just didn't want to participate in such a demeaning stunt. That was one thing he could control.

Some descriptions of what it was like to visit Pompton Lakes and watch Louis spar became preoccupied with the scene more than the fighting. While Louis' trainer Jack Blackburn sent out an all points bulletin to gyms for tall sparring partners so Louis could get used to jabbing up, others were less focused on Louis' task. If those thousands of fans who came to check out Louis got hungry or thirsty they could purchase hot dogs or cold drinks. Vendors actually sold souvenirs of the trip to New Jersey. The newspaper demands on Louis increased exponentially over anything else he had ever faced.

Although many nicknames had been appended to Louis before the world settled on "The Brown Bomber," the arrival of the king-sized Carnera on the fight scene gave other ink-stained wretches the opportunity to play with the language. Besides "The Ambling Alp," Carnera was also referred to as "The Merchant of Muscle" and "The Vast Venetian," among other listings. One writer seemingly lost all control in describing Carnera as "The Tall Tower of Gorgonzola." Pretty cheesy.

At the weigh-in, Carnera made his mark on the scale at 260½ pounds, while Louis was measured at 196 pounds. Louis was just a young man and he later admitted that when African Americans began tying him to Ethiopia and making it seem as if a victory over Carnera was going to have international repercussions, he didn't know what to make of all that. "Blacks put a lot of burdens on my shoulders," he said. "I was only 21 and I didn't know if I could carry that kind of weight. I didn't know how to handle acting for all my people. I just wanted to fight."[6]

When the two fighters stepped into the ring, announcer Harry Balogh offered an unusual preamble to his introduction of the combatants. With a nod to current events and Italy's impending threat to Ethiopia, he offered a plea for comportment.

"Ladies and gentlemen," Balogh said, "tonight we have gathered here to watch a contest of athletic skill. We are Americans. That means we have come from homes of many different faiths and that we represent a lot of different nationalities. In America, we admire the athlete who can win by virtue of his skill. Let me then ask you to join me in the sincere wish that regardless of race, color or creed, the better man may emerge victorious. Thank you!"[7] In other words, on behalf of management, Balogh implored the 64,000 or so fans to not take sides in the Italian-Ethiopian political drama and start pounding on one another. Stick to the sporting aspect of the event, he urged.

In retrospect it seems surprising that Louis was not the unanimous favorite among writers. Anyone who saw Carnera picked apart by Baer should have wondered if he could ever stand up to such punishment again. Louis was young, in shape and talented. Doubters couldn't get past Carnera's size, experience, and the fact that he had held the title.

African Americans, naturally, supported Louis in great numbers. They had literally taken a beating for centuries and with war looming between Italy, a white country regarded as a bully, and the black country of Ethiopia, they wanted Louis to provide a whupping to Italy's emissary. American blacks were just starting to get to know Louis, but in the pre-fight run-up in New York, Louis toured Harlem, appeared on stage there at a club performing an act with a comedian, and made sure to appear at the Cotton Club. At this fabulous bastion of black entertainment, he met Cab Calloway, Duke Ellington and Lena Horne. Later, Louis and Horne became a sizzling item, though mostly out of the public eye.

Louis was on the cusp of being hailed as the biggest sports star and hero for members of the American black community. With each fight more fans were made, and he percolated to the forefront of their consciousness. When fight time came, Jacobs, Louis, and his team were rewarded for the manner in which Louis had been presented and for what he had achieved with his fists. This was the biggest heavyweight title fight in some time and it was good box office. Thousands of fans came from afar to New York to witness the spectacle, and thousands of them were arriving from the big industrial cities of the north that had been the destination work places of the displaced Southern blacks. Besides the New York locals who scraped together the ticket prices, fight fans streamed into town from Chicago and Detroit, where Louis already had followings, and Pittsburgh and Cleveland. It was an occasion for black royalty to see and be seen and some took note that among those sitting at ringside were Duke Ellington, Congressman Adam Clayton Powell, Jr., and Ralph Bunche. Bunche became a Nobel Prize–winning diplomat.

Also leading up to the Carnera fight, Louis' manager, John Roxborough, had to fend off Owney Madden, who sought a cut of Louis' hide, and somehow Roxy was able to do so. The most astute boxing writers also recognized how critical success was to both fighters. They were at crossroads points and the winner would be ascendant, more Louis than Carnera, who had already been to the summit. Still, if he could defeat Louis, Carnera might yet get another shot at the title. Nat Fleischer, *The Ring* magazine editor, said promoter Mike Jacobs had a good view of the future. "He realized that he and his colleagues had a mint in the Bomber and that if Joe could get by Primo, his fortune would be made."[8]

Although Louis had some experience on his resume, the Carnera bout was his first truly big fight. The hype was 10 times as much as he had seen. The arena was the huge Yankee Stadium. More than 60,000 people showed up. He was told he was the savior of his people. For someone that young, that was indeed a lot to handle. A less focused athlete, no matter the level of his physical skill, might have had his head turned and been too distracted to give his best performance.

However, physical talent is not all it takes to become a champion. What a man has upstairs in terms of smarts, instincts, and an ability to rise to the occasion all play parts. Louis was well-equipped to become a champ. "That was the best night in all of my fighting," he later said. "I couldn't believe that crowd. If you was ever a raggedy kid from the country and you come into something like that night, you'd know. I don't thrill to things like other people. I only feel good at certain things. I felt the best I ever felt that night."[9]

The insight offered by Louis was intriguing. Louis was able to control his emotions in the ring, even after satisfying wins, because of his natural tendencies to be subdued. It wasn't that difficult for him to adapt to Roxborough and Black's orders because he leaned that way anyway.

The Louis strategy for the Carnera fight was to stay in close on the big man and not permit him to wind up. Carnera was a powerful man, if not artful in the ring, but he always had a puncher's chance and with those big mitts he could clock a guy. So in accordance with Blackburn's instructions Louis approached Carnera cautiously. If anything, the way things unfolded, he gave him too much respect. In the first round Carnera's jab was revealed as little more than a pawing gesture.

For the first four rounds Louis stalked Carnera carefully, picking his spots, landing some of his stinging jabs. There was a moment in the fifth round when Louis astonished Carnera. The Italian had long been used to throwing his weight around. He was always the stronger of the two parties in the ring. However, when the men were emerging from a clinch, Louis lifted Carnera off his feet and threw him aside. "I should be doing this to you," Carnera said.[10] If he hadn't realized it before as Louis' sharp punches penetrated his defenses, Carnera had to understand then how much trouble he was in.

The end came in the sixth round with Louis swarming Carnera with both hands. Once, twice, three times Carnera was sledge-hammered to the canvas, and after the third knockdown referee Arthur Donovan declared the fight over.

Louis' pre-fight appearances in Harlem might not have been necessary, but his post-fight arrival was. After the fight he was exhausted and all he wanted to do was sleep. But Harlem glowed with joy, Louis' fans snake dancing in the streets, celebrating the victory of their hero over the big white man by downing copious amounts of booze. Louis slipped into the Savoy Hotel totally committed to hitting the sack. His public clamored to see him, but Louis resisted. Finally, at 2:30 in the morning, with a malfunctioning microphone set up to broadcast his words, he appeared before the cheering throng for a few moments. It didn't matter what he said, the people merely wanted to view him.

On this night, Louis was spectacular and his showing under the clear night sky was electrifying. It can be argued that when Louis dismantled Carnera his future was written. The boxing world was taking a close look at the soon-to-be heavyweight champion. That was for those who recognized the best in Louis. Not everyone did.

One of the most memorably insulting passages ever written about Louis was concocted in the description of the bout's ending by a sports writer named Davis J. Walsh, employed by the International News Service. Decades earlier, sports writers felt that Jack Johnson's habit of smiling down at his decked foes was distasteful. Now Walsh took the opposite tact. "Something sly and sinister, and perhaps not quite human, came out of the African jungle last night to strike down and utterly demolish a huge hulk that had been Primo Carnera, the giant. And high above the clamor over the knockout Joe Louis, the strange, wall-eyed, unblinking Negro, administered in the sixth round there rose a cry that smote upon the ear drums and left them shivering. It was the primitive, unnatural shriek of the Harlem belle, reacting to the emotions of centuries."[11]

Clearly, the chord struck in Walsh was the same thing touched in the smarmy mutterings of white sports writers a generation earlier who used their sharpened pencils to mock Johnson. Behind the words lay an unspoken fear. Just maybe black men were equal to whites. Just maybe this Joe Louis guy (or Jack Johnson) was superior to the white boxers he knocked out. For some like Walsh the notion was too much to bear and so he portrayed Louis as something less than human. Louis was not only on his way to becoming heavyweight champ, but also a champion of his people, and a symbol of greatness, equality, and heroism for them.

Nothing would ever be the same for Joe Louis after he knocked out Primo Carnera in the sixth round. He was now a national, even international, figure, a champion-in-waiting if allowed to fight for the title without his skin color getting in the way. And nothing would ever be the same for Primo Carnera. He kept fighting into 1946, but less actively. The gangsters who silently oversaw his career looted his earnings and left him broke. His career record was 88–14, though there are doubts about the legitimacy of many of his early fights.

Later that same year Carnera switched to professional wrestling. He was a hit on that circuit and 'rassled 188 times, winning the vast majority of the time, into the 1960s. He died in 1967 at age 60. At no time did Carnera ever admit any awareness or belief that some of his boxing matches might have been fixed. His conscience was clear and his mind uncluttered by doubts.

Long into retirement when he wrote his autobiography, Louis said he was never scared of Carnera, never believed that the giant's size would thwart him. At the fight weigh-in in a New York state office building, Louis said, "For all his big self, I wasn't the least bit intimidated, although Carnera kept making faces at me, saying all kinds of silly things. He looked foolish to me."[12]

Of course, in the ring, it was Louis that made Carnera look foolish. "He never hurt me once," Louis said. "I felt ready for any heavyweight in the world — Jimmy Braddock, Max Baer, anybody."[13] That's exactly what Mike Jacobs, John Roxborough, Julian Black and Jack Blackburn felt, too. The closer they got to the top, the road narrowed, and the choices of whom to fight were limited. Only a handful of potential opponents on the scene could advance Louis' career now and help him attain the dream of gaining the heavyweight crown.

10

Showdown with "Killer" Baer

They said Max Baer was a killer in the ring and Joe Louis better watch out.

Louis signed to meet Baer on September 24, 1935, at Yankee Stadium. The event was sold to the public as a battle between two punchers. Louis was the hotshot of the moment, but with a 41–8 record and a reputation built over the dead bodies of two unfortunates, Baer had considerable respect as a legitimate foe for the Brown Bomber.

Baer was known for his hard punching and his bout with Frankie Campbell on August 25, 1930, in San Francisco ended tragically. There was a messiness to the fight that underscored what occurred. In the second round Campbell landed a shot and Baer slipped to the canvas. Campbell believed he had scored a knockdown and adjourned to a neutral corner.

While pausing there Campbell made the ill-advised choice to wave in celebration to the crowd at Recreation Park. Unknown to him, because he was showboating, the referee did not rule the contact a knockdown. So while Campbell was under the impression that Baer was being watched and counted over, Baer was actually scrambling to his feet. Enraged by the slip and Campbell's histrionics, Baer ran at Campbell, who was half-turned away, and smashed him in the back of the head with a hard blow. That knocked Campbell down. Worse, Campbell soon began complaining to his cornermen that something in his head did not feel right. Yet he continued to fight.

Complicating matters, before the fight, Kid Herman, who had been Baer's handler, jumped ship and betrayed his friend by joining forces with Campbell. As the bout went on Herman screamed at Baer and taunted him. Baer took it to heart and became furious. This did not do Campbell much good. Because Herman was out of reach on the other side of the ropes, Baer released his fury on Campbell.

Campbell, who used the anglicized last name that his baseball-playing brother did not employ as Dolph Camilli, took a fearsome beating from Baer's bludgeoning fists. The fifth round was the denouement and it was ugly. Baer pounded away at Campbell, who rather than fall to the ground was trapped partially upright along the ropes. That left him open to more and more punishment, and when he did eventually fall he dropped into unconsciousness and did not rise.

Once his anger and passion were spent, Baer calmed and became compassionate and sympathetic when he viewed the sorry state that Campbell was in. He waited by his side for a half hour before an ambulance carried away the stricken opponent. Baer later visited Campbell's bedside at the hospital, keeping vigil with Campbell's wife. However, Campbell passed away.

Baer broke down and cried at the news of Campbell's death. Doctors attending to Campbell made a point of saying that Baer's unscrupulous blow to the back of the head was not a factor in Campbell's demise, but that more damage was done from repeated punches to the jaw and that likely displaced Campbell's brain.

Still, when Campbell died authorities brought charges of manslaughter against Baer. Distraught from the incident and reportedly suffering nightmares for some time, this heaped more stress upon Baer. The California Boxing Commission suspended him from ring activities within the state's borders for a year.

Compounding Baer's image as a dangerous man in the ring was the pummeling he delivered to Ernie Schaaf in September of 1932. Schaaf had decisioned Baer in Madison Square Garden in 1930 and Baer achieved vengeance with a majority 10-round decision. It was what occurred later that affected Baer's reputation. Five months later Schaaf died after a fight against Primo Carnera, but doctors said he had suffered considerable long-lasting damage when he lost to Baer.

In some corners of the boxing universe Baer was blamed for two ring deaths. In a sport looked upon as the closest thing to war, that was not all bad because it might instill fear into opponents. But Baer did not relish the image. In the movie *Cinderella Man* Baer is played as a boorish man given to gloating about the power in his fists and his ability to destroy and pound a man to death.

That seemed to be an extreme characterization. Baer was a member of the Hollywood set. He was a wavy-haired, handsome man who dated starlets and seemed more likely to act out his masculinity in the bedroom with babes. The thunder in his fists certainly gave him confidence when going up against the best heavyweights, but he was not the brute of a killer he was cast as.

Even in the 1930s, as moviemakers shifted their focus from silent pictures to talkies, big-time athletes were in demand. They were already entertainers in a sense displaying their talents to the public and they had name recognition. Baer was a natural choice to try out for films. He was good-looking, well-known as a top heavyweight contender, and he was very much intrigued by what the spotlight in Hollywood could do for him. Baer ended up making 20 movies during his lifetime, the first one in 1933 called *The Prize Fighter and the Lady*. Carnera was also in that movie, along with more accomplished acting presences Walter Huston and Myrna Loy.

At a time when promoters often seized upon opponents representing different ethnic groups facing one another as a gimmick, Baer was listed as a Jewish boxer. He was part–Jewish, but never disavowed that heritage, even if no one would mistake him for an Orthodox believer. He wore a Star of David symbol on his trunks when he fought. Eating ham may not have been kosher, but indisputably Baer was a ham of a personality. Besides making movies, he played the vaudeville circuit and later in life performed on TV variety shows. His son Max, Jr., was a full-time actor and was known for playing Jethro on *The Beverly Hillbillies*. Max's brother Buddy also fought for the heavyweight crown.

In 1933, around the time the 6-foor-2 older fighting Baer was baring his chest in his first movie, he faced Max Schmeling in the ring. Baer became popular with the American Jewish community by defeating by technical knockout the German known as dictator Adolf Hitler's favorite fighter at a time when the Nazi leader was consolidating power and his anti–Jewish policies were taking hold. In a backdrop of the early awareness of what type of world view Hitler was promulgating, Baer was inspired to continue displaying the embroidered Star of David on his shorts when he fought.

The next year Baer won the heavyweight championship by decimating Carnera. He knocked him down 11 times to capture the crown. It was as thorough a beating as any heavyweight title-holder ever took. Baer held the title for a year and lost it in one of the division's greatest upsets of all time when James Braddock, an 8–1 underdog, lifted the crown from Baer's head. It was a stunning result. Braddock had not long before been seen merely as cannon fodder for prospects. Baer seemingly had overwhelmed lesser opponents.

But Hollywood Baer became distracted by the finer things in life, partying too much, and did not train wisely. Braddock trained like a demon for what he recognized as the biggest chance of his life. Baer advertised his foolishness and how lightly he took Braddock by joking around at training sessions and at the weigh-in. The deadly serious Braddock won a unanimous decision in Long Island City, New York, on June 13, 1935.

Baer was accustomed to his anvil blows paying dividends. Braddock was no defensive genius, but by comparison Valentine's Day is short on heart. Braddock had been battered by life and he stood up to Baer's tangible blows with equal courage. He returned fire just enough to sway the judges.

By the time a match was made with up-and-coming Joe Louis, Baer was after redemption. He sought to regain the heavyweight title, and to get another shot, he had to wade through the other contenders. No one loomed as a larger obstacle than Louis. Baer was only 26, still in his prime years as a fighter, and should have loomed as a serious threat to Louis.

Baer liked the high life, but he had not come from privilege. His father was a butcher and he worked in the family business. It was said that when he was in his teens he built his strength by swinging a meat ax at a dozen hogs or calves per day and then hoisting the meat on his shoulders to move into refrigeration.

That hard work laid a foundation for him, but as he moved up the boxing ladder and met fine looking women and sampled the champagne lifestyle, he tended to avoid the hard training necessary to stay in top shape. He could get by with raw power against some contenders, but Louis was a different sort of challenge. At the weigh-in the numbers confirmed a certain group of apparent advantages for Baer. He was an inch taller than Louis at about 6'3". He weighed 211 to Louis' 199. His reach of 81½ inches was five-and-a-half inches longer. Baer also had more experience.

Baer's match against Louis was intensely promoted by Mike Jacobs. Louis, at 21, still relished long-distance running and hard training. He had a hunger and ambition in him that was unfulfilled. He was chasing the heavyweight championship of the world and at that point in his life nothing could distract him.

Not even getting married a few hours before the fight. Almost insanely, against the wishes of his handlers, in the lead-up to one of the most important bouts of his career, Louis insisted on marrying Marva Trotter, the woman he had once spied in his training camp. The ceremony took place even as the under-card was playing out before the crowd jamming Yankee Stadium a few blocks from the apartment house where he stayed in Harlem.

As Jacobs was banking a $1 million gate, 1,000 curious Louis supporters who probably did not have the cash for a ticket to the main event gathered in the street, hoping for a glimpse of Louis and his bride. Trotter was only 19, though a mature woman for her age, when she married Louis at 381 Edgecombe Avenue. With only a few witnesses, the ceremony was performed by the Rev. Walter Trotter, Marva's brother.

Rarely is there a juxtaposition of two such widely disparate events in the life of a leading American sports figure within such a short period of time.

Usually, personal business takes a back seat to professional business. It would have been more commonplace for Louis to fulfill his appointment in the ring with Baer and then fulfill his date with Trotter. But he was the one who insisted on the order of events. This way his honeymoon could begin immediately after the bout.

At the apartment building, Louis put on a white shirt and a business suit and then realized he had forgotten a tie. He insisted that the crowd outdoors was merely waiting for him to appear for his fight and did not know he was getting married. Given the way gossip travels, that was probably naïve of him.

Many of the formalities associated with that joyous milestone in young people's lives were ignored. No cake, no music. Julian Black served as Louis' best man and his coterie of boxing mentors was present. The maid of honor was Trotter's sister Novella. Once the ceremony was completed there was no lingering. Louis estimated they were out of the apartment 15 minutes after he said "I do."

The ceremony was a quick one and when given permission to kiss the bride, Louis did so, but then he was immediately hustled away to the stadium where he could change into boxing trunks. From a lovey-dovey mood, Louis had to transfer his focus to the potentially dangerous foe awaiting him with fists curled.

Baer had done his job promoting the fight with showmanship, and that helped hype the gate, but it was later reported that when fight night arrived he suffered a panic attack and almost refused to come out of his dressing room. Suddenly, the idea of going one-on-one with Joe Louis did not seem so appealing for a fighter who had shirked his training.

The source of this insider information was former heavyweight champ Jack Dempsey, serving as a Baer cornerman. He later revealed he had to plead, cajole and threaten Baer to get him to move from the locker room to the ring. Baer, he said, wanted to run for the hills and not risk a beating. So much for the future image of killer Max. Dempsey's tale bordered on the surreal.

Baer, who had goofed off in training, had suffered a genuine hand injury in workouts that could have been employed as grounds for postponing the fight if he had thought of it a day or two earlier. When he flipped out in his dressing room he said he could only fight one-handed and that Louis might kill him. "I don't care if they're both broken," Dempsey said. "You're not quitting now." Neither man would be able to stand the humiliation. "I let him know in very direct language that he had to get out there and fight," Dempsey revealed long after the fight. "No choice."[1]

Stage fright does not become fighters. They convince themselves that they are invincible and survive on that raw belief, and as a byproduct they convince boxing fans that they have the heart of a lion. If a boxing crowd sniffs out fear it worries the fight is fixed. They lose all respect for a boxer if they sense he is scared. It is one thing to be beaten to a pulp while putting up resistance. That is seen as noble. It is quite another to appear cowardly. That will ruin a fighter for life. "Fighters know fear," Dempsey said in a moment of candor. "It's like a lump in your chest. But you learn how to live with it. You don't talk about it and you try not to show it."[2]

As always during the 1930s, any time Louis, the African American contender, fought a white heavyweight, it was pointed out in the press. There was no racial animosity between Louis and Baer. Louis looked at Baer as just another guy in his way on his journey to the heavyweight crown. It was difficult to tell exactly what Baer thought given his colorful, joking antics leading up to fight night, but he seemed more self-absorbed than conscious of Louis. The combatants did not make a big deal about race, but the sports writers always made note of it in their reports in case any boxing fans missed the fact that Baer was white and Louis was black.

Maybe Baer had reached an "Oh, my God, what have I done moment?" in his dressing room during the period of quiet before he trudged to the ring to face Louis, but Louis did not waste time introducing himself once the bell rang. "When I climbed into the ring I spotted Marva at ringside," Louis said. "I wanted this to be a quick fight. I wanted to start being a married man as soon as possible, but I put all those thoughts out of my mind and concentrated on Baer."[3]

Years later Louis said that when Baer moved to the middle of the ring in the first round he looked petrified. Trainer Jack Blackburn advised Louis to jab and keep Baer off balance as he sounded him out, but Louis slipped in a powerful right uppercut and later said that when that punch landed, he recognized immediately he had Baer. It was only a matter of time.

Although that is a bold statement to make based on such brief observation early in the fight, Louis proved correct. This September match was scheduled for 15 rounds, but Louis pulverized Baer, taking him out in the fourth round. There was plenty of time for Baer to go look at falling autumn leaves.

A wire service account of the destruction said observers "saw [Louis] mow down the once magnificent Max Baer with a punching blast as deadly as machine gun fire. Mercilessly, methodically, never wasting a blow and rarely slackening a punching pace that has had few equals in heavyweight history, Louis knocked out the former champion in the fourth round of a 15-round match that revived all the glamour of the prize ring in a near-million-dollar spectacle at Yankee Stadium."[4]

Louis knocked Baer down three times, twice in the third round when he was saved by the bell. When Baer was counted out in the fourth he rose as far as one knee. There were suggestions Baer was able to stand again and fight on, but refused to do so. Baer's own words damned him on that count when he said, "I could have struggled up once more, but when I get executed, people are going to have to pay more than $25 a seat to watch it."[5]

Grantland Rice, the nationally syndicated columnist and preeminent sports columnist of his era, reported from ringside in his "The Sportlight" column, writing, "Max Baer left the primrose path, wandered into the jungle and came near losing his life. He happened to run across a jungle cat by the name of Joe Louis, the greatest fighter of his generation, and, just before the finish of the fourth round, Baer finished his ring career on his knees, with spurting blood streaming from mouth and nose, the worst beaten and the most badly battered heavyweight that ever came to the end of the road."[6]

During this period of Louis' rise through the ranks of heavyweights, sports writers were getting used to him and getting used to the idea that a black man might be the best fighter in the world. But quite often the writers employed jungle analogies to sum up Louis' performances, making sure readers understood that he was a black man who most certainly owed his ancestry to darkest Africa. "Dead-pan, sleepy-eyed Joe Louis, with the half-lidded look of the jungle cobra, shuffling out to his night's work, took charge of the job from the first move," Rice continued.[7] Rice referred to Louis as being from jungle country or Baer making his misstep into the jungle several additional times in his story. At one point Louis, previously compared to a snake, was compared to a leopard.

More extreme than Rice in his summation of Louis as being straight from the jungle and exaggerating offensively was the prose by another prominent sports writer, Paul Gallico, who among other accomplishments in life wrote the dramatic novel, *The Poseidon Adventure*. On Louis, Gallico said, "Louis, the magnificent animal. He lives like an animal, untouched by externals. He eats. He sleeps. He fights. He is as tawny as an animal and he has an animal's concentration to his prey. Eyes, nostrils, mouth all butt forward to the prey."[8]

Perhaps Rice believed that no one could absorb such a beating and continue in the ring, but his pronouncement that Baer had fought his last was considerably off base, even if Baer's wife also expected him to retire. He did no such thing. He laid off until the following June and then embarked on a 19-fight winning streak. Baer continued boxing six more years, until 1941, before he retired with a 68–13 mark. He never again fought for the heavyweight crown, however.

When Louis' domination of Baer was complete, with his beaten foe resting on one knee in the ring and the fight declared over, he was thrilled. Louis had made a statement of reckoning to the rest of the heavyweight division. He was coming and everyone else better get out of the way or be trampled.

"I'd knocked out my second ex-heavyweight champion," Louis said. "I've always considered the Baer fight my greatest. I've never had better hand speed. I felt so good I knew I could have fought for two or three days. When I knocked out Max Baer, I knew in my head that this was the turning point. All my fights had meant nothing until Baer. I said to myself, 'Maybe I can go all the way.'"[9]

Dempsey was no happier with Baer after the fight than he was beforehand in the privacy of the dressing room. He praised Louis and he disparaged Baer. "Louis is good, there's no doubt about that," Dempsey said. "It will take a really great fighter to beat him and there's no one around now capable of turning the trick. Baer is all washed up. I told him he ought to quit. He simply hasn't got it anymore. At the finish he was knocked absolutely senseless. He didn't know where he was until we dragged him back to the corner."[10]

As was starting to happen with regularity, Joe Louis' black fans in Harlem turned off their radios and celebrated in the streets, dancing until dawn, according to one report. The account was written with both a breathless and patronizing style racist in word choice.

"Delirious screechings arose from Harlem, the largest Negro city in the world," the story went. "The brown panther man from Detroit stood all but canonized in the eyes of his wildly enthusiastic racial brethren. His feats seemed to shed some white light of glory and triumph down on the thousands of shining black and brown faces that, distorted with excitement and gaiety jammed all the thoroughfares for many blocks above the Harlem River. 'Joe Louis wins! Joe Louis wins!'"[11]

Now Joe Louis had the confidence to match his skills. Also, by this time Louis' celebrity had grown to tremendous proportions within the American black community. When he won a big fight such as the Baer match, his supporters flooded the streets, dancing and partying with joy. This was especially true and common in Harlem, the capital of black America. Joe Louis was their guy. He was the Man who took it to the Man. With Louis' ascension his popularity would only grow.

11

An Eye for the Ladies

Joe Louis had what some people describe as "bedroom eyes." He may have been soft-spoken, he may have been shy as a boy, and he may not have been glib, but he had a powerful aura that attracted women. For all the time, energy, money and effort they knew they would have to invest and for all of the obstacles they knew they would have to face to guide the young black fighter to the heavyweight championship, they did not want to be derailed by the condemnation Jack Johnson attracted by mingling with white women.

Louis was much less of an outgoing personality than Johnson, anyway. His natural inclination was to avoid flamboyance. When he responded to reporters' questions his natural tone of voice was soft, not bombastic. It was not in him to brag, boast and draw the spotlight to himself with loud proclamations. To a very large extent early in his career, Louis let his fists do his talking for him.

However, Louis was very much of a sexual being. He was easily attracted to the fair sex, found little reason to hold back when women flirted with him — as so many did — and he had a roving eye. While Louis seemed to embrace the idea of marriage, there was never any point in his life (at least until nearing the end of it) that monogamy came easily to him, or was even much sought-after.

Louis not only liked a pretty face and a pretty body, but he seemed to have no resistance to whoever came along. Although his team worked hard to promote a clean, All-American reputation for him as a good boy who loved his mama, in reality Louis could be swayed by anything in skirts. The one major difference between Louis and Johnson — a monumental difference — was that Louis with few exceptions was discreet. He did not flaunt his conquests. He had no desire to gossip about his dates or his bedroom partners. He worked hard to keep his relationships secret and out of the public eye.

If Louis had any interest in girls as a youngster in Alabama, he did not report on that. He didn't admit it to anyone who recorded it, anyway. Detroit was another matter. From the time he was 14 he hooked up with a young lady named Bennie Franklin. They were a low-key couple for some time.

When Louis and his friends sought avenues of entertainment they spent hours at the movies, sometimes with only one guy buying a ticket and then waiting until an usher was not around and then opening an exit door for others to spill inside in a group. They then splurged on candy, drinks and whatever was offered behind the concession stands.

"Oh, and the girls," Louis said. "I always loved beautiful girls and I had me one, too, a real pretty girl named Bennie Franklin. She was the only girl-friend I had in Detroit from the time I was 14 till I was practically married. Now I won't say there wasn't a little fooling around here and there, but Bennie was special. In fact, she was too special."[1]

By that Louis meant that Franklin, who also had roots in Alabama, was a step-daughter of one of his sisters. Although he was knowledgeable enough to recognize that their relationship did not count as incest, he was sensitive about the family connection to want to keep it secret from his relatives. "She was a small, brown-skinned beauty with long, shiny black hair," Louis said. "She was kind, sweet and smart. The two of us would sneak around to the movies, and I'd visit her practically every chance I got. No one noticed because it looked like I was going to see my older sister."[2]

In their teens Louis and Franklin went to amusement parks and on picnics, as well as the movies, and right up until the moment he married Marva Trotter, Louis hung out with Franklin. In his autobiography Louis said he regretted breaking her heart. She was astonished that he had found another when he informed her. "I wish I had broke up with her in a nicer, kinder way," Louis said more 40 years later.[3]

Louis had been infatuated with the attractive Trotter from the moment he saw her at his fight camp. At the time she was only 18. By the time they married she was 19 and he was 21. Louis' handlers liked the idea of him getting married. It demonstrated a certain maturity and they thought it was great for Louis' image with the public.

If Louis was ever faithful to Trotter for more than 10 minutes, it was doubtful. Marriage appealed to him. He loved Trotter. But to Louis that didn't mean she was the only fish in the sea. Louis was handsome and muscular and he bared a good percentage of his body when he performed in his sport. All of that contributed to his sexual appeal to women in general, women who just decided they wanted a piece of him, or women he got to know well. He had no governor on his actions to hold him back. He was ready for action if the woman was.

Louis was lucky he was not the heavyweight king in modern times with cell phone cameras and the Internet prepared to disseminate any photograph of him going somewhere he wasn't supposed to go, or going somewhere with someone he shouldn't be with. Louis would have been found out much more easily these days.

Trotter was pursued by Louis. At the time she was a secretary taking courses at the University of Chicago. She was mature for her age, but still naïve in the sense that she misread her husband. She thought she was enough for Joe Louis, not only in the bedroom, but in life. Once he captured the heavyweight title, Trotter believed, Louis would give up boxing and retire to a quiet life with her and whatever number of kids they had. It was a colossal misjudgment. Louis was never going to be all hers. He already belonged to the world and he had not yet approached the peak of his fame.

Leading up to his first bout with Max Schmeling, Louis and Blackburn set up training camp at his favorite Pompton Lakes, New Jersey, location, but it was more circus than serious workout camp. In defiance of most common sense rules of boxing, Louis brought his wife to camp and she stayed at the Stanley Hotel only two blocks, away. Insatiable in his desire for her, Louis made constant visits to her abode. However, Louis also was not above bedding any other woman who happened to wink at him while visiting training camp.

Blackburn and his other handlers prevailed upon Louis to ask Trotter to return to New York City until the fight. She did. But that didn't mean Louis calmed down. He started making side trips to Atlantic City and had encounters with other babes. He was young, vigorous and full of himself— and if he didn't think that way there were plenty of pretty, sexy women around to tell him so.

Trotter seemed to enjoy being Mrs. Joe Louis. They were the most prominent African American couple in the country, and when they walked down the street in Harlem, especially once Louis' victories grew in stature and he became the champ, they were like royalty. Fans trailed them on the sidewalks. It was heady stuff. For the most part, at least for some time, Trotter seemed oblivious to Louis' straying.

Eventually, Louis, who was mostly an absentee father to his children and a roaming husband, performed disappearing acts with his old friends like Freddie Guinyard. They jumped in the car at a moment's notice and began driving to parts unknown even to them. It was a lark. They went gallivanting around to different cities, spending time with women, just having a grand time. Indeed, once they were gone for so long with no flight plan filed, a low-key search was begun for them. Word traveled slower in the 1930s. It didn't even seem that Louis was working to avoid being found, just that he was too busy having fun to stop until he ran out of money.

"Joe was never a constant husband," said Louis' friend Truman Gibson, choosing a rather curious way to describe his pal's marital status. "Especially in the early years when he'd be away so much." Other women "were always slipping him pieces of paper with their names and phone numbers on them and chasing after him. Of course, we all know Joe couldn't run too fast."[4]

Trotter also liked the lifestyle being married to a heavyweight contender, and then the champ, brought her. Louis made a fortune for his title defenses by the standards of the day, but he was a spendthrift. He always picked up the check when he was out for the evening and he gave away money by the hundreds and thousands of dollars at a time to anyone who had a sob story, to those he knew well, to those he just met. Trotter probably never came close to understanding how freely Louis dispensed the money he earned in the ring. He did buy her a classy place to live, an apartment building that she spent considerable effort on making a home out of the place with her decorating and design talents.

While he is certainly not remembered for his connection to horses, Louis actually had a great fondness for riding and participated in the first United States Negro Horse Show in 1938. He was good enough as a show horse rider to take a third place and win prize money. Through Louis, Trotter developed an interest and spent weeks taking lessons. Louis purchased a farm where he kept horses.

As time went on, though, Trotter wised up to Louis' philandering. Through a combination of his own carelessness and then her sleuthing, more than once she caught him with another woman. Louis' most foolish transgression was bringing a woman to the farm when he thought Trotter wasn't around, only to have her show up and remind him that they were hosting a rather large dinner party there that night.

At other times Trotter creatively confronted Louis in public, once showing up at an event where he was scheduled to receive an honor and literally elbowing aside the date Louis brought and accepting the award for him. Louis more or less showed remorse on these occasions, demonstrated by buying her gifts, but he never changed his habits. He loved Marva, but that didn't mean he was going to be an every-day, homebody husband.

Louis moved in circles of the wealthy and famous and inevitably came into contact with women who were likewise described. He had numerous one-night stands with women he met everywhere and anywhere, but he knew the Hollywood set, as well, and that led him to some trysts that were quite daring for the era and that above all, for both parties' sake, had to be kept quiet.

Although the white women rule was paramount on the list Louis' team

One of heavyweight champion Joe Louis' hobbies was riding horses. He competed in some equestrian events and owned horses that he kept on a 477-acre farm in Michigan (Special Collections, Detroit Public Library).

wished him to adhere to, he had affairs with Sonja Henie, who first gained notoriety of her Olympic figure skating prowess and then acted in Hollywood, and also with Lana Turner. It was very much in all of their interests to stay quiet about any liaisons.

Henie, who was born in 1912, was a child prodigy in the figure skating world, and like Louis, one of the most famous athletes of her time. She won the Norwegian senior championships for the first time when she was only 10. Henie was not quite 16 when she made her Winter Olympic debut in St. Moritz, Switzerland, in 1928. She captured the gold medal there, again in 1932 in Lake Placid, and still again in 1936 in Garmisch-Partenkirchen. Henie also won nine world championships.

After the 1936 Olympics, as Louis was rising to prominence, Henie turned pro and began making a living in ice shows. Then she shifted to moviemaking in Hollywood, where she crossed paths with Louis. Henie's entrée to movies was skating in them. She became a regular at Fox Studios and at the tail end of the Depression era Henie made as much as $2 million a year. Henie was way ahead of the curve in marketing, endorsing everything from jewelry to dolls for little girls.

In 1939, Henie appeared on the cover of *Time* magazine — and that was after her amateur skating career was over. Awkwardly, given the way Germany treated Norway, and Joe Louis' own involvement with the United States Army, at one point Henie appeared to have an ill-advised connection to Adolf Hitler. She was once seriously criticized for offering a Heil Hitler salute in 1936. After Henie won gold for the third time in the Winter Olympics that year, she had lunch with Hitler, who presented her with an autographed picture that included a personalized inscription.

Louis once (much later) described Henie, who was originally from Oslo, with almost a brotherly appreciation, although that was not their relationship. "She was a pug-nosed blonde with a bright blue eyes and one of the best sports I've ever known," he said. Then he added a little bit more to indicate the relationship went beyond platonic. "We had a nice thing going, but she was a smart woman and so we kept everything 'undercover.'"[5] Henie was only 57 when she died in 1959 while traveling on an airplane.

The Louis-Turner affair was a torrid one, but apparently of limited duration. That may have been for many reasons. Their lives did not regularly intersect. They may have satiated their curiosity. Also, Louis' romantic life was quite entangled. Not only was he married to Marva, but he was in the middle of a steamy romantic relationship with Lena Horne, too.

Turner was one of the goddesses of the American screen world and was married seven times. A spectacular blonde beauty, Turner was discovered by MGM when she was only 16. Always in demand, Turner appeared in such well-known films as *The Postman Always Rings Twice*, *The Bad And The Beautiful*, and *Peyton Place*. She has been described as renowned as a femme fatale and was the love interest leading lady in many films. Nominated for an Academy Award for best actress, Turner played opposite many well-known leading men, including Clark Gable. Turner's eye-turning physique and the Hollywood attire she donned gained her the nickname "The Sweater Girl." Although she did not like the nickname, there is little doubt her physical attributes earned her the appreciation of many movie-going males. Turner passed away at age 74 in 1995.

By far the most complex of Louis' affairs with well-known actresses was his much lengthier off-and-on connection with Horne, who like him was also considered African American royalty. Horne was beautiful, a famous singer whose success crossed over into white America. Horne also fell in love with Louis and wanted him to leave Trotter and marry her. Louis said he came close to doing so. If he had, it would have been understood by his public because Horne was not a white woman and she seemed to come from his social strata.

Horne fell for Louis long before she knew him. She was one of the many rabid fans who was devoted to him because of his brilliance in the ring and who came under his spell via radio when he fought. Horne was eloquent in her description of what Louis meant to the American black community and how he carried the hopes of millions on his shoulders. It was therefore incredibly devastating when he lost to Max Schmeling in their first fight.

Already well-known for her pipes, Horne had a singing engagement in Cincinnati on the night of that fight. She was performing with a band and they all listened to the bout. "I was near hysteria toward the end of the fight," Horne said, "when he was being so badly beaten and some of the men in the band were crying." Louis, she said, "carried so many of our hopes, maybe even dreams of vengeance." Horne could not contain her emotions and had tears running down her face as she sang. Her mother chastised her for it, saying, "Why, you don't even know the man." Horne grew angry at her mother's indifference, yelling, "I don't care. He belongs to all of us."[6]

She was right. A little bit later on Horne wanted Louis all to herself. She fell for him completely and almost fell apart over him because he wouldn't be true to her. Horne was light-skinned, with dark hair, and a sex symbol as well as a torch singer and Louis would have been the envy of many men if the knowledge of their coupling became well-known. They were such big stars in their own right and it made a certain kind of sense that they would gravitate toward one another. They first met at either the Cotton Club in Harlem, where the bold Horne began working as a 16-year-old, or when her father, a racketeer named Teddy Horne, brought her to Louis' New Jersey training camp once.

Unlike Turner and Henie, Horne was not given to keeping her feelings under wraps. She wrote a love letter to Louis that he imprudently saved and it was discovered by Marva. Trotter used the letter as a galvanizing reason to split up with Louis. Although she dumped his clothing out on the street, they reconciled, but only for the moment. A divorce court case began, they reunited, but still ultimately divorced. When they were together Trotter bore two children, son Joe Louis Barrow, Jr., and daughter Jacqueline.

Horne was most admired as a singer, but she also appeared in numerous movies. In her remarkably long life (from 1917 to 2010), Horne was often a fiery, demanding, commanding presence. She campaigned vigorously for Civil Rights and was outspoken when snubbed because of the color of her skin. On any short list of the greatest American nightclub performers, Horne would have to be mentioned. Although Horne wanted Louis to herself—and Louis was tempted to marry her—there is no reason to believe that he would have been monogamous with her either.

Louis did not exactly harbor a liberal outlook when it came to marriage. He had clear ideas what he wanted in a wife and he just as clearly felt he was not confined by many boundaries. He once told Marva, "All you have to do is just be beautiful, gracious, a good mother and a good wife. Just be my doll-baby."[7] It is impossible to picture Lena Horne as such a cooperative shrinking violet, and it was not any easier for Trotter, who eschewed the public eye.

Trotter had to accept a large amount of humiliation from Louis. She caught him cheating on her enough times. She caught him in public with other women. Multiply those occasions by many, many other times where she heard whispers or merely held suspicions and her tolerance level was exceeded. She still loved Louis, but she got sick of his ways. He may have been loving and attentive when he was with her and showered her with gifts, but that wasn't enough. He was Joe Louis, the most important man in black America. There were standards to uphold when she was out with him in public and pressures to deal with. Trotter did not want to have to cope with his infidelities, as well.

"Eventually you tire of it, the crowds knocking your hat off and pushing you out of the way to reach him," she said. "Fame is the most difficult thing that can happen to a relationship. Your life is just not your own. You always have to be up and on the scene."[8]

Louis and Trotter were divorced in March of 1945. Although he gave away great sums of money, Louis always provided for his wife's needs, spending lavishly on her, even if sometimes the most expensive of gifts were offered as apologies. But Trotter wanted love more than money. "Joe thinks I ought to be happy because I've got all the material things any woman could want," she said. "But it's no fun being alone all the time."[9]

For his part, Louis said he brought Trotter many fancy gifts out of a guilty conscience. Like many women who are flattered when a man buys something special for them, she would say, "You shouldn't have." However, Louis admitted, he had to in order to assuage his own guilt, whether she knew or not.

Louis didn't divorce Trotter to marry Horne, as she had hoped. But there was a high-voltage attraction between Louis and Horne. They got together, left one another, but as soon as they saw each other they got the hots for each other again. Throughout their relationship Louis was more open about seeing Horne, though he did so under the guise of friendship when he visited her on a movie set, or they were photographed in public. He gave her a mink coat as a gift, though, and he did confess to certain friends that Horne was much more than a pal.

They were quizzed about their connections by newspaper reporters. Horne said, "Sergeant Louis and I have been friends for several years and to me, like 50 million others, he's a symbol of greatness. I can certainly admire him and be in his company without hopping off to the altar.[10]

Once, when Louis believed Horne was seriously involved with another man, he thought it was OK to see her just to talk. But when they saw one another sparks flew. "She was more beautiful than she'd ever been. Nice and sweet, but Lord she had a filthy mouth. Could cuss better than any sailor wished he could. We started talking and talking. Next thing I knew we were getting real serious. We were planning all kinds of places and ways we could see each other."[11]

After Louis and Trotter reconciled from her initial divorce filing, but before their actual divorce, Louis was on the West Coast, visiting Hollywood. Marva had only recently given birth to the couple's first child. Horne was in California making a movie. But so was Lana Turner. Both Horne and Turner were sending word that they wanted Louis to come be with them. "By this time I really felt I was in love with Lena, but I was feeling like a dog," Louis said. "I wanted to marry Lena, but I didn't want to leave Marva."[12] At the time Louis solved his dilemma by ignoring entreaties from both Horne and Turner and staying with Trotter.

Louis and Horne had a messy falling out that finished their relationship. Horne was scheduled to score a golf match that Louis was involved with to benefit the U.S.O., but changed her mind, saying she was on her way to Arizona for a different gig to entertain the troops. They began arguing and an angry Louis peeled off a gold ID bracelet Horne had once given to him as a gift and let it fall from his arm into her suitcase.

"Well, then Lena started cursing me like nobody ever had," Louis said. "Before I knew it, I hit her with a left hook and knocked her on the bed. Then I jumped on her and started choking her. The thing, thank god, that saved her, was that her aunt was in the apartment. Lena was screaming and her aunt ran in and started trying to pull me off."[13]

The aunt threatened to call the police and that penetrated Louis' anger-addled brain. When he calmed, Louis was very frightened that he had almost killed Horne and was shocked by his own behavior. He could compare the raw emotions he felt when Horne got to him to nothing else he had ever felt. When Louis said he telephoned Horne to apologize she hung up on him.

That was the end of their tempestuous time together. It was remarkable that word of their fierce encounter did not leak out. And fortunate for Louis since his carefully crafted image as a good guy would have been destroyed along with his reputation and he may well have gone to jail. This was an aberration in Joe Louis' behavior and it could have cost him dearly.

"I had never known such a feeling," Louis said. "What the hell made me do something like that? I'm not that kind of person. Passion can mess you up."[14] Louis confessed this sordid story in his 1977 autobiography, but Horne did not confirm it, even then. She admitted to just one aspect of it — her ability to swear like a sailor. At the time she blamed his co-authors who had "probably concocted lies" to help book sales.[15]

Louis stuck with Trotter, divorced her, and then they remarried. A second divorce, this one final, followed as Louis neared the end of his boxing career.

12

Working His Way to the Top

Joe Louis battered Primo Carnera and blitzed Max Baer. He was now a legitimate, generally perceived genuine contender for the world heavyweight championship. In-between his match with Baer that he didn't sweat enough to worry about getting married on the same day, and the one with Carnera, Louis had wiped out King Levinsky in the first round of a scheduled 10-round fight on August 7, 1935.

Although Louis' triumphs over Carnera and Baer were considered more significant because of their high standing, his demolition of Levinsky was also illustrative. Levinsky was a top-ten heavyweight, but what was so striking about his bout with Louis was just how frightened the fish seller from the Jewish ghetto in Chicago appeared to be.

Levinsky battled many of the best heavyweights around, from Baer and Carnera, from Jack Sharkey to Tommy Loughran. He even fought an exhibition with Jack Dempsey. In a long career he compiled a record of 75-36-7. But probably the worst night of his boxing life was his brief appearance in the ring against Louis. He was later accused of "freezing" from fear and indeed Levinsky showed none of the skill, endurance and bravery he exhibited in other fights.

This may be a case of Louis' reputation preceding him. He was undefeated, he was knocking everyone out, and he reduced Levinsky to just another wannabe with a two-fisted attack that ended the fight quickly. King may have only been a king in his own mind, but he was closer to royalty ranking than he displayed versus Louis.

Whatever got to Levinsky, he was clearly scared of Louis during the last run-up to the trip to the ring. Promoter Mike Jacobs did a routine stop-in to Levinsky's dressing room at Comiskey Park and was so alarmed about what he saw that he demanded that the starting time for the main event be moved a half hour earlier. He was worried that Levinsky would flee into the night. When boxing commission officials asked why the change, Jacobs looked upward to the clear sky and made the deadpan comment, "It's gonna rain."[1]

To Jacobs' relief he had his two opponents in the ring when the bell sounded. Louis knocked Levinsky down twice and the fight was over 2 minutes, 21 seconds into the first round. The Kingfish was a dead mackerel and he embarrassed himself by being quoted at the scene by pleading with the referee to stop things. "Don't let him hit me again," Levinsky said. "Please don't let him hit me again."[2]

It was a payday for Louis. He made $53,000 for the short outing. Louis had also bet his handlers that he would finish off Levinsky inside of a round — and if he did fulfill the prognosis they would have to stop drinking for six months. It was trainer Jack Blackburn he was most concerned about. Blackburn had been guilty of some heinous sins when under the influence of drink. The genesis of the bet was an uncomfortable walk that Blackburn took accompanying Louis into the ring. Blackburn said he didn't feel very well and cited the reason that he had had too much to drink lately.

By the time Louis pulverized Carnera, Levinsky and Baer, there was not a fight fan in the country who did not believe that he was going to become the heavyweight champ sooner or later. It did seem only a matter of time. Under careful management, Louis had been guided into prominence. He was getting closer to making all of their dreams come true.

Louis had been scrupulous in at least publicly following all of the rules laid out for him by managers John Roxborough and Julian Black. He did not lord it over fallen opponents. He had not been seen in the company of white women. He projected the image of a polite, self-effacing, yet confident athlete who was stable through marriage.

Although in 1935 there were no other mainstream African American athletes of prominence (track star Jesse Owens would grab the nation's attention a year later and the best players in Negro Leagues baseball competition were not universally known) the country was getting used to the idea of Joe Louis, a black man, beating up on white opponents. They could tolerate him because they saw him as a pretty nice guy, a humble man, and as someone who was physically clearly superior to the white opponents he finished off.

There had been some other changes in Louis' life, too. His handlers got him a tutor and Louis learned some of the school lessons he had skipped earlier in life through poor instruction, his own lack of interest and because he dropped out as a teen.

When reporters first interviewed Louis after his fights he sometimes mumbled his answers and he kept them very short. He offered no insights and he didn't trust the fast-talking sports writers who quizzed him about his skills.

Louis was uneducated, but not stupid. He was deft at avoiding any verbal traps laid for him by clever talkers. He had a very strong sense of self. He believed in his abilities and he was not a show-off. He did his job in spectacular fashion and those who loved boxing thirsted for a new and worthy champion after the up-and-down state of the heavyweight division following the stardom of Dempsey and Gene Tunney.

In every possible way that they could, Roxborough and Black burnished Louis' image. It was no publicity trick that he bought his mother Lillie a new house with his boxing earnings, but the duo made sure that Louis' largesse was not kept secret. It was widely reported that mom gave Louis a Bible when he left home and that he dutifully read it. Did he really? It's not clear how much time Louis spent on reading the religious words, but it didn't matter so much to his handlers if the world believed he was a student of the Word. Years later, in his autobiography, Louis said he made himself read some of the Bible every day. He did not say how long he kept up this routine.

Public relations and marketing were the name of the game to Roxborough and Black and Jacobs, even in the 1930s. They wanted to make Louis as socially acceptable to the prejudiced as was possible, win over those in neutral territory, and didn't mind at all that he was considered the greatest hero on the planet to the black community.

The background men wanted to build Louis into a popular New York figure. New York was the center of the universe as far as they were concerned. The biggest city in the land was the place where everyone from the hinterlands came to make it big. It was true for the fight game, as well as on the Broadway stage. New York was the media capital of the world, which meant newspapers and magazines at the time, with a nod to radio.

To that end, Louis, who was by nature no more of a song and dance man than Franklin Delano Roosevelt, performed at the Harlem Opera House. He appeared onstage with a comedian named Dusty Fletcher. Fletcher made most of the jokes. Louis was his straight man, which everyone thought should have come naturally to him since he was always poker-faced after a fight. Louis skipped rope and punched the speed bag to the accompaniment of the song "Anchors Aweigh." It was like a light workout in front of a crowd of people, only on a stage, not in his usual training camp. As the wind-up to his act, Louis knocked the speed bag into the crowd.

The African Americans in the audience ate it up. Louis was getting bigger all of the time in the entertainment world, though this was not his medium.

Louis was much like the white baseball stars who dabbled in vaudeville in the off-season.

The more men Louis knocked out, the more people wanted to be around him. He was amazed that famous people he had only read about in the newspapers thought it was a pretty special thing to meet him. "Can you imagine people I always admired were seeking me out?" Louis said. "Bill 'Bojangles' Robinson, the dancer, took me around one night."[3] He met Duke Ellington, Cab Calloway, and all of the other biggest names among African American entertainers. Gradually, Louis' name got mentioned with theirs. It is difficult for the sports fan of the 2000s to imagine, but Louis was the only black sports star on the American scene that most white Americans were familiar with unless they were extremely dedicated and serious baseball fans. Those in the know recognized Satchel Paige and some other black baseball stars, but it was years before they were celebrated in everyday American life.

There were various clues that Louis tripped over to inform and remind him of just how big he was getting to be in the black community. One Christmas he went to church with his mother and was stunned at the topic of the sermon. "The Reverend J.H. Maston preached a powerful sermon that day," Louis said, "and it was about and around me. He talked about how God gave certain people gifts and that these gifts were given to help other men. My gift was fighting and through my fighting I was to uplift the spirit of my race."[4]

What a remarkable thing for a young man to hear in his house of worship. The good reverend announced to the congregation that Louis was one of God's chosen people and he had a responsibility to show the world that the black man was tired of being pushed around. "I thought to myself, 'Jesus Christ, am I all that?' Louis asked himself. "After that I thought many times of my responsibilities and I worried. I just wanted to fight and make some money and have some fun with pretty girls. Now I knew there was more."[5]

That sermon heaped considerable pressure on Louis' shoulders. As he became a more thoughtful and mature man he seemed to welcome it, though at first certainly only in the context of his broader ambitions in the ring. Louis was growing on many fronts and expanding his interests, too. He was always going to be attracted to a pretty girl and that would never change. Monogamy was not in his makeup, and an otherwise good man who proved his generosity and character in so many other ways was beset by this character flaw. He was hardly tormented by it, but that was one aspect of Louis' way of life that was not going to be altered.

From the time the once poor boy began making money, however, he was generous to a fault with his gifts. He might give a sister a car. He paid college tuition for another sister. But he gave money away to strangers on the streets and that big heart and tendency to give big was established early and never waned.

Louis was a big baseball fan — he loved the Detroit Tigers — and if practical he would have played more often. Once, on a return visit to Detroit he saw many of his old friends doing nothing in the neighborhood. He ended up funding the Brown Bomber Softball Team primarily for them, but he also suited up when he got the chance.

The fighter bankrolled the team and sent it off touring on the road in a bus. When he could play with the club he did. Other times he coached first base. Roxborough, Black and Blackburn felt it was an unnecessary risk to dabble at softball. He might be injured. Louis said they were right to worry because he did eventually hurt an ankle, but hanging around the softball team gave him pleasure.

After disposing of Baer, Louis and his crew were angling for a shot at the heavyweight title — soon. Team Louis believed in keeping their man busy and as Jacobs kept working to position Louis for a chance to win the crown, he took on more bouts to stay sharp. A couple of months after Louis pummeled Baer he met Paulino Uzcudun at Madison Square Garden before 19,945 fans in a scheduled 15-round fight. At that time some important bouts were scheduled for the championship distance even though no title was at stake.

Uzcudun, of Basque heritage from Spain, had challenged Carnera for the heavyweight title, but lost. Nicknamed "The Basque Woodchopper" and regarded as a solid fighter, his lifetime record was 50-17-3. Uzcudun was a sound defensive fighter and when he faced Louis on December 13, 1935, many in the crowd thought his main goal was to stay upright and preserve his record of never having been knocked out.

To that end Uzcudun seemed overly cautious, although some of those scoring gave Uzcudun the first round. For Louis, Uzcudun was a puzzle that had to be solved while exposing himself to the least amount of danger. Louis was patient, trying to penetrate Uzcudun's awkward style where he bent forward in a crouch with a cross-arms style and his face protected. Louis jabbed and moved, jabbed and moved, all the while studying Uzcudun's unorthodox methods. It took a few rounds for Louis to figure out his best approach, but when Louis saw his opening and slammed Uzcudun with a strong right, he knocked two of his opponent's teeth through his lower lip. "After the fight, trainer Whitey Brimstein, who worked in Uzcudun's corner, told me that he never saw anybody hit a man as hard as I hit Uzcudun that night," Louis said. "I was ready for the world."[6]

The United Press account of the bout began, "Terror spread among the heavyweights again today in the wake of Joe Louis' latest conquest — his knockout of rugged old Paulino Uzcudun, iron man of the ring, who was hammered into helplessness by the destructive fists of the 21-year-old Negro." Uzcudun had never been knocked down in 69 fights until the blow from Louis' right hand decked him, "a right which landed with such impact it ripped open a gash in the Basque's face large enough to thrust a finger through."[7] Uzcudun rose on shaky legs at a count of eight, but Louis landed three straight haymakers to finish him off.

Louis may have been ready for the world, but he had to settle for Charley Retzlaff, originally a North Dakota farmer who relocated to Minnesota. Retzlaff was nicknamed "The Duluth Dynamiter," and he was a hard enough hitting puncher that Louis' cornermen warned him to be careful around Retzlaff's fists. There proved to be nothing to worry about, though, when Louis finished off Retzlaff in the first round of their January 17, 1936, bout at Chicago Stadium.

Retzlaff did not play defense. He came out to slug with Louis and it took only one minute for Louis to analyze his opponent's style. Boom, down went Retzlaff from a left hook. Abruptly, Louis was in command and Retzlaff, although on his feet by a seven count, was not steady on his legs. Retzlaff was game, but his pins were looking for a reason to fold. Louis provided it when he trapped Retzlaff on the ropes and belted him with lefts and rights and finally one more big right to end things.

Louis was 24–0. His team wanted to mop up the heavyweight ranks so there would be no one who could make a claim on a title bout before Louis. Just as Louis continued to prove his mettle by besting ex-champions like Carnera and Baer, there was one more ex-champ hanging around, still active, still hoping for another chance to win the heavyweight championship.

German Max Schmeling was aging. Roxborough and Black felt his best days were behind him. From their standpoint there was no reason not to fight Schmeling as one of the final steps prepping for the big moment when Louis obtained his opportunity to fight for the most valuable and prestigious individual title in sport. There was every reason to believe that Louis could handle Schmeling easily. What occurred next was totally unanticipated. Unforeseen at the time were swiftly changing world developments creating a political climate that would impose their will on the fight.

Not only was Louis' encounter with Schmeling terribly important to his future as a boxer, but the bout morphed into something far more important than a sporting event for the principals and the nations they represented. By the time Joe Louis and Max Schmeling squared off in the ring on June 19, 1936, their title fight had become a symbol of a mini-war as a real shooting war loomed, and the combatants were categorized as symbols of two diverging ways of life.

The irony was dense. Joe Louis, a black man, became a representative of an America that treated African Americans as inferiors. He was chosen to defend the land of the free and the home of the brave from a man who represented what soon was revealed to be one of the ugliest and most evil empires in world history. The opponents were boxers merely seeking a crack at the heavyweight crown, but circumstances threw them into much broader roles on the world stage.

13

Max Schmeling

Given the length of his birth name, it is no wonder that everyone knew him as Max. The protagonist in two major dramas in Joe Louis' career was born Maximillian Adolph Otto Siegfried Schmeling on September 28, 1905. The German heavyweight fighter was the best European boxer of his time.

He was considerably older than Louis and made his pro debut in Nordrhein-Westfalen, Germany, on February 8, 1924. Louis had not yet turned 10 years old at the time.

The story goes that Schmeling became enamored of boxing when his father brought him to a theater to watch a film of the Jack Dempsey-Georges Carpentier July 2, 1921, title fight, but that's not how Schmeling tells it. Boxing was practically an underground sport in Germany in the years immediately after World War I. The public paid it little attention. But Schmeling was smitten with the sport after watching that heavyweight-bout film and returned to watch it several times in the same week. In his autobiography he says that he took his father to see the film after he had already seen it a few times and reports that his mother said his constant talk about the fight and his own fresh ambitions in the sport "started to get on everyone's nerves."[1]

Dempsey became Schmeling's sporting hero, and he decided he would grow up to be just like Dempsey. He did his best and later sparred two rounds with the aging Dempsey in an exhibition. Schmeling later told sports writers that Dempsey had whispered to him that he was someday going to be champion of the world. He beamed with pride at those words, and some years later when he was fighting out of New York Schmeling got to know Dempsey better and reminded him about what he had said.

"That's what I told all the young boxers I met back then," Dempsey said.[2] Schmeling could laugh about the comment then, but originally it had the desired effect of giving him some confidence. It was a courteous thing for Dempsey to do and he had nothing to lose by encouraging young fighters with such statements, and once in a while, as in Schmeling's case, he would be proven correct. Actually, with his thick head of black hair, his thick eyebrows and sturdy build, Schmeling looked quite a bit like Dempsey, and on occasion he was mistaken for him in public.

That relationship with Dempsey lay in the future, but only days after he repeatedly viewed the Dempsey-Carpentier film, Schmeling acquired some boxing gloves and began his career.

Then, and throughout the 20th century, with few exceptions, the best heavyweight boxers were to be found in the United States, not overseas. If a man wanted to get somewhere in his profession and he weighed more than the light-heavyweight limit of 175 pounds (or later the 190-pound limit of cruiserweight), he pretty much had to campaign in North America to build his resume and reputation. It didn't matter if he was undefeated, the Missouri mantra of being the Show-me State prevailed when it came to big-time boxing. The only way to get recognition and be taken seriously as a contender for the heavyweight crown was to fight in front of the critical United States audience.

Initially, Schmeling gained his seasoning close to home, competing in his first 17 matches in Germany. By the time he embarked for a bout in Belgium, he had a 14-2-1 record. Schmeling scored a draw in Brussels and then it was back to the comfort of Germany, site of his next eight fights. Schmeling had a bout in Poland and then resumed his busy schedule in Germany once more, clicking off 17 additional fights on home ground.

As he progressed, Schmeling said that he gained wisdom, as well as experience. He applied his brainpower to figuring out fighters whom he had never seen box before. Also, by hooking up with and marrying the actress Anny Ondra, his social horizons expanded. Schmeling became friendly with painters, singers, sculptors, actors and actresses. He posed in the nude for two sculptors taken with his muscular physique and got to know Marlene Dietrich. The more cerebral arts set was fascinated with Schmeling, who represented success in the realm of the physical. In his own way Schmeling brought boxing into the mainstream of German society as his own career advanced.

This was the Berlin and Germany between the world wars, as it groped for an identity and sought pleasures and outlets in a wide variety of forms. Schmeling penned his autobiography in the late 1970s and reflected on the capital city of the time period.

"As I look back from the distance of a half a century to Berlin ... I see a city of enormous energy, a hectic lust for life as if the whole world knew that it stood before an approaching catastrophe," Schmeling said. "Berlin was an open city, a city of cafes and bars, revue and dance palaces. Everything happened in public and no four walls could contain it."[3]

In late 1928 Schmeling traveled by sea to the United States for his first fight across the ocean. He was European heavyweight champion and was disturbed to discover that meant nothing to New Yorkers. He was short on contacts, was unable to get a fight, and was running low on money when he linked up with the man who became the guiding force in his career.

Thus began a partnership with American manager Joe Jacobs, who had the New York and American connections to get Schmeling bouts and to help improve his reputation. Jacobs was a transplant from Hungary to New York, of Jewish heritage, and excelled at the art of the deal, something Schmeling sorely needed assistance with at the time. On November 23 of that year Schmeling made his American debut and knocked out Joe Monte in eight rounds of a scheduled 10-rounder to raise his record to 38-4-3.

Schmeling probably shouldn't even have been in the ring. He was suffering from a fever from some flu-like condition, but he was desperate for a bout and felt as if he would miss out on a big chance if he postponed. "For a second I saw his [Monte's] unprotected chin in front of me," Schmeling said. "With my last strength I let go with a short right. Joe Monte suddenly collapsed as if his legs had been ripped out from under him."[4]

While Schmeling's overall record was impressive, it took more than numbers to make an impact on the boxing scene in the U.S. Schmeling picked off a couple more wins in New Jersey and New York and then on January 2, 1929, he elevated his profile with a technical knockout of Johnny Risko in the ninth round of a scheduled 15-rounder. In that bout Schmeling displayed the thunder in his right hand by knocking down Risko four times, in the first, seventh, eighth, and ninth rounds. *The Ring* magazine — then a young publication but steadily growing in influence until in future years it became known as the Bible of Boxing — chose the contest as its Fight of the Year.

Schmeling's record was 41-4-3 and his showing retroactively gave luster to the wins accumulated in Europe. Paulino Uzcudun, closer to his prime years than when he engaged Louis later on, was Schmeling's next foe and the Basque boxer carried Schmeling through all 15 rounds. Max won on points despite injuring his powerful right hand in the fifth round. The Uzcudun fight was huge for Schmeling. It was billed as an elimination bout to fight for the crown. Jacobs had worked wonders in maneuvering Schmeling into position for advancement.

Jacobs was also shrewd enough to obtain exposure for Schmeling outside of the ring. He sent him to any and all offbeat events to build name recognition. He counted on Schmeling's right hand taking care of the boxing business and he took care of the public relations business. Schmeling was pretty much on a nationwide tour. One thing he excelled at was mingling with movie types because he already had friends of an artistic nature. Once invitations were wangled to exclusive Hollywood parties, Schmeling made the most of it in saying hello at the least to stars such as Douglas Fairbanks and Gloria Swanson, Clara Bow and Mary Pickford. Elsewhere, he crowned a beauty queen in Chicago. That made little sense, but it was good PR.

At this point Schmeling had achieved the goal that caused him to set sail for America. He was on the radar screen in the sport, world-ranked, and now positioned for a shot at the vacant heavyweight title. He was matched with Jack Sharkey on June 26, 1930, at the Madison Square Garden Bowl on Long Island, with the winner destined to walk away as the new title-holder.

Sharkey was not his foe's real name, but adapted from Joseph Paul Cukoschay. He was Lithuanian by heritage, but was born in Binghamton, New York. Sharkey had a good resume, with wins over Harry Wills, Young Stribling, Tommy Loughran and Mike McTigue, but he was not a large heavyweight and he was not a consistent one. He was dangerous and gutsy, but could be had by a lucky punch. He sometimes seemed off for an entire night in the ring. Sharkey nearly had Dempsey knocked out, but when the champ hit him with what Sharkey claimed was a low blow, he forgot the cardinal rule of the ring to protect oneself at all times. Instead of focusing on Dempsey, Sharkey complained to the referee that no foul was called. While he was voicing his displeasure, Dempsey decked him and ended the fight.

For whatever motivation, Sharkey chose to be antagonistic to Schmeling. He adopted the Muhammad Ali strategy of later decades of taunting his opponent, perhaps trying to distract him. Schmeling did not verbally retaliate, but basically ignored Sharkey.

"First, I'll cut his face to ribbons," Sharkey said leading up to the bout, "and then around the seventh round I'll knock him out. What does he have going for him other than his resemblance to Jack Dempsey?"[5] That wasn't a bad line really. But Sharkey did not stop there, saying that Schmeling didn't even deserve a shot at the title. "He pokes his nose into our country and gets a title shot just like that. If our leading boxers demanded that when we were coming up, we would have been slapped right down, and with good reason. This German comes over here, and expects that, with two ridiculous elimination bouts, he has earned the right to face me."[6]

The June 12, 1930, bout was scheduled for the championship distance of 15 rounds, but it ended in an unsatisfactory manner in the fourth round when Sharkey was disqualified for delivering a low blow. The decision — and the title — were handed to Schmeling. It is the only time that a fighter has won the heavyweight title by disqualification (Evander Holyfield retained the title in June of 1997 when foe Mike Tyson was disqualified for biting him on the ear). The New York State Athletic Commission and the National Boxing Association recognized Schmeling as the champion.

It was an awful way to win the heavyweight title. While officials were expressing disgust with Sharkey's low blow, Schmeling was writhing on the canvas in pain as if he had been knocked out. So he gained the crown lying on his back. It was not a satisfying ending for the 80,000 fans who bought tickets to obtain entrance to Yankee Stadium. Nor was it satisfying for Schmeling. Initially he actually tried to reject the title, though his handlers told him it was his whether he wanted it or not.

Both Sharkey and Schmeling were depressed, not the usual post-fight emotional situation. "In the dressing room I was examined by the ring physician, who confirmed the damage of the low blow," Schmeling said. "This was announced over the loudspeaker, which unleashed a new round of boos and whistles. Even Sharkey himself didn't protest. After I had more or less come around, I realized that I had realized the goal that I had always wanted, but in a way that could only make me new enemies.... My crown was without glory."[7]

Almost immediately, Schmeling's handlers began to work on him about accepting the title with grace. To them it was crazy talk he would consider giving up the heavyweight championship because he didn't like the way he won it. Their answer to him was to lay low, recover from the fight physically, and then go out and defend the title with honor to prove that he was the rightful owner of the crown. No one was pleased with the result — not that Schmeling won — but how the fight was settled, so there was no question that there would be a rematch between him and Sharkey.

First, however, Schmeling signed up for a defense in Cleveland against Young Stribling on July 3, 1931. Born in Georgia, Stribling was nicknamed "King of the Canebrakes." Turning professional at 17 in 1921, Stribling was an almost hyperactively frequent fighter who competed in 289 fights. He won 256, lost 16 and had 14 draws. He had enough power in his fists to score 125 knockouts.

Stribling came from a family of acrobats who appeared on vaudeville stages all over the world. The clan finally settled down sufficiently for him to play high school basketball, in which he excelled. When he decided his future lay in boxing his mother trained him and his father managed him. It was all in the family business, which they had been used to operating. Stribling became a professional fighter while in high school and totaled about 75 bouts before graduation.

The family rented a bus and Stribling went on the road fighting exhibitions. These were often all-comer bouts with $10 at stake if a local could best the young boxer. Few could. It was a colorful, offbeat life. Stribling married by age 21, and he died tragically from injuries suffered in a motorcycle accident at 28 in 1933.

Before that Stribling fought as often as some people took out the garbage, about once a week, and included were some very serious opponents, such as Schmeling. Stribling was no pushover for Schmeling. It is claimed that in all of those fights, in all of those rounds, Stribling was never stopped, except one time. His bout with Schmeling concluded with him on the losing end of a technical knockout in the 15th round. That win solidified Schmeling's hold on the title and gave it legitimacy in his own mind.

Schmeling said he gained a grasp of Young Stribling's daredevil nature in the weeks leading up to the bout when daily for a period of time Stribling buzzed his foe's training camp in a small airplane.

The match was not an easy one for Schmeling, a self-described slow starter. Stribling seemed aware of this and pressured the champ hard in the first round. More alarmingly for Schmeling after he repelled Stribling's charge, the title-holder said he kept getting thumbed in the eye and couldn't see his opponent. On the advice of his corner, Schmeling retaliated with the same method and the thumb-sticking hostilities ceased.

Schmeling felt in control of the fight from the seventh round on, but could not put Stribling on the canvas. "I came at him with combinations that drove him all over the ring," Schmeling said. "And while his legs buckled a number of times, Stribling refused to go down. Then came the bell for the 15th round. Determined to end the fight, I hit Stribling with a devastating left hook to the chin. As if paralyzed, his arms dropped and he fell slowly to the canvas. He managed to rise by nine, but then staggered and fell back on the ropes. There were 20 seconds left in the fight when Stribling's father threw in the towel to end the fight."[8]

It was a proud moment for Schmeling. He had vindication. He was in against a tough foe and proved his mettle. He defended the title with his fists, not through an official's ruling. This was a tremendous milestone in Schmeling's life and it was even more important than he could have imagined, because soon after he did meet Sharkey in a rematch with unhappy results for him.

Schmeling-Sharkey II took place on June 21, 1932, at the Madison Square Garden Bowl. It went the 15-round distance and although most experts at ringside felt Schmeling was the victor, the split decision went to Sharkey. Schmeling was no longer heavyweight champ. When the official announcement was made in the ring that Sharkey was the new world title-holder, Schmeling was shocked. "I couldn't believe my ears," he said.[9] Schmeling said he was dazed, tearful, and completely stunned and had to force himself to march across the ring to congratulate Sharkey.

It was at this moment that Joe Jacobs, Schmeling's manager, uttered one of the most famous phrases in sport, one that stuck in the lexicon, and is still repeated, though the source of the original comment is probably not known to the person saying it. "We wuz robbed!" Jacobs proclaimed.[10]

It was one of those bad decisions where everyone else watching a fight believes they saw a different outcome than what was officially ruled. Former champ Gene Tunney told Schmeling that he won. New York Mayor Jimmy Walker sought him out to console him and said he believed he won the fight. Jacobs ran around telling anyone who would listen that the fight had been stolen from Schmeling. Nonetheless, the result stood, and Schmeling was the ex-champ. That meant he had to rebuild his reputation, rejuvenate his stature, and as the title bout went elsewhere, prove his ability all over again.

A resurgence did not come so easily for a dejected Schmeling. He did not fight again for three months and then stopped Mickey Walker. A good win. However, his next showing did him some harm in public perception. Schmeling met Max Baer on June 8, 1933. Clearly, the winner was going to rise in the ratings. In front of 53,000 fans at Yankee Stadium, Schmeling was stopped by technical knockout in the 10th round of the 15-rounder.

Worse, Schmeling lost again to Steve Hamas and in Spain was entangled in a draw with Uzcudun. Schmeling's rep took a beating more than his face did. In his previous five fights his record was 1-3-1. That is a fine number if a team is playing a zone offense, but not if it represents wins, losses and draws. Schmeling's career was on the ropes. People were saying he was washed up, that he had suddenly got old.

Distressed, but not ready to retire, not ready to give up, Schmeling redoubled his training efforts and dedication and embarked on a series of wins, gaining revenge over some of those who had just taken advantage of him. Schmeling first won fights back in Germany over the new crop of contenders, Walter Neusel and Hamas. Then he bested Uzcudun on points in 12 rounds, this time in his own country instead of Uzcudun's.

Victories over Henry Thomas, Ben Foord and Steve Dudas restored some of Schmeling's credibility. The vulnerability shown during Schmeling's five-fight mediocre stretch, however, stuck in the minds of John Roxborough, Julian Black and Jack Blackburn, Louis' backers. They felt their man could easily handle an aging Schmeling and could gain in stature because Schmeling had a sound 48-7-4 record and was the former champion.

Schmeling rated as the seemingly perfect opponent for Louis. He was a step up in class, he had a name, but he did not seem terribly dangerous. And Louis wanted to eliminate any other contender who might loom as competition for him to attain a title bout.

Schmeling was back in America when Louis met Uzcudun. While every-one raved about the force of Louis' knockout, Schmeling tried to contain a secret smile. When questioned after the fight about how he might do against Louis now that their bout was a sure thing, Schmeling came away from the overwhelming Louis performance not frightened one bit.

Periodically, he let slip a view of what transpired that was different from everyone else's. Speaking in accented English, Schmeling said, "I zee zome-thing."[11] He said it more than once and what he saw, this little sly observation revealed later, was that Louis dropped his right at inopportune times and if a man could stand up to Louis' punishment, a well-timed punch could cause tremendous damage.

Schmeling came away with this view at a time when the rest of the boxing world was pronouncing Louis as super human. This knowledge that he pos-sessed was what sustained Schmeling as he trained for the big fight and his showdown with the man that everyone believed would become the next heavy-weight champion by walking right over Schmeling.

14

Schmeling, Hitler
and the Nazis

The difference between Max Schmeling of 1928 when he first sailed to the United States and Max Schmeling of 1936 when he signed to fight Joe Louis was twofold. In-between Schmeling won and briefly held the heavyweight title. The other major difference was his seemingly budding relationship with Adolf Hitler and the changing status of Germany in world opinion.

When Schmeling began his professional boxing career almost no one in Germany cared about the sport. By the time he won the heavyweight championship in 1930, however, Germany was more enthusiastic about embracing him because he had become a worldwide name and his success represented reflected glory.

That lasted only so long since he held the title only briefly, but as Schmeling once again rose in the rankings to become a serious contender and prepared for his bout with Louis, internal changes in the country affected how the world saw him.

Hitler's strident extremism and his consolidation of power was a hallmark of 1920s and 1930s Germany, reeling from the aftereffects of World War I and harsh sanctions placed on the country by the victors, including the United States. Hitler and his emblematic swastika became ubiquitous beginning in 1922. Year by year, step by step, appealing to the worst instincts of the masses seeking someone to blame for ongoing poverty, unemployment and inflation, Hitler's power expanded.

His political party was officially called the National Socialist German Workers Party and for short they were referred to as the Nazis. In the infamous Beer Hall Putsch of 1922 in Munich, Hitler sought to overthrow the government. Instead, he was arrested and sent to prison. While in jail he wrote his memoir, *Mein Kampf,* which spelled out his own brand of extremism.

Once released, Hitler put on a full-court press to take over Germany by any means. He was a vigorous, inflammatory, and emotional speaker who swept up listeners in his causes of nationalism, anti–Semitism, and anti–Communism, and found receptive audiences when he railed against the Treaty of Versailles, the post-war document that was so onerous to Germans.

In 1933, the Reichstag parliament building erupted in a blaze. Although it is now universally believed that Hitler had the fire set himself, at the time he blamed Communists for the conflagration and used that as a pretext to speak ever more loudly against them. By 1933, Hitler's gathering strength was too powerful to ignore and he was appointed chancellor. He used the legitimacy of that office as a jumping off point to assume complete authority. Hitler replaced the Weimar Republic with his Third Reich and became a dictator who ruled by tyranny and violence.

For the most part the rest of the world turned a blind eye. Other war weary countries either didn't care or didn't want to know what Hitler was up to in Germany. No one imagined that he would become one of the greatest evil forces in world history. No one had the stomach for intervention and no one understood Hitler's grand expansionist ideas.

Only the most politically attuned figures inside the nation comprehended the nature of his destructiveness, the violence he at first subtly, and then with an iron hand, began propagating on German Jews as he systematically stripped them of their rights and property.

By the time Schmeling was ready to meet Louis in June of 1936, enough evidence had been accumulated for the world to see what type of leader Hitler was and was becoming, but there was little in the way of protest of his actions. All the while, Hitler was turning German manufacturing production into a war machine and rearming a military that had been stripped of its might after World War I.

Schmeling had always been popular with New York sports writers. He was genial, engaged them in friendly banter, and was cooperative. The writers liked Max and he showed he was better than the average European fighter, someone who was definitely in the mix among the best heavyweights.

But when Schmeling returned to New York to prepare for his 1936 fight against Louis, the climate had changed. Although anti–German feeling was not running high as of yet, and the writers who already knew Schmeling did not closely identify him with Hitler, he did face questions about the new regime. And Jewish organizations in the city and Jewish writers were skeptical about his politics. This was all at a minimum, but it was percolating near the surface of Schmeling's give-and-take during the publicity building to the fight.

It was not a siege of negative publicity given the limits of Americans' comparative naivety about Nazi Germany at the time, but some articles did refer to Schmeling as "a Nazi puppet." Also, many close watchers of the boxing world felt Schmeling was simply over the hill.

Years later, when he reflected on the rise of Hitler and his wickedness, Schmeling marveled at his own blindness. He said he was immersed in his own career and did not get involved in politics, indeed barely noticed when Hitler became chancellor and had no conception of what it meant for the future of the country. While his friends informed him about demonstrations in the streets in favor of Hitler, only a few miles away where he lived on the other side of town, nothing of the sort was happening.

"After the fact people spoke of an awareness of history in the making, but it wasn't like that at all," Schmeling said. "Surviving newsreels give the impression of a city and a people wild with excitement and change. But in reality the celebrations were limited to the inner city and a few neighborhoods controlled by National Socialists. Still, you could sense that something new had begun, a bustling energy had come over the country, new confidence, new hope. But it wasn't as if the country had been divided into two opposing camps — followers and opponents of the regime. We were so used to frequent changes in the government ... that no one viewed Hitler's appointment as a 'final chapter.'"[1]

Schmeling said that he met Hitler for the first time near the end of April, less than two months before his first bout with Louis. He was eating dinner with some auto racing friends when an SS officer arrived at the restaurant with a message for him. Schmeling was being summoned to the reich chancellory for an audience with Hitler.

Schmeling was deposited into an empty room, but was swiftly joined by Hitler and some of the other high-ranking Nazis, Joseph Goebbels and Herman Goering, as well as other cabinet officials. Hitler genially welcomed him and they spoke for about 20 minutes. At the end of the meeting, Schmeling said Hitler told him, "I've heard that you're going to America. If anyone over there asks how it's going in Germany, you can reassure the doomsayers that everything is moving along quite peaceably." Hitler added that if Schmeling ever needed anything not to hesitate to contact him.[2]

It may not have been clear to Schmeling immediately, but it was later when he reviewed the session, that Hitler wanted him to be a public relations figure for the regime on his visit to the U.S. Reassure everybody that things were OK. If Schmeling says it, it must be true, had to be the hierarchy's thinking. Schmeling said he "couldn't help but feel a little flattered. Let's face it, one can also be bribed by small favors."[3] In addition, he noted, in his years-long career, as owner of the European title and the world heavyweight crown, previous government officials had completely ignored him. Hitler made time for tea with other athletes and artists. For the first time Schmeling was made to feel by officialdom that he had done something special on par with other countrymen in the arts or sports. Schmeling admitted that having the head of state provide such personal attention was heady stuff.

The same year Hitler rose to chancellor, Schmeling and actress Anny Ondra married. In the early stages of their marriage Schmeling received considerable criticism because of suggestions he was pointlessly going on as a fighter when he had nothing left. There were also rumors of him having an affair with another actress. Both distractions passed and Schmeling and Ondra remained married for 54 years.

Hitler seemed entranced by their union and taken with the attractive Ondra. He worked to charm her and invited the Schmelings to various outings. Once, the couple accompanied Hitler to a dinner at the home of the publisher of the Nazi party's main newspaper, and as they drove along Hitler pointed out the sights and highlights of the landscape in Bavaria.

Once, soon after, Schmeling did take advantage of Hitler's promise to help him out if he was in need. Back in Berlin Schmeling was stunned by a piece of mail from the government that brusquely informed him that he had been accused of a currency violation and was being sentenced to six months in jail and a 10,000-mark fine. The root of the matter was Schmeling's purchase of some gold bars and stock from an American he knew and then depositing them in a safe deposit box.

Schmeling did not realize he had done anything wrong, but some government officials released the findings to newspapers and he was embarrassed by the to-do. Schmeling called Hitler for aid and after he visited him the angry chancellor picked up the phone and made the entire matter go away instantly. Schmeling heard Hitler's side of the call that included the phrase, "There will be no discussion. Take care of the matter immediately."[4] And that was that. Poof, the problem disappeared. At this moment Schmeling could not help but think about how nice it was to have friends in high places.

Hitler extracted some assistance from Schmeling as well. One way Germany wanted to show off to the world that it had bounced back from the devastation of World War I was by making a splash in hosting the 1936 Winter Olympics in Garmisch-Partenkirchen and the Summer Olympics in Berlin.

Although official commentary from the administration of President Franklin Delano Roosevelt about what was taking place in Germany was extraordinarily restrained, there were enough rumblings of discrimination that Avery Brundage, who would later become head of the International Olympic Committee, but then was the chief of the U.S. Olympic Committee, wanted to know what was going on. He was concerned, he said, about how Jewish and African American athletes would be treated. Hitler enlisted Schmeling to deliver a letter of reassurance from the German government to Brundage when he returned to the United States.

Beyond acting as messenger, Schmeling personally assured Brundage that blacks and Jews would be treated equitably in Germany. Later, he wondered if he had been too reassuring because he had no authority to speak so forcefully on behalf of Hitler and could do nothing to assure that those athletes would be well-treated. At that point the U.S. Olympic Committee was considering boycotting the games in Berlin, but in a close vote decided to participate after hearing about the letter. In actuality, Hitler did clean up his act and his administration's during the games, putting his plans for extermination of Jews on hold. His purpose in hosting the games in the first place was to garner good will. So if he had to live with sham policies for a couple of weeks, it was no big deal. There was plenty of time later on — and there would be time bought — in showing off German's athletic prowess and its capabilities as a perfect host to the rest of the world.

For a time leading up to the Louis fight, the German press spouted racist dogma about him, dismissing him as a jungle creature and as stupid, but as the fight and the Olympics drew near, the disparagement ceased. Schmeling said he never insulted Louis in such a manner and he also never joined the Nazi party, although other prominent Germans of the period were pressured to do so.

Schmeling was in an awkward position. He was going to risk his reputation against a black man, supposedly his inferior. In the United States his affairs were handled by a Jewish man, supposedly his inferior. He did not adorn his clothing with a swastika or carry such a flag. While admittedly pleased to be invited into the inner circle in the halls of government, if only socially, he seemed to be a man willing to go along to get along rather than a true believer in Hitler's cause.

He left Germany with limited fanfare for New York by ship for the final training sessions, with well wishes from German officials who knew when he was departing. In the 1930s, well before the age of the Internet and other convenient electronic devices, reporters greeted arriving vessels in major city harbors to glean news as quickly as they could before their subjects went through customs.

A gaggle of sports writers and photographers swarmed Schmeling's ship. He posed for pictures with his arms around manager Joe Jacobs and promoter Mike Jacobs, both of whom were Jewish, and smiled broadly. He submitted to two hours of questioning from the writers. On the passage across the Atlantic Ocean, Schmeling ran 12 miles a day on the decks.

It was clear from the beginning of the conversation with the writers that there were going to be political overtones to Schmeling's return to the United States and his participation in the fight with Louis. Schmeling was asked if Hitler saw him off and he replied, "Why should he? He's a politician and I'm a sportsman."[5] While that might have been an oversimplified, disingenuous answer, it was also true and accurate. But it illustrated the perception among others that Schmeling was pals with the dictator.

In the midst of all the chit-chat Schmeling predicted he had sailed the ocean blue for the purpose of defeating Louis. "I guarantee you," he said, "if Louis makes the same mistakes with me that he did with Baer, I shall knock him out."[6]

For his part, Louis, a burgeoning American celebrity, had already been embroiled in a fight that brought political issues to the forefront. When Louis battered Primo Carnera it was supposedly as much about defeating Italy and a symbolic stand for Ethiopia. Louis was not really thinking about defending democracy from the Nazis at this time. But there was a groundswell of fan support from people who might not typically back a black fighter because of the beginnings of suspicion of and distrust of Germans.

It was not going to be merely two heavyweights in the ring. Although the full extent of Adolf Hitler's intentions would not be revealed for a few years, and World War II also lay in the future, the symbolism was emerging. As much as they tried to defuse and ignore such labeling, the fight was going to be between Joe Louis American and Max Schmeling German.

15

Louis-Schmeling I

By the time the bout with Max Schmeling rolled around there was every indication in the worried Joe Louis training camp at Lakewood, New Jersey, that the protégé was believing every word being written and said about him suggesting he was an invincible fighter, a superman of a boxer.

For the first time in his professional life, Louis was not listening as hard to trainer Jack Blackburn as he should have been. For the first time he was not working out as religiously as he always had. Camp was becoming too much like summer camp for Blackburn's taste. The key to success in the boxing world is to take every opponent seriously, to prepare for the underdogs as energetically as the champions.

Of all things, Louis was distracted by the game of golf, a sport he had recently taken up as a hobby, but which began dominating his thoughts and interfering with his workouts. Blackburn frowned on golf. One reason was the amount of mental energy Louis poured into it. He repeatedly told Louis to cool it because playing golf also developed different muscles than throwing punches. But Louis did not heed his admonitions.

Golf was a kind of new toy for Louis. Ed Sullivan, later a household name in American homes because of his television variety show, was then a writer for the *New York Daily News*' sports department. Just before Louis began training for his Charley Retzlaff bout, Sullivan and Louis became friends and it was Sullivan who introduced the fighter to golf. They were both obsessed with the game to the point Sullivan and Louis would whip out their putters and alternate shots inside Louis' apartment.

One other benefit of Louis' growing fame, though it could also be perceived as a distraction, was his invitation to make a movie in Hollywood before the Schmeling fight. He spent some time in California filming *The Spirit of Youth*. Everyone from Marva to managers John Roxborough and Julian Black, kept Louis company in Los Angeles.

Louis had always loved watching movies, and although he got to play a character something like himself in the film — a boy who washed dishes who grew up to become a world champion — he took note of the working conditions for other blacks in Hollywood among those trying to be professional actors. "Black women certainly weren't playing any heroine roles in those days," Louis said. "If you were a black actress who was good-looking, you were lucky if you got the role of the maid. Many times you had to be big, fat, talk with a heavy Southern accent, bug your eyes, and act stupid."[1]

Typical of Louis, where there were sexy young women he was the focus of flirting. And typical of Louis, even though his wife was on the trip, too, he didn't resist. He jokingly called himself the example of the real weaker sex because he was no match for all these feminine wiles. "I didn't resist one pretty girl who had a sparkle in her eye," Louis said.[2] This is when Louis made the acquaintance of Sonja Henie.

Leading up to the Schmeling bout also, Louis turned 22 and held a big birthday bash. Everyone from friends and relatives to Nat Fleischer, editor of *The Ring* magazine, and other boxers such as Tony Canzoneri, Tommy Loughran and reigning heavyweight champ James J. Braddock were in attendance. There was a little byplay between Louis and Braddock. The winner of the Louis-Schmeling fight was almost guaranteed the next chance to fight for the belt against Braddock.

Braddock knew that it was likely his best payday would come against the increasingly popular Louis, and he took advantage of their proximity to not only wish Louis a happy birthday, but to needle him slightly. "OK, Joe, you must be running from me," Braddock said. "I mean I'm the champion and all. Now here I am coming to you."[3] Louis assured Braddock that as soon as he beat Schmeling he could sign to fight him for the crown.

By most accounts, Schmeling was an 8–1 underdog against Louis for their 1936 fight at Yankee Stadium. Most boxing observers felt that Schmeling was past his prime at 30, going on 31, and that Louis was too rugged, too strong, and on an unstoppable train to the top. Later, Louis admitted he took Schmeling lightly in the lead-up to the fight. "I didn't give the German a second thought," Louis said. "He was washed up and had never been much. I was a big shot, the best in boxing, and everybody knew it, especially me. I didn't even want to train. I just wanted to have a good time."[4]

About as bad as the golf was in the mind of Blackburn was the fact that Marva, Louis' wife, accompanied him to training camp. In a famous line in the movie *Rocky*, trainer Burgess Meredith harshly directs a comment at his fighter Rocky Balboa, saying, "Women weaken legs." There always has been such a feeling, a superstition, that wives and girlfriends are no good for boxers in training. Better that they should refrain from sex, so the appearance of Mrs. Louis at training camp made Blackburn growl and scowl.

After a short stay, Blackburn got his way and was able to persuade Marva to leave. He still had his hands full with Louis, however, both because of golf and female camp followers. Louis was not one to pass up a night in the sack with any babe who crossed his path and many were willing.

Years later, when he wrote his memoirs, Louis said he was too full of himself at the time. "Now I look at me in May, 1936," Louis said from the vantage point of four decades later. "I look back and get mad at myself. I think I'm Mr. Big Shit. I know I'm going to win anything I want. My record speaks for itself. I married a fabulous woman, I bought a beautiful home for my mother, I'm sending my sister Vunice to Howard University to study teaching, women are running me crazy, big, important people are my friends. Shit! I can't go wrong. I got the money, I got the power."[5]

Still, Blackburn felt the golf was the worst evil for Louis' preparations. Louis spent hours in the summer sun being drained by the heat. While he was a good golfer to a point he had a penchant for being suckered into big money games by superior players and routinely lost large sums of money. This went on for the rest of his life. The period in New Jersey while training for Schmeling was only a sneak preview of that weakness.

With 20–20 hindsight and self-recrimination after the fight, Louis said of his behavior at the Jersey camp, "I acted like a little boy."[6]

This was uncharacteristic of Louis. For the first time in his ascent all of the praise and attention seemed to feed his ego and sidetrack him from taking care of business as he had so scrupulously done before all his previous bouts and on the run that made him 24–0 leading into the Schmeling fight. By his own admission Louis acted foolishly before the match with Schmeling. Schmeling was deadly serious, aware that this was likely his last chance on the big stage if he didn't win.

Yet Louis did not shirk training altogether. When he was a young man he relished his early morning runs. He came to camp weighing 216 pounds, his walking around weight, and worked hard enough to drop to a fit 204. He ran six miles a day, but he cut sparring from six rounds to three some days because of golf games with sports writers. They should have been suspicious that Louis had time for them. But they also probably believed their own hype that Schmeling was not a foe to particularly worry about.

Blackburn, whom Louis still referred to as "Chappie," was the voice of reason, but his was not a voice that Louis was listening to intently. Instead, he was tuning him out on occasion. Blackburn warned Louis that Schmeling had a dangerous right hand, but Louis reacted more or less like "Yeah, yeah, yeah." Louis felt he was in perfect peak form for the fight—five days ahead of time. While Roxborough and Black wanted to take him away for some deep sea fishing so he could relax and escape the crowds that always surrounded him, Louis instead went golfing one more time.

The weigh-in took place in New York at the Hippodrome on a rainy day. Schmeling weighed in at 192 pounds and Louis at 196. Louis frequently reposed before big fights in New York at an apartment at 381 Edgecombe Avenue. It was a popular residence for several major African American personalities.

Although Adolf Hitler's reign was in its early days, enough word of his prejudices and hatred of Jews had filtered out of Germany that American Jews began lobbying against Schmeling's appearance. New York is one of the largest enclaves of Jewish people in the world and even in the 1930s, years before creation of the state of Israel, they had some political clout. Jewish organizations began a campaign trying to convince fans not to buy tickets because Schmeling was a representative of Nazi Germany. "The whole thing made me uneasy," Louis said.[7]

The fight was postponed briefly because of rain, but on the new date it was also cloudy, damp, and there were occasional flashes of lightning. Come fight time the air was clear enough, but the threatening weather held the crowd down to around 40,000, about half of what might have been expected. Was it the weather or the Jewish boycott, or a combination of the two? Whatever the reason for the lower turnout, the gate fell far short of the rare $1 million level that was anticipated by Mike Jacobs.

While Louis had been goofing off, trainer Blackburn had been as focused on preparation as ever. The strategy he devised for his fighter was built around jabbing and probing in the early going to feel Schmeling out and to tire him out. Keep that left jab flicking in the older man's face and pick your spots with the overhand right. For the most part Louis followed instructions, but when he unleashed a left hook that he firmly believed in, he was surprised that Schmeling was able to counter over it. This was the weakness that Schmeling had spied in Louis' fight against Paulino Uzcudun when he mysteriously said, "I zee zomething." Louis was dropping his protection when he threw the punch and while Schmeling had to seize the opening swiftly, he felt it was possible to breach Louis' defenses this way.

Louis thought he had developed the advantage and was setting Schmeling up for a finishing hook. He had already cut Schmeling under the right eye with one of those fearsome left hooks, and in the fourth round he thought he saw the same kind of opportunity. But when Louis threw the hook this time Schmeling responded with a perfectly placed right that dropped Louis to the canvas.

This unexpected development brought the roaring crowd to its feet, partially in surprise and partially in response to the sudden shift in momentum. Louis, who at that point in his career had never been down as a pro, fell over backwards from the blow. The smart move for a fighter who has been staggered enough to be knocked down is to clear his head by waiting to rise to his feet and use up much of the 10 seconds allotted. It's typical for fighters to rejoin the battle after eight seconds.

But this was new territory for Louis. He was not only shocked that he had gone down, he was embarrassed and he jumped to his feet immediately. It was a mighty hit and its effect was significant on Louis, not something that could be shaken off in a few seconds. He was hurting. "I couldn't believe it," said Louis. "I staggered right to my feet, but my eyes were blurred and my mind was blurred and I saw everything blurred from then on."[8] In an ill-advised move, since he was not used to being in such a position, Louis was up at the count of four.

Schmeling sensed the trouble Louis was in and chased him promptly. Louis was able to gain a clinch and forestall additional punishment. He had hit the deck with just 20 seconds remaining in the round and was able to fend off Schmeling long enough for the bell to ring. Louis retreated to his corner hopeful that Blackburn had a remedy for the big punch. It was too late for Blackburn to work magic, though. Perhaps Louis had left his best shot on the fourth hole when he was playing golf instead of in the fourth round. The best that Blackburn could do was soak him with water to revive him and then implore him to keep his hands up and to protect himself.

But this was only the beginning of the beating Schmeling was about to administer as he turned the fight around. It was Schmeling on Louis like a tiger, pouncing like a jungle cat, in the fifth round. The pressure was telling. Schmeling did not give Louis either time or space to recover. Another big right hand wobbled Louis in the fifth round, though he did not go down this time.

To some degree the crowd swung its support behind Schmeling, sensing an upset. Among Louis' friends and family at ringside, come to watch the usual Louis pugilistic artistry, they instead were viewing a vivisection by a seasoned pro tearing apart their loved one. Freddie Guinyard drew the unenviable task of escorting Louis' mother, Lillie Barrow, out of the area as she cried. Marva sat at ringside watching her husband's beating and she was also in tears.

Louis' last line of defense was Blackburn. Blackburn employed every trick he knew to revive Louis, to rejuvenate Louis, and try to shift him into being enough of a counter-attacker and mover so as to avoid more punishment and fight back strongly. Louis was game and gutsy in this significant test of his fortitude and will, but Schmeling's best punches had sapped him. Although Louis swung with all he had and landed a fair share of rights to Schmeling's body, he was simultaneously being drained of energy. Some of Louis' attempted body punches — his focus trying to wear down Schmeling — were below the belt and referee Arthur Donovan subtracted points from his score, twice giving rounds to Schmeling for the low blows.

Fighting for his dignity and his future, as well as his reputation, Louis did strike Schmeling with big rights and Schmeling did seem to tire a bit. But when Louis sought to seize the moment with another left hook in the 12th round, once again Schmeling exploded a right hand to Louis' jaw and the impact drove Louis backwards into the ropes. Louis was almost helpless and Schmeling moved in to finish him off. Right after right smashed into Louis' head until he could no longer stand up and plummeted to the canvas. Donovan stood above Louis counting him out at 2 minutes, 29 seconds of the three-minute round. The winner by knockout was Schmeling in a stunning upset.

"I heard the counting as if it came from far away," Louis said later. "But I was sleepy and it didn't mean nothing to me. If I tried to get up, it was instinct. I didn't know what was happening. I just wanted to lay there and sleep."[9] After 10 seconds passed the result was official and Louis could sleep as long as he wanted to because it was no longer any concern of Schmeling, Donovan, or the 40,000 fans.

In some minds, Schmeling had accomplished the impossible. He had made the powerful Joe Louis look mortal. Astonishment reigned on press row and some writers almost immediately began writing Louis off for good. The headline on syndicated columnist Grantland Rice's piece read, "German Hits Louis Often and Easily Defeats Him." The sub-head read, "Ring Myth of Superman Is Exploded as Schmeling Wins." Rice's lead read this way: "The atom has been taken apart. The myth of the superman has been exploded completely."[10]

Rice pointed to the fourth round knockdown via Schmeling's right hand as the key moment in establishing his command over Louis, and the scribe said of Louis that he "hit the floor and bounced like a 200-pound rubber ball." And Rice called the result "the greatest upset in heavyweight history."[11]

There was no such thing as computer punch counts in those days, but Schmeling's repeated pummeling of Louis with his sledgehammer right hand is what stuck in the minds of writers and also stuck in the head of Louis. To

Rice, after the fourth round, Louis was able to stay on his feet and fight back only through ingrained training instinct.

From the fourth round through the 12th, when Louis toppled for good, Rice said, "Louis took one of the worst beatings I have ever seen in any ring."[12]

Joe Williams, renowned sports columnist for the *New York World–Telegram*, concurred with Rice's surprise and with the severity of Louis' beating in his own dispatch from ringside. "Some day the sphinx will talk, the pyramids will crumble, the oceans will stand still, and very likely the scientists will be able to explain the phenomenon," Williams penned. "Something loosely akin to this was recorded when Max Schmeling knocked out Joe Louis in 12 rounds under a frowning sky at Yankee Stadium last night. And so today you will read that the greatest upset in ring history took place, that the impossible happened, that the condemned man electrocuted the warden."[13]

Schmeling's phenomenal performance completely transformed his career. From being perceived as a fall guy on the way down, he flipped things around and he was now seen as the near-certain No. 1 contender for Braddock's title. At home in Germany, Schmeling had been an admired athlete, someone who succeeded at a sport that few attempted. But besting Louis elevated his stature. It didn't hurt any that Louis was a black man and the hierarchy of German government's cornerstone policies revolved around boosting white Germans as a superior race over dark-skinned people, but the magnificence and thoroughness of Schmeling's triumph was broader based. He truly had represented his nation superbly.

It was intriguing that many fight observers felt that the bout belonged to Schmeling once he plastered Louis in the fourth round because he could not tell. Schmeling recognized that Louis was a great fighter and he did not promptly realize that his blow was so damaging because Louis kept fighting back with great courage and determination. Schmeling had waded in on Louis and took hard lefts to his own face for the trouble. His left eye was closed by Louis' fists and Schmeling could not see clearly when he landed his haymaker. "With all this," he said, "I hadn't noticed how hard Louis had been hit by me. He was in such incredible shape that he showed no effect and seemed to continue the fight with the same sharpness and intensity as before."[14]

Schmeling and his trainer, Max Machon, both recognized the significance of the punch, although they did not understand how badly Louis had been hurt. To them, the importance was confirmation of their fight plan, that Schmeling could sneak his right hand over Louis' defense and catch his foe with big punches.

After Schmeling polished off Louis in the 12th, it wasn't until he watched the film again that he remembered raising his arms in the air in triumph.

Braddock climbed into the ring, congratulated Schmeling and told him he now deserved a shot at his title. At least as satisfying was a visit to his dressing room by Jack Blackburn, the vanquished second meeting the victor. "You were great Max," Blackburn said.[15]

Leaving Yankee Stadium, the car transporting Schmeling to his hotel passed through Harlem. Where before Louis' fans partied in the streets to celebrate his wins, this night they were rioting instead, pounding on cars being driven by white men. This was the night when Lena Horne broke into tears in the middle of her act because Louis lost — and she didn't know him yet. Schmeling's hotel room was filled with flowers. He had won no title this night, but something almost as difficult to acquire — respect.

Schmeling was awake all night. He was able to call long distance and reach his wife, Anny, who asked when he was coming home. Schmeling returned to German soil on June 26. His mode of transportation was not by the usual ship this time, but by an air ship that was supposed to be a herald of the future. Schmeling secured passage to Europe on the Hindenburg.

The disastrous wreck of the Hindenburg lay ahead, but Joe Louis' career experienced a disaster of similar proportions. Once he had completed his obligation for the fight, Louis' family informed him that two days earlier his step-father had suffered a stroke. The close relations did not want the illness on the fighter's mind when he stepped into the ring. So he got that bad news immediately after he absorbed his defeat. Louis went to his step-father's bedside. Paralyzed by the stroke, Pat Brooks died soon after. Louis, who considered the man to be his real father, cried at the loss. He was doing his share of mourning, both for the lost step-father and the lost undefeated record.

Initially, Louis did not want to go out in public. He did not want to be seen by the same people who adored him. He felt he had let down the entire black race and his face wore the welts and scars of his beating. Louis could barely look in the mirror, never mind show his face to the masses. He hunkered down in a Harlem apartment for three days. Marva treated his physical wounds, the puffy face and swollen jaw, with compresses. When Blackburn asked him if he wanted to watch the fight replay, Louis declined. "No," he said. "I saw the fight."[15] He had seen it up close and personal, from too good of a vantage point, actually. It was not an experience he wanted to relive. The physical damage would not take long to heal. The psychological damage was a question-mark.

If African Americans were disappointed so dramatically by Louis' loss, sports writers in the Deep South who at best merely tolerated Louis because of his dark skin quickly pounced on his failure. O.B. Keeler, who wrote for the *Atlanta Journal*, had always been borderline insulting when describing

Louis and reached new depths at this moment. He termed Louis "The Pet Pickaninny," and said Louis "was just another good boxer who had been built up."[16]

Suddenly, Schmeling was a German hero of international proportions. There was reflected glory to be had here and Hitler seized the moment to associate himself with the victor. Any good news for Germany was considered to be good news for Hitler's regime. The German chancellor sent a telegram of congratulations to Schmeling in New York and sent flowers to Schmeling's wife Anny in Germany.

When Schmeling returned to his country, Hitler summoned him to a celebratory lunch and Schmeling brought his mother as well as his wife. Promoter Mike Jacobs, who did not foresee the outcome and thought Louis would make short work of Schmeling, had given the visitor from overseas the European film rights to the bout. Combined with footage of the two men training, and Schmeling's immensely popular victory, the film made for a full-length movie and Schmeling made good money from its distribution, particularly in Germany.

There were some sports writers who believed that Louis would never get over the defeat. They thought he would be perpetually demoralized and never recover sufficiently to become champion. If they had over-praised Louis before, they underestimated him now.

It took courage to stand up to Schmeling's heavy blows, to continue battling when the cause was lost. If Louis was truly a special fighter as all had proclaimed, then he had it within him to recoup and recover. The mark of a great champion is often how he responds to adversity. For the first time in his professional career, Louis was in that position. He could give up or he could respond to the seemingly dismal circumstances and rebuild.

The world waited. Louis' handlers didn't wait long at all to begin repairing the damage. Once Louis was ready to exit New York, he and Blackburn took a train to Chicago. It was in private moments like this together, the man who also shared the nickname Chappie with his protégé also showed he was a friend.

"Everything happens for the best," Blackburn said at a time when it was difficult for Louis to picture how anything good could come out of this debacle. "This'll make you a better fighter. It'll learn you that you can't take a thing lightly when you walk into the ring. He took advantage of a mistake you made. Well, you're young and you make mistakes. All you got to do is learn from your mistakes and not make them again. You're better than him and you'll be ready for him and you'll beat him when you get him again."[17]

It was soothing talk and it was accurate. Blackburn knew his man. He knew Louis had the right stuff and wasn't going to give up, but rather rebound with determination, and just as importantly, with knowledge earned the hard way.

Better times were coming. Blackburn was sure of it. Louis had to be convinced of it. It may have been that on the occasion of what he called the worst night of his life and the most embarrassing and devastating defeat in his life, Louis matured into manhood.

16

Joe Bounces Back

Bruised and battered, puffy-faced and sad, Joe Louis woke up as a different man on the morning of June 20, 1936. It was as if Humpty Dumpty had taken a great fall, but Louis had a team of supporters — from wife Marva and trainer Jack Blackburn, to co-managers John Roxborough and Julian Black — behind him to make sure all of the pieces got put back together again, and he came out of his disappointing experience stronger than ever.

One shattering loss can ruin a boxer. But that is not an automatic thing. One of the great things an undefeated fighter has going for him is an aura of invincibility. A beating such as Louis took wipes that out. It is possible to rebuild, however, if the boxer is of singular fortitude and is adaptable enough to learn from defeat.

A very distinctive characteristic that became apparent as Joe Louis' career wore on, but which was not yet known, was that each time he fought an opponent for the second time Louis got better. If it was a close fight the first time it was not likely to be a close a fight the second time. Same thing for him with defeat, or near defeat; Louis would assess and analyze and fix his mistakes.

Up until Max Schmeling beat the stuffing out of Louis he was on a fast track to a shot at the heavyweight title. Now it seemed Schmeling had replaced him as the No. 1 contender and earned a shot at James J. Braddock's championship ahead of Louis.

One thing was working in Louis' favor, though. Braddock, nicknamed "Cinderella Man," was a spectacular underdog who had endured hardship and poverty simply trying to feed his family and recover from tough losses that had all but finished his boxing career before he stunned the universe by capturing the heavyweight title from an underachieving and under-trained Max Baer in a 15-round decision at Long Island City on January 13, 1935.

Braddock was in no hurry to defend the crown against contenders who

127

might lift it from his head. Instead, he milked the championship as if it was a generous cow, going for all it was worth, making money for appearances, fighting exhibitions and making up for the harsh period of not-so-long-ago when his family was on welfare. Braddock wanted to enjoy the benefits of his remarkable triumph for as long as possible and then wanted to make as much money as possible for any defense of the title.

These delaying tactics by Braddock and his camp gave Louis time to rebuild his own resume as a frustrated Schmeling sat around idle at home in Germany.

Louis' handlers bought into the if-you-fall-off-a-bicycle, get-right-back-on-it school. They did not waste time. Almost as soon as Louis physically recovered, they matched him with former heavyweight champ Jack Sharkey. They did not want Louis sitting around brooding. So the fight was set for just two months after the Schmeling loss at Yankee Stadium. This was a critical fight for both men. If Sharkey lost he was pretty much finished near the top of the rankings. If Louis lost it might mean the same, although he was still young. Louis needed a good showing to demonstrate that Schmeling had not beaten him gun-shy.

Louis had the motivation he needed, but he also spurred his preparations along by blaming himself for the letdown against Schmeling. He understood that he probably blew the fight with lackadaisical training and by being too cocky. He wasn't going to make that error again. He knew he needed to show well for fight observers and fans to regain belief in him and he needed to put on a good show for his own confidence.

Still only 25 fights into his hurry-up career, Louis understood how the boxing world worked. Everyone had viewed him as invincible. Well, those days were gone. He could still improve, but he had more proving to do now.

"I had to be resold to the public," Louis said. "It was like I had climbed up a steep flight of stairs and fallen halfway down. I wanted a return match with Schmeling as soon as possible. I could taste the blood, but my managers said no."[1] Of course Schmeling had nothing to gain from a rematch. He had already done yeoman work to score the upset and seemed to be perfectly positioned to fight Braddock. He didn't need another Louis fight for anything except the payday. And the prestige of winning the heavyweight title outweighed the amount of money he might earn for meeting Louis again. From his standpoint, any rematch was pointless and only deflected him from his real goal.

Mike Jacobs was the promoter, and he devised a plan for Louis to work his way back into the picture. Sharkey owned a 37-12-3 record. He was past his prime but was a name, and if he could manage a win over Louis his career might be rejuvenated. Sharkey had retired, but was lured back because a victory over Louis could change everything for him.

Sharkey was 33 years old and for someone fresh out of retirement he seemed notably unimpressed by Louis. The newspapers leading up to the weigh-in were full of bravado attributed to Sharkey indicating that he could defeat any black fighter. Sharkey was quoted as saying he had an "Indian sign,"[2] whatever that meant, that would enable him to beat any African American fighter, saying it as if it was a curse of some kind acquired from a medicine man. It sounded cockamamie.

There were some expectations of tensions between the men surfacing at the weigh-in, but nothing happened. There was a minor polite hello exchange and that was it. Sharkey weighed 197¼ pounds and Louis weighed in at 199¾.

The hostilities were scheduled for 10 rounds, but Louis was fit and angry and he wiped out Sharkey in the third round. The loss sent Sharkey back into retirement. It was a good win for Louis. Sharkey's name was respected and the win was precisely what Louis needed to follow up his devastating defeat. *The Ring*'s Nat Fleischer called the fight Sharkey's "last stand. He was determined. He came through with a quick rally, but the infuriated Louis was at him in a flash and the rally quickly ended. In went Joe. He disregarded Sharkey's rush. He met him with a stinging left to the face.... Jack went down for a third time, face forward, his body striking the lower ring strand."[3]

Louis made new friends and rekindled old relationships with his domination of Sharkey. The United Press account of the event noted how impressive Louis was in defeating his third ex-heavyweight champ after Primo Carnera and Max Baer. "Another turn of boxing's wheel of fortune whirled Joe Louis back into the select circle of heavyweight challengers today, the only man in his division ready to meet all comers," the report's lead read. "Louis, the stigma of his Schmeling defeat only a hazy memory, swiftly smashed down Jack Sharkey, a hollow shell of the once magnificent boxer."[4]

Most importantly for the witnesses, as Fleischer summed up, they saw Louis rebound from his defeat with no apparent lingering effect. "...the crowd went home thoroughly convinced that the knockout of the Bomber in the only setback he had suffered since starting his professional career ... had not affected Joe Louis as a fighter. They were satisfied that he could still reach the top."[5]

That was the critical impression Louis wanted to leave, and having someone as influential as Nat Fleischer notice and conclude that fact was important for the mission of the night. Equally important, the same message got through to Louis' management team.

It was like learning to walk again. Louis was taking baby steps to rehabilitate his image. He could never make everyone forget the loss to Schmeling, but he had to overcome it. Roxborough and Black huddled and came up with a strategy similar to the one they followed when Louis was just starting out. They wanted him to stay busy, to take fights often, and keep piling up the wins.

On September 22, 1936, Louis stopped Al Ettore in the fifth round of a scheduled 15-rounder. Considerable attention was paid to this fight. Sports writers who had written Louis off following the loss to Schmeling were intrigued after his demolition of Sharkey. Ettore was next in line. After this one, the United Press seemingly forgot all about Schmeling: "Joe Louis once again is America's ranking challenger for the heavyweight title. Safely past Al Ettore, Philadelphia's highly touted blond tiger man, Louis is back where he was before he met Max Schmeling."[6] That was a sunny assessment, but the fact that anyone would write such a comment showed Louis was definitely making strides to regain his prior stature. "Last night's crowd turned out to see how Louis would stack up against a rugged fighter of his own age, a youngster who simply exuded confidence and whose boasting had made many believe he really had a chance to upset the Brown Bomber. They saw Joe take the test in his stride."[7] Ettore may have shown promise up until then, but was never a serious factor in the heavyweight division afterwards.

Even the famed Grantland Rice dragged himself to Philadelphia to take another gander at Louis, whom he had proclaimed finished after the Schmeling defeat. Rice did not seem quite so convinced of that prior conclusion after Louis stopped Ettore.

"A Joe Louis who looked 200 percent different from the dazed and bewildered fighter who lost to Max Schmeling, stopped Al Ettore of Philadelphia in the fifth round," Rice wrote. "Louis looked to be far keener and sharper than against the German a few months ago. If he [Louis] had used his right against Schmeling as he did against Ettore, there might have been a different story."[8]

On October 9 Louis knocked out Jorge Brescia in the third round of a scheduled 10-rounder. Next, he blasted out Eddie Simms in the first round of a scheduled 10-round fight and then overpowered Steve Ketchel with a second-round knockout on January 11, 1937. Louis had won five fights in a hurry, upping his record to 29–1. He had not only fought in New York, but gone on the road to Philadelphia, back to New York, then to Cleveland and Buffalo. Louis was taking care of business with ruthless ferocity. He still loved Marva. He still loved women. And he still loved golf. But he did not allow for anybody or anything to interrupt his training again.

Chappie and Chappie were working together again, all of the moving parts synchronized and in harmony. Louis won back the faith of his handlers and won back the faith of his public. Mike Jacobs certainly did his part to supply opponents and venues for Louis to stay occupied and regain universal respect.

Louis needed time and wins. Braddock was the sole proprietor of the heavyweight crown — things were not then as they became much later in the century with the title divided up into pieces by competing governing authorities that each recognized a different fighter. The heavyweight division revolved around Braddock and that was an amazing thing in itself, given how he had been perceived only a short time before the Baer fight. He was seen as washed up, a one-time scrapper who was injury prone, who always seemed to have something go wrong when he got a big chance to advance his career. Braddock was completely written off.

Braddock and his loyal manager, Joe Gould, who stood by him in the worst of times, even when the Depression almost completely ruined both men, controlled the heavyweight division, and not a soul could blame Braddock for squeezing as much money for his future and family's security out of his reign. Although he had fought with the heart of a lion to defeat Baer, not many fight people felt Braddock would successfully defend the crown whether he fought Schmeling, as expected, or Louis.

The behind-the-scenes workings of boxing have long been rife with shenanigans, secret deals, and strange developments which make little sense to the average boxing fan. Once Schmeling demolished Louis it seemed clear that he would catapult into position as the man Braddock must fight when he defended the title.

In the 1930s it was not uncommon for a heavyweight champ to do what Braddock was doing, however. It was expected that title defenses would come at a spare pace and that the champ, whose hard work had earned him the distinction of holding the coveted crown, would be able to gain some recognition, fame, and fortune from his time at the top.

Schmeling was impatient. He thought he had done what needed to be done when he clobbered Louis and he wanted his shot at the title. There were occasional suggestions that he keep busy with some minor fights while Braddock paraded around America soaking up adulation and money, but Schmeling refused to fight anyone else.

Concurrent with Braddock's delaying tactic in coming to an agreement with Schmeling were the changing currents in international politics. The more Adolf Hitler solidified power and the more his repugnant his policies became, the more word spread across the Atlantic Ocean about some of the nasty things he was up to despite his regime trying to hush them up.

Gradually, a groundswell of American opinion was forming against the German government and as a by-product, against Schmeling, as well. Schmeling had spent considerable time in the United States and especially New York as he advanced his career. He was friendly with many of the sports writers and when he knocked out Louis, fans in New York had cheered him. But now every day that passed seemed to make him more unpopular.

Louis kept up a relentless pace and Schmeling sat around worried in Germany, waiting to hear that his manager, Joe Jacobs, had made the long-awaited match with Braddock for the title. Finally, Schmeling, concerned that things were moving so slowly, jumped on another ship and sailed back to the United States.

In the summer of 1936, Germany was tossing the biggest party it had ever thrown. Berlin was hosting the Summer Olympics and Hitler very much wanted to make a good impression on the world. He backed off from his racist and violent programs while the world came to visit and instead hoped that his well-trained, well-prepared sportsmen would demonstrate Aryan superiority.

Instead, this became the Olympics forever remembered as the games of Jesse Owens, the African American sprinter and jumper from Ohio State University who won four gold medals in the long jump, 100 meters, 200 meters and relay, for an unprecedented haul of rewards. Hitler had been greeting and congratulating gold-medal winners, but made himself scarce when Owens won. This was permanently catalogued famously as a snub of Owens. Overnight, however, Owens had become an American sporting hero and took his place alongside Joe Louis as one of the two most famous black men in the nation.

Owens, like Louis, had been born into poverty in Alabama and with his family later moved north for better opportunity. Over time, since they were a club of two, naturally enough Louis and Owens became friends, and remained so for the remainder of their lives.

Schmeling was in Berlin for the opening of the Olympics, but left for the United States with the games underway under the assumption that a deal was being finalized for him to fight Braddock. A plan was being hatched for the two to meet, but Braddock asked the New York State Athletic Commission to postpone the fight because he was suffering from arthritis in his always-troublesome right hand.

This delay boosted Mike Jacobs' scheme to propel the active and now-impressive Louis back into the top spot as the most deserving challenger for Braddock's crown. When Schmeling returned to New York he found much public sentiment being generated against Germany, Hitler, and the Nazi party. No longer was he so warmly embraced.

There was a growing recognition that a Braddock-Louis fight would command a bigger gate than Braddock-Schmeling and produce much more revenue. Braddock's manager, Joe Gould, thinking of a sly way to make a buck, proposed a Louis-Braddock exhibition, but when he suggested this to Roxborough in a meeting he also asked for a 50 percent stake in Louis' contract. Roxborough bluntly rejected that idea.

As the nationalism being spouted in Germany spread, a gnawing worry began to take hold among boxing officials in the United States. Mike Jacobs, Madison Square Garden and the New York State Athletic Commission envisioned a scenario where Schmeling won the title from Braddock and then disappeared in Europe. He would carry the crown with him, out of their reach and sight, and not even appear in the U.S. again or fight American boxers, in essence hoarding the title indefinitely under the sway of the Nazis.

That background fear also played into Jacobs' hands and his plans. While Schmeling smoldered and sweated, Jacobs played politics. He also had the power to make certain things happen that would enrich several of the interested parties. Jacobs held pow-wows in quiet places while Louis kept on punching his way past fresh opponents in public ones.

On January 29, 1937, Louis met Bob Pastor in Madison Square Garden for a 10-round fight. In a bit of a surprise, Pastor, who ran like a rabbit for most of the night, escaped without being knocked out. Louis won by unanimous decision, though he was irritated by Pastor's tactics. Running was not the entire repertoire of unusual tactics employed against Louis that night.

Garden boxing chief Jimmy Johnston was trying to hold onto his matchmaker job at the most prestigious fight venue in the world, but Mike Jacobs was encroaching and trying to take over the position (he eventually succeeded). Johnston felt the key to his own future was a Louis loss, so shortly before Louis left his dressing room for the ring Johnston and some henchmen burst in and made the sham accusation that Louis was using quick-drying cement in his gloves. Roxborough was outraged and shouted Johnston and his men down with the threat that he was going to call off the fight. The troublemakers backed away and there was no proof Louis was really distracted from his assignment.

Johnston ordered Pastor to dance and run away from Louis and stay on his feet. Pastor survived and landed enough jabs to fool some observers into thinking he had won the fight. Louis wanted a great showing and wanted to knock out Pastor, but he had never met anyone with a style quite the same. Pastor rarely stood and fought, and always tried to stay out of range of Louis' lethal overhand right and left hook.

"I felt like a goddamn fool trying to chase this mosquito," Louis said afterwards. "Chappie kept telling me to try and trap him in a corner. Impossible. I never fought anyone like him. I was clumsy. When I reached out to give him a good punch, I might just graze him. He must have run 12 miles that night."[9]

After that ridiculous bout, Louis halted Natie Brown, the second time he engaged the cute fighter, in the fourth round of a scheduled 10-rounder in Kansas City. That fight took place on February 17, 1937. In the eight months since Louis fell to Schmeling, he had won seven fights and raised his record to 31–1.

Enough time had passed to give Mike Jacobs time to outmaneuver Joe Jacobs. Even if Schmeling thought he had won the right to fight for Braddock's title, he had lost that seemingly guaranteed opportunity in a smoke-filled room. Mike Jacobs struck a startling deal with Joe Gould to convince him to break the contract signed to fight Schmeling and instead fight Louis. All of those concerned knew that a Louis-Braddock fight would provide more money all around. There was enough doubt that Braddock could fend off Louis, so Gould wanted an insurance policy to guarantee that he and his guy could still have cash flow even if Braddock lost.

Remarkably, as part of the deal to fight Louis, in case Louis won, Mike Jacobs guaranteed Joe Gould and Braddock 10 percent of his net profits for the next decade for all of the heavyweight title fights he promoted. That was the sweetener that clinched the agreement.

Paid either $500,000 or half the live gate and radio revenue for this fight, Braddock stood to gain financially regardless of the result. If he won, he was still heavyweight champion with all of the glamour and fortune that label brought. If he lost, he still shared in the profits of Jacobs-promoted heavyweight deals until he was long into retirement.

It was quite the arrangement for Braddock, fulfilled the dream for Louis, and shut out Schmeling temporarily, no matter how loudly he cursed and complained.

17

And the New Heavyweight Champion of the World

The thing about boxing is that you only get two men in the ring fighting at once. It is not tag-team wrestling. So although heavyweight champ James J. Braddock signed separate contracts to fight Max Schmeling and Joe Louis, he was only going to fight one of them at a time.

Once the Mike Jacobs ploy worked offering the best financial terms, Schmeling was out of luck. Although he went to court to stop the Braddock-Louis bout and the court fined Jacobs, it had no impact on the fight schedule. Schmeling was shut out and for the moment out of the picture. No one ever said the boxing world was fair. Schmeling was shunted aside and not as many boxing people stood up for him as might have if he were not associated with the Nazi regime in people's minds.

Louis had recovered from his beating, won seven fights in a row, and the fight New Yorkers and Americans wanted to see was a Braddock-Louis showdown. Everyone liked Jimmy Braddock and everyone admired Joe Louis. Besides, they both were Americans and the heavyweight title was not going to be shipped overseas regardless of who won. It was going to stay right there in the United States.

The date, June 22, 1937, and the place, Comiskey Park, home of the Chicago White Sox, were set. It was a fine pairing. Braddock was the underdog champ, a man who through force of will and grit had rejuvenated a moribund career. He had suffered in his sport, been down and out during the Depression and he, his wife and children, had barely survived the depths of poverty. He scrambled to keep a roof over the family's head, hustling to put enough food on the table.

Braddock represented one of the sport's most uplifting tales. It was remarkable how far he had traveled in a short time, from the welfare rolls to Broadway, from being destitute to being on the top of the world. Braddock was an overgrown light-heavyweight, barely even big enough to be considered a heavyweight. He was a symbol for those wearing threadbare clothing, eating soup for dinner, and standing in lines begging for work. He had been through the most discouraging of times, so when the average Joe saw him he could think there was hope for him, as well.

"Like so many of them," wrote his biographer Jeremy Schaap, "he had been devastated by a system that he assumed was stable. Like so many of them, he had been forced to ask for help. The decline in his personal fortunes mirrored the national collapse."[1]

Cinderella was the fairy tale character whose foot fitted the glass slipper carried by the rich prince who rescued her from poverty. Damon Runyon, the famous New York newspaper columnist, is the one who dubbed Braddock "Cinderella Man." Braddock's life pretty much paralleled the fictional circumstances.

Braddock was born in New York City's Hell Kitchen neighborhood in 1905, but he lived much of his life in northern New Jersey, across the bridge. He was a Jersey City guy and he was a rough, tough fighter being guided to the light-heavyweight title by manager Joe Gould when he ran into a series of unfortunate injuries that are regular byproducts of his sport. Braddock's main problem was that he kept breaking his hand and then taking fights anyway for money at less than full strength.

His stock dropped rapidly and the Depression nearly killed him. Braddock showed up for work on the docks each morning, hoping to be one of the men picked to make a day's pay. Sometimes he was chosen, sometimes not. The dock work actually turned out to be beneficial, building up Braddock's strength, so when Gould was finally able to land him a fight, Braddock was fitter than anyone supposed. It was supposed to be a hallelujah payday.

Those who manage young prospects who they believe can become contenders try to maneuver them through the minefield of early opponents, stepping up gradually in class, and with luck timing matches so that their boy can fight a name on his way down. Joe Louis had already beaten three ex-heavyweight champs. The handlers of a fighter named Corn Griffin were in the market for just such a bout for their young buck. Braddock, they were assured, was a has-been, a fighter out of shape. For one thing, Braddock took the fight on only two days' notice. That was the catch, take it or leave it. Braddock was going to give his best, but had no illusions. He knew he could make enough from the fight to keep the gas and electric companies at bay and to buy milk for his youngest child.

So the match was signed and Braddock, to the surprise of all, made the most of his last chance and knocked out Griffin in three rounds in Long Island

City, New York. The unexpected win reignited Braddock's career. He told Gould, "I did that on hash, Joe. Wait till you see what I can do on steak."[2]

A few months later, when he had trained and taken his fitness to a new level, as well as dined better, Braddock handled John Henry Lewis in 10 rounds. Then he bested Art Lasky in 15 rounds. Braddock's replenished reputation provided him with a shot at Max Baer's heavyweight title. Baer completely overlooked Braddock, who fought gamely and courageously and wrested the crown from him in an unlikely upset. It was unfathomable how far Braddock had come in such a short time.

Although the bout went the distance, there seemed little doubt that Braddock won. When the decision was announced, Braddock looked down from the ring to Gould at ringside and said, "We did it. We did it."[3]

For the first time in a long time Braddock made some decent money, $31,244. He promptly went down to the relief office (as the welfare agency was called then) and paid back the cash he was given when broke. Then Braddock fattened his bank account by fighting exhibitions for two years, avoiding any genuine defense of the crown until the deal was sealed with Louis.

Actually the first thing Braddock did was go to a pet store to buy his kids a turtle. When he went off to fight Baer he was leaving from his own home, not some fancy nearby hotel, and when his children asked where he was going, he said he was going "to get the title." The kids thought he said he was headed out to get a turtle, so he felt he had better not come home empty-handed.[4]

No black man had fought for the heavyweight title since Jack Johnson lost it in 1915, but little protest seemed to attend this match-up because of race. Louis was the preferred contender over Schmeling. Not that there was any shortage of general racist observation in the sporting press. Bill Corum, a New York columnist, authored a stunning paragraph about Louis that read this way: "There isn't an ounce of killer in him. Not the slightest zest for fighting. He's a big, superbly built Negro youth who was born to listen to jazz music, eat a lot of fried chicken, play ball with the gang on the corner and never do a lick of heavy work he could escape. The chances are he came by all those inclinations quite naturally."[5]. One had to wonder what Corum's sources were for such outrageous comments other than his own suppositions.

Whether he actually wrote the story that appeared in *Boxing News* under his name, dictated it to someone, or allowed a sports writer to pen it for him, leading up to the Louis bout Braddock stood up for himself in print: "I can still hit and I can still box," he said. "Corn Griffin found out about the punching. Maxie Baer and John Henry Lewis found out about the boxing, and in a short time Joe Louis will find out about both."[6].

Schmeling refused to give up his claim on fighting Braddock until the last minute. He returned to the United States and set up a training camp in Upstate New York. It was almost pathetic in its silliness. He may have worked out hard, but Schmeling-Braddock was a faux fight. It didn't exist and wasn't going to happen. Some fight fans actually bought tickets, but their money was refunded. Louis and Braddock were busy in Chicago on June 22, 1937. The Madison Square Garden Bowl on Long Island didn't even turn on the lights for the alleged Schmeling-Braddock bout that night.

Somewhere between 45,000 and 65,000 fans (depending on who did the writing, though it was probably closer to the lower figure) got the right address and attended the Louis-Braddock bout in Chicago, including former heavyweight champs Jack Dempsey and Gene Tunney. On their walk in the dim light to the ring, Louis, in step with trainer Jack Blackburn, was told, "Chappie, you gonna be champ tonight."[7]

Louis paid a high price being battered around the ring by Schmeling. He was now as dedicated to his trainer as he had been when he first turned pro, and he devoured every word of advice Blackburn uttered. They were on the cusp of something great. His moment had come and he was ready for James J. Braddock.

Speaking of pre-fight preparation, Louis said, "The next few months Chappie and I were almost one person. He was completely devoted to his task and I was just as blindly devoted to mine. If he had told me to jump off the Empire State Building during this period, I would have done it. I had total faith in him, especially after the Schmeling defeat. Chappie wasn't drinking and I wasn't fooling around."[8] Louis probably didn't even read the results of major golf tournament in the newspaper that summer, never mind pick up a club.

Louis went on a 30-day exhibition training tour by train and lived with his handlers and sparring partners, killing the dead time by playing cards and playing music. His main respite was playing records and grooving to tunes by Duke Ellington. That was even before settling into a stationary training camp at Lake Geneva, Wisconsin, the resort town just north of the Illinois-Wisconsin state line.

Jack Johnson was still alive and whatever his motive, he tried to sell his services to Braddock to provide advice and all of the so-called secrets he knew that would help the champ defeat Louis. Perhaps Johnson wanted to maintain his status as the only African American heavyweight champ. Perhaps he was just looking to remain in the spotlight. Or perhaps he just needed some money. He didn't get the job.

Nat Fleischer was an interested observer as Braddock first postponed the bout with Schmeling complaining of arthritis. Then he said he couldn't fight because of an injured thumb. Then Gould made the lucrative deal to cut Schmeling out. Shenanigans aside, it made sense, *The Ring* editor said. "In Louis, Jimmy knew he had one fighter with whom a fortune could be obtained."[9]

Any time there is competition one side wins and one side loses. Upsets happen every day in sports. That's why they play the games. Although Joe Louis was heavily favored over him, Jimmy Braddock had to look no farther back in history than Louis' loss to Schmeling or his own victory over Baer to be buoyed and reminded that this was all true.

When Braddock was quizzed by the press leading up to the bout he did not seem nervous or intimidated by Louis. "It's just another fight to me," Braddock said.[10] That could hardly be the truth because he was putting his coveted prize on the line and risking the title for the first time. It should have been no real surprise that Braddock said something like that. He had been the underdog in every fight he had been in for some time, but won all of them. People cheered for him, but they didn't risk their bankrolls betting on him. Same thing this time.

Somewhat more bizarrely in the time-honored tradition of April Fool's jokes, the NEA (Newspaper Enterprise Association) service wrote a fictional story about a bout that never happened between Louis and Braddock date-lined Stamford, Connecticut. "James J. Braddock knocked out Joe Louis last night in a savage bout fought 'secretly' in an old barn near here. A small, select gathering of 500 millionaire sportsmen witnessed the affair, paying $1,000 apiece for the privilege. The battle was fought on a winner-take-all-basis." The story reported that the fight ended in the 13th round. For those who made it all of the way to the end of the story, it signed off with the phrase, "It's April Fool's Day."[11] It didn't say much for what most thought of Braddock's chances if it took a made-up article like that to give him the win.

Unlike occasions when Louis fought at Yankee Stadium and could spend fight day at a nearby apartment, he remained at his training camp right through the day of the bout. He woke at about 10 A.M., ate a hearty breakfast and entertained his entourage with some playful shadow boxing and fancy footwork that he likened to a poor imitation of Bill "Bojangles" Robinson's skills.

Then the group went by car to a train station in Zion, Illinois, and took that mode of transportation into Chicago for the midday weigh-in. Louis registered 197¼ pounds on the scale and Braddock 197. Limited chatter between the fighters was polite. Braddock facetiously had a record titled "You

Can't Take That Away from Me" delivered to Louis at Lake Geneva. It wasn't a bad gag.

The fighters had been placed in the same corridor at Comiskey Park and their dressing areas were separated by only a wooden partition. It was all business in Louis' private area. The time for instruction was past, but Blackburn kept up a steady stream of reminders, basic advice such as "Keep your hands up" and "Don't get careless."[12] Nothing too complicated. Presumably Louis was in his own zone by then, anyway.

Louis was slow to leave his dressing room and in a rare departure from form, Braddock, the champion, preceded him into the ring. He got tired of waiting for Louis to appear, it seemed. He also seemed unwilling to wait for Louis to mount an attack when the bell rang for the first time. Braddock charged across the ring and swung big at Louis' head, though he missed. After that there was a feeling-out process with minor exchanges until Braddock unleashed a sneaky right hand that hit Louis flush on the jaw and dropped him to the canvas for a shocking knockdown.

The crowd screamed in surprise, awed by the blow. They had not expected to see Louis deposited on the seat of his pants. Louis bounded up so quickly that referee Tommy Thomas did not even start a count. "It took me off my feet, but it didn't hurt me all that much," Louis said. "I was surprised by it and I didn't know what to think, but I could think. I wasn't jarred out of my senses like in the Schmeling fight and I jumped right to my feet."[13]

Any time a boxer goes down in a big-time fight the crowd is energized. There is borderline pandemonium. The same type of excitement seizes those broadcasting the bout. So the entire country was frenzied when Louis went down. He did not lose his head, however, and immediately fought back. It was the high point of the fight for Braddock, though he did use his jab to good effect and pick his spots well in the first five rounds.

As the three-minute rounds passed, Braddock faced a new problem. He had not been engaged in a real bout in two years, so he had not been tested beyond exhibitions. His stamina was fading. Louis began to impose his will in the sixth. After some exchanges, Braddock was left with a badly cut mouth because of a split lip. Braddock's face was so bloody that his manager and friend Joe Gould informed his man that he was going to ask the official to step in. But Braddock refused to go along. He didn't want his reign to end while sitting on the stool in his corner.

In a famous exchange, Gould said, "That's it, Jim. I'm going to have the referee stop the fight." To which Braddock replied, "The hell you are." Gould said, "It's time." And Braddock said, "If you do, Joe, I'll never speak to you again." So Braddock went out for the seventh to accept more punishment and dream of a puncher's chance that he could catch Louis.[14]

Braddock tried to be the aggressor in the seventh — no running for Braddock — but Louis landed the better punches and the way Braddock seemed wobbly on his legs it was clear Louis was draining the starch out of him. More and more of Louis' rights were landing and Braddock got shakier.

The end came in the eighth round. Although Braddock's cornermen soaked up his blood in the one-minute intermission between rounds and tried to cool his brow, it was all for naught. As soon as the round began Louis caught up to the champ again and peppered him with rights. Then he landed a left hook followed by a right to the side of the head that dropped Braddock to the ground. Braddock fell flat in the middle of the ring and Thomas counted to 10 standing over him, even as he made an effort to stand after five seconds. The contest was over at 1 minute, 10 seconds of the eighth.

It was an extraordinary moment in American sport. An African American man was the new holder of the heavyweight championship. Joe Louis was the possessor of the most prestigious individual title in sport. It had taken many years, but a black man followed in the footsteps of Jack Johnson. And Louis' victory was hailed far more than assaulted. No one doubted that Louis had won the fight fair and square. Everyone who knew the sport (except for Max Schmeling) recognized that the best fighter now held the biggest title. At that point in the 20th century, Louis, at 23, was also the youngest heavyweight champ of all time.

When Braddock could not continue, the announcement that sang through the in-ring microphone was the sweetest of all possible lyrics for Louis. "The winner and new heavyweight champion — Joe Louis!"

Braddock explained what happened as best he could and recognized it was a missed opportunity when he put Louis on the canvas in the first and was unavailable to follow up. Braddock believed that for the rest of his life. "If I'd hit him a good one after I knocked him down I'd have had him," Braddock said. "But I didn't. Joe was always in trouble with punches to his head, but he was always getting out of trouble. He was smart enough to keep covered up."[15]

The occasion should have been one of unadulterated for joy for Louis, and certainly his fans around the country celebrated with fervor. But when asked the simplest of questions, how it felt to be the world champion, Louis almost snarled. "Don't nobody call me champ till I beat that Schmeling," he said.[16] He actually pronounced it "Smelling," though naturally, not as an insult.

Just as Schmeling had felt unfulfilled because he won the title on a foul in his bout with Jack Sharkey, Louis could not fully accept the glory that was due him in beating Braddock and improving his record to 32–1 because of the blemish on his record from the Schmeling loss. He would not sleep well until he avenged it.

In the dressing room, Jack Blackburn, who understood the vagaries of the fight game much better than his young fighter, felt the satisfaction of training a man to victory in a heavyweight title bout. Certainly there had to have been a bit of extra satisfaction since his man was an African American. Blackburn told Louis he was taking the right glove off his fist and keeping it as a souvenir because he had earned it. Louis didn't disagree with that.

On the streets, on the way home, thousands of black residents of Chicago greeted and feted Louis. It represented a fresh burst of adulation. Everyone felt Joe Louis had vindicated himself by winning the title except Joe Louis. He was the champ and that felt good. But he needed victory over Schmeling to be at peace, no matter what anybody else said.

18

Being the Champ

Joe Louis never pretended that beating James J. Braddock to lift the heavyweight crown was going to be easy, or was easy. After only a few hours of sleep, he woke at 6 o'clock the morning after the bout because his hands were throbbing. Everyone always said that Braddock was a hard-headed dude. They meant stubborn. Louis learned it was for real.

To remedy the pain Louis soaked his hands in hot water, not once, but several times, and then adjourned to a Mike Jacobs–organized press conference. Everyone wanted to hear from the new champ. Louis' presence was greeted with applause at the Morrison Hotel in Chicago, but more striking was the heap of telegrams of congratulations from all over the country. And even more surprisingly, Louis was being presented with offers to appear in movies, on the radio, and on the stage. It was estimated by Louis and others that the offers were valued at $500,000 if he accepted everything.

This was symbolically significant because, in case anyone forgot, Louis was a black man. He had just usurped the prized sporting title from a white man. Rather than being vilified as Jack Johnson had, he was being feted and rewarded. It was naïve to believe that racism had suddenly abated in the United States, but something was different. It seems that the careful managing by John Roxborough and Julian Black in portraying Louis to the public in a certain way had been as wise as they believed. The American people — as a whole — liked Joe Louis.

To a degree. Not all coverage of the fight made it seem as if Louis had achieved much of anything. Braddock was a popular champion and had been a boxing and life underdog for years. He was portrayed as a fallen hero. Nothing to quarrel about there. He had been game and spirited and fought the best he could. There were still members of the press, though, who could not get past the fact that Louis did not show emotion in the ring. To those writers he was a cold-blooded killer, inflicting cruelty with his fists. Given that it was a boxing match, it was an odd way of looking at things. The nature of boxing is that two men throw punches and the best man wins. It was almost as if these sports writers wanted Louis to smile as he worked. Of course when Jack Johnson did that, he was vilified. The white press was still getting accustomed to Joe Louis the man.

There are always some writers in the press corps with better vision than others and the well-respected scribe Dan Parker understood the situation better than most. "How wrong everyone has been about Louis," he wrote. "They called him dumb. They said he was a sucker for a right. They questioned his courage — all after a lucky combination enabled Schmeling to score a knockout over him a year ago. I think it was lucky for Mr. Schmeling he wasn't in there Tuesday night instead of Mr. Braddock."[1] Parker may have been generous in saying that only a lucky group of punches stretched out Louis against Schmeling. Even Louis never asserted that. Louis blew that fight in training and Schmeling was brilliant in his preparation. The rest of what Parker wrote was indisputably true.

There was no immediate outcry that some Great White Hope would have to be found to avenge the white race against a marauding black man. Not everybody in the country was going to invite Louis to dinner, but some kind of progress was being made.

The single most amazing thing that happened to Louis in the immediate aftermath of his capturing the heavyweight championship had nothing to do with boxing at all. He got word from authorities in Alabama that his natural father, Munroe Barrow, was actually alive and residing in a mental institution. Louis had long before gotten used to the idea of Pat Brooks as his father. So did his mother, who was technically a bigamist if Munroe Barrow was alive. Louis had not seen his birth father since 1915 and everyone in the family had presumed his death ages earlier.

When one of Louis' siblings traveled to Alabama and confirmed that the man inside the institution was really their father, Louis began paying for his care, and the next year, when the elder Barrow died, Louis paid for his funeral. But he never visited the man and there was no reunion. To Louis, Munroe Barrow was an estranged and insane stranger, not his dad.

As a side note to the Comiskey Park bout, Jacobs was always in the business of making the most money possible from a promotion. But Louis had quietly asked him to scale down his price range. Not everyone could pay ringside prices of $50 and many of his fans were poor. Louis made it a standing request of Jacobs to price some cheap seats at $5 to $10, and for the Comiskey bout, in a large baseball stadium, the bargain tickets were $3.50. Louis wanted black people to get the chance to see him fight live, not always be stuck with hearing about his exploits on the radio.

Everyone in the Louis camp felt the champ needed a vacation. So Louis went off to play softball with the team he founded for his friends, touring the Midwest for games. Sometimes he played a little bit. Sometimes he just coached. But Louis loved baseball and this was the rough equivalent. Rather than tour making thousands of dollars performing boxing exhibitions, Louis preferred hanging out with his friends having fun for a little while. Instead of making money, Louis was spending money, a habit he never broke in his life. The team probably cost him $50,000 to run and Louis always emptied his pockets of cash when eating out with friends, passing beggars on the street, or being hit up for money more discreetly by those he knew, or those he just met. Louis was literally a meal ticket for many regularly, and many others by happenstance.

Louis had always responded well to a busy fight regimen. Roxborough and Black also believed that the boxing world was not ready to maintain its support for an inactive black champion who squirreled away the crown while he gallivanted around fighting exhibitions and padding his bank account as Braddock had done. Jack Dempsey had done the same. But if Louis just parked the championship belt without risk, the public might turn on him, his managers felt. So Louis signed a new five-year contract with Jacobs with a commitment to fight four times a year.

Max Schmeling couldn't have been more ticked off if his house had been robbed. He felt he deserved the shot against Braddock and he had plenty of support for that argument. He wanted to fight Louis for the title now. Certainly, after his impressive victory he wasn't afraid of the new champ. Now that he owned the title Louis felt that gaining revenge for his only loss would legitimize his reign, so he wanted to fight Schmeling in his first defense.

But just because logic suggests a match should be easy to make, just because the combatants want to make the match, doesn't mean that the match will be made. It is the same today. There is always some peripheral matter that can come into play when scheduling a big fight. In the case of Louis-Schmeling II, Jacobs said he tried to negotiate a deal, but that Schmeling wanted too much money, too large a share of the gate, against the champ. Louis was indeed the title-holder, but Schmeling did not want to undersell his worth. He figured he was 1–0 against Louis so that should count for something.

Not as much as he thought, though. The talking ceased and Louis agreed to make his first title defense versus Tommy Farr at Yankee Stadium on August 30, 1937. If Schmeling wanted to scout Louis he could buy a ticket.

Farr was from Wales and is still considered one of Great Britain's best heavyweights. He engaged in 126 bouts and won 81 of them against 30 losses and 13 draws. He had two bouts ruled no contest. Farr was no soft touch and he was admired for his fearlessness, a reputation that was only enhanced after he met Louis as a significant underdog.

Schmeling had hoped to fight Farr as a tune-up for Louis, but Jacobs swooped in with a better offer of $60,000 and 25 percent of the movie and radio rights. Farr decided a trip to New York was worth his while. Farr was a miner, a tough guy, and he was unflappable when Louis sought to take him out. His strategy was to crowd Louis and prevent the champ from getting good leverage with his jab. It was an intelligent plan and at times Farr perplexed Louis.

Farr's credibility going into the fight was limited. He was not a big name on the U.S. side of the Atlantic Ocean and Jacobs could only sell 30,000 tickets, leaving plenty of empty seats at the stadium. The pre-fight hype didn't help much, either, since sports writers told anyone who would listen that Farr was going to be easy prey and would be knocked out. Although Louis clearly scored better and won a unanimous decision on points, those who skipped the contest missed a pretty good fight. Louis was tested.

Not only did Farr avoid a knockout, he was not knocked down. However, Louis still punished him, drawing blood from cuts on his face as early as the third round and exploiting them the rest of the night. The Associated Press scored the fight eight rounds for Louis, five for Farr and two even. It was a very respectable showing for Farr, but ultimately he was just another Louis victim as Joe raised his record to 33–1.

When Louis was examined after the fight it was obvious that his bruised right hand was injured sufficiently to warrant the use of a cast for a couple of weeks. While it was not broken it was harmed as the result of a punch that broke Farr's nose.

Only days later, while Louis was nursing his aching hand, Jacobs announced that the long-awaited Schmeling-Louis second fight was on. Schmeling capitulated for less money than he originally sought. Jacobs had the upper hand and threatened to cut Schmeling out of the picture altogether and conduct an elimination tournament to name a new No. 1 contender. But Schmeling and Louis would still have to wait a while longer. The fight was announced for June of 1939, nine months from the Farr bout. During that era, mega fights were only held outdoors in ballparks or football stadiums to accommodate the anticipated crowds. There were no really large indoor arenas the way there are in the 2000s with domed stadiums. The outdoor fights had to be scheduled for the summer. It was already September. Louis couldn't even train, and Jacobs wasn't going to either risk an autumn bout or rush things.

The way Joe Louis looked in his prime as heavyweight champion. With 25 title defenses spread over 12 years between 1937 and 1949, Louis held the title longer than any other man (Special Collections, Detroit Public Library).

The schedule gave Louis time to heal completely and squeeze in a couple of more defenses against less-threatening foes. For Louis' second defense, Jacobs rounded up Nathan Mann, who had been born Natalie Menchetti in New Haven, Connecticut, and was a year younger than Louis. Mann was a 5-foot-10 bruiser, but did not figure to give Louis the same competition as Farr had when they met on February 23, 1938, after Louis enjoyed a several months' rest.

Like all title fights, this was scheduled for 15 rounds, but Mann did not make it out of the third. Madison Square Garden was the site and 19,490 turned out to watch what the United Press called "Mann slaughter."[2] This was after Louis, who had the inconvenient habit of starting slow, was on the receiving end of several good, right-hand shots thrown by Mann. That three minutes represented Mann's moment of glory. After that Louis was in charge.

Mann recklessly assumed he could hit Louis as he pleased. Louis proved he was mistaken. Louis' combinations took over and he knocked Mann down three times by the third before he was counted out on a fourth knockdown. Rights, lefts, Mann was introduced to everything in Louis' weapons arsenal. The United Press observer concurred, "Louis could not have been more effective if he had carried an axe in one hand and a blackjack in the other."[3] During the Louis onslaught, Mann's nose bled and he was once knocked halfway through the ropes. In the second round a Louis right connecting with the side of Mann's head knocked the challenger sidewise first and then down. He took a nine-count. That was the prelude to the conclusion in the third.

Louis impressed the usual boxing observers and syndicated writer Bob Considine thought he looked magnificent. "All of the merciless cruelty that brought him to the top of the fight game came back to the fists and heart of Louis Wednesday night when he knocked out the young Connecticut heavyweight after 1 minute and 56 seconds of the third round. One again the merciless stalker, Louis, leaner and meaner than the night he destroyed Primo Carnera, floored his game foe four times before Mann, giddy and gory from punches, was counted out by referee Arthur Donovan. The Negro has regained the old fire that was sadly lacking when Max pinned his ears back two summers ago."[4]

After wiping out Mann, Louis still had five months to wait before he could get his chance against Schmeling, and so to fill the time his handlers scheduled another defense, April 1 against Harry Thomas of Eagle Bend, Minnesota. Schmeling had knocked Thomas down seven times in a December 1937 fight in Madison Square Garden. Thomas was a space-filler for Louis and a yardstick of sorts.

Thomas, who retired in 1939 with a 41-13-2 record, met Louis at Chicago Stadium in a scheduled 15-rounder. Any challenger given hope by Louis' occasional first-round carelessness watched in awe as Louis eliminated that problem. He was on Thomas from the first bell, dominating him with his jab and pushing him around with the periodic right hand that gave the challenger a headache.

One Louis right hand to the head near the end of the third round spun Thomas completely around and left him with blurry vision. Thomas was sinking to the canvas in his own corner when his manager, Nate Lewis, reached through the ropes and placed a stool under Thomas as if the round had ended rather than there still being seconds on the clock. Louis stood at center ring surprised by the goings-on. Referee Davey Miller began to admonish Lewis, who pointed at the timekeeper just as the bell rang.

In the post-fight discussion Lewis explained that he thought the round had ended and he had just not heard it because of the crowd noise. Thomas was subject to being disqualified because of his corner's action, but Miller let the action continue. He may have done Thomas a favor if he had halted it because Louis knocked the challenger down four times in the fourth round before the fight ended in the fifth. Having been beaten up by both Schmeling and Louis, Thomas had an expert eye view to compare the two men. "Boy, can that Louis hit!"[5] Thomas said with some difficulty through damaged lips from the blows he took when the bout was over.

Inevitably, Thomas was asked who would win between Schmeling and Louis when they met with the title at stake. "Joe Louis will knock out Max Schmeling when they meet again," Thomas said. "I am willing to bet every penny that I got in my purse ($4,699) last night that Louis will knock out Schmeling."[6] As far as is generally known, no one checked back with Thomas months later to see if he followed through with his betting claim.

Louis had already defended the heavyweight title three times in 10 months and his record was 35–1. He was bugged by that "1" on the chart, but he couldn't erase it. He was more anxious than ever to avenge it. Farr, Mann and Thomas had been disposed of and nothing lay between April and the June date with Schmeling but time and training. "Right around this time I felt perfect," Louis said, "absolutely perfect. I was finally the fighting machine Chappie had promised to make me."[7]

Louis couldn't wait for the rematch with Schmeling.

19

Louis-Schmeling II

Max Schmeling was well-liked in the United States as an individual. Sports writers enjoyed his personality and conversations. He was also admired because he had won the heavyweight championship and because he had knocked out the formidable Joe Louis.

But Schmeling's image and reputation were no longer in his own hands and he could do nothing to control world events and the powerful political currents shaking his home country of Germany like a massive earthquake.

Although Adolf Hitler still was putting on an act for the international community, pretending that he harbored no plans of expansionism and he still cared what others thought to enough of a degree that he kept his diabolical plans to wipe out his nation's Jewish population a secret, hints, reports, and stories filtered beyond the Third Reich's borders.

More and more to Americans, Schmeling became identified with a repugnant regime. He was caught in the middle, seen as a favored son bringing glory to his country by Hitler, and seen as a sympathizer and tool of an administration that was gaining enemies by the day to Americans.

The United States was Schmeling's second home. He had been traveling back and forth between Germany and the U.S. for years. The U.S. was the scene of his greatest boxing triumphs. His manager, Joe Jacobs, was based in the U.S. If Schmeling was surprised by his reception when he arrived in May of 1938 by ship after crossing the Atlantic once more, he shouldn't have been.

It did not help any that Schmeling had been quoted in German newspapers making inflammatory racial statements indicating a prejudice against blacks. He denied making them and said the quotes were fabricated, but they followed him to the United States.

"The black man will always be afraid of me," Schmeling was reported as saying (there was some supposition that Hitler's propaganda minister Joseph Goebbels made up the comments). "He is inferior." He also said, "I am a fighter, not a politician. I am no superman in any way." That sounded more like him. Schmeling was in no position to complain about Nazi comments attributed to him and in less of a position to defect, even if it occurred to him at the time, though it was only 1938 and World War II had not begun. His wife and mother did not accompany him to the states and he would not abandon them.[1]

Before the first Louis fight Schmeling was asked if Hitler personally gave him a send-off to the U.S. and he said no, that there was no reason for the country's leader to do so. This time Schmeling did receive a hearty, party sendoff before he sailed.

Schmeling was greeted by protestors waving signs calling him a Nazi and saying he should not be allowed into the U.S. Even Louis took note. "Man, did he catch hell," the champion said.[2]

By 1938, Schmeling was not under any illusion that Hitler was going to be the kind of leader he, his family and friends, wanted to see running Germany. On his own and through his actress wife, Schmeling was tight with the artistic set and they were free thinkers who despaired as they saw Hitler's so-called enemies being forced out of jobs and being rounded up and never seen again.

"In our sphere we came to know this regime's other face soon enough," Schmeling said in his autobiography. "Each of us had at least one person we were close to who had been forced to leave the country. Others had been forced out of a profession or simply made to live in fear. And we all knew — or at least knew of — persons who had already been arrested."[3]

By the time Schmeling left for the second Louis bout, he was viewed skeptically by some in the Nazi hierarchy. Schmeling had never become a member of the party and he had refused a specific honor that Hitler wished to grant him. He had delicately avoided accepting an award called "The Dagger of Honor" knowing it identified him with the leadership. There was risk in turning down the offering, too, but Schmeling did so. Against his will, on both sides of the ocean, Schmeling was being drawn more and more into a political world he wished to duck. It was like running in quicksand.

Schmeling never forgot his tumultuous reception at the docks before the second Louis fight. "The posters that they held over their heads called me an 'Aryan Show Horse' and a representative of 'the master race,' while they shook their fists at me," Schmeling said of the protestors. At his hotel there were other protestors with signs, too, including one reading, "Boycott Nazi Schmeling."[4] It got worse. When Schmeling went for a walk in Manhattan, on streets he knew well and had always been hailed fondly on, strangers instead raised their right arms and gave him sarcastic "Heil, Hitler" Nazi salutes. Some friends lobbied him to stay in the United States permanently.

"For the previous 10 years New York had practically been my home," Schmeling said, "so of course I was bothered and hurt by all of this. There was Hitler, who was filling the world with hate and fear. Among the demonstrators were surely many who had been forced to emigrate." No one wanted to see him win, Schmeling said, because, he admitted, "I was a showpiece for the Nazis." During his training time in the U.S. Schmeling received "thousands of hate letters signed Heil Hitler."[5]

It was very apparent that this was going to be one of the most unusual boxing matches of all time with out-of-the-ring international repercussions seemingly of greater significance than the simple matter of who won and who lost. Even after he retreated from New York City to his training camp upstate in the Adirondack Mountains, Schmeling was stalked by sign-waving picketers.

Louis had had a taste of this once before, drafted as an African American to uphold the honor of Ethiopia when it was about to be overrun by Italy when he fought Primo Carnera. The magnitude of this match was so much greater. Louis was being drafted by all Americans to represent the country's ideals, not just his race. Given the amount of prejudice still prevalent in the United States, given the depths of hatred still rooted in the Deep South and tentacles that reached elsewhere, the irony could not have been denser.

Until this moment Joe Louis had been a celebrity by virtue of being the world's heavyweight champion. Now he was assigned the task of using his fists to fight for the honor of the nation and to uphold its pride and dignity, as well as the principles it had been founded upon. Louis was morphing into a hero character.

After he won the title, but before Louis was lined up for another go-around with Schmeling, he attended a Washington, D.C., dinner at the invitation of President Franklin D. Roosevelt. Louis arrived by private car sent from the White House. In a meeting with FDR the president reached out and squeezed Louis' biceps, saying, "Joe, we're depending on those muscles for America."[6] The United States was years from being involved in a shooting war in Europe, but likely FDR saw the inevitably of the future clash.

"Let me tell you, that was a thrill," Louis said. "Now, even more, I knew I had to get Schmeling good. I had my own personal reasons and the whole damned country was depending on me."[7] Some doubted that FDR ever had that exchange with Louis, but it was reported in many publications and Louis recounted it in detail in his autobiography.

Louis was not unaware of the political hubbub, the amount of abuse being heaped upon Schmeling and how Americans were taking sides based more upon his citizenship than his skin color. Some might not have liked being aligned with an African American, but almost all Americans were suspicious of Hitler and even if Louis was a "Negro" he was their Negro and thus the lesser of evils. That was one way of looking at it if you didn't like black people. Louis had his own legions of fans, in the black community and among all boxing fans. He earned those with his talent, personality and demeanor, making friends as he rose through the ranks of contenders, and by the way he handled himself as champion. Louis had been around long enough for the public to get to know him and know what he was like. Even before he plunged his nation into war Hitler made it easy for people to despise him with his beliefs of the inferiority of blacks and Jews and other minorities set as a cornerstone of his platform.

Democracy versus Nazism was a backdrop for the fight, but Louis retained his single-minded focus and motivation. Schmeling had beat him badly and cost him his only defeat. The only way to clean the slate was to return the beating. More than anything, symbol of his race, representative of his country, all aside, Louis wanted to redeem himself in his own eyes. He couldn't avoid being drawn into comments about the broader issues, however, when he was constantly peppered with questions from sports writers about the topic. "I fight for America against the challenge of a foreign invader, Max Schmeling," Louis said on the radio, although it didn't really sound like him. The second part of the statement did. "This isn't just one man against another, or Joe Louis boxing Max Schmeling. It is the good old USA versus Germany."[8] Rather remarkably, the interview drew a response from the German government, alleging that Louis was trying to exploit the fight for racial propaganda reasons. That was a comment that made a lot of Americans blink.

Louis prepared in deadly earnest at his Pompton Lakes, New Jersey, training camp. He did not play golf. He left Marva at home. He did not take fun trips to New York or Atlantic City. Being in top form for Schmeling was the main thing on his mind. Trainer Jack Blackburn and his assistant, Mannie Seamon, plotted carefully to bring Louis to a fine peak at just the right moment. Once he was in training camp, removed from the exterior noise of the political din, it became easier for Louis to narrow his focus and look at the Schmeling bout the way he had approached 36 others — it was a fight.

In late May, Louis, Blackburn and the others in his entourage went on a field trip from camp to Long Island City where they watched Henry Armstrong and Barney Ross fight for the welterweight title. Although this was surely first-rate entertainment, there was a broader educational purpose to the mission. Blackburn wanted Louis to watch Armstrong implement his style and possibly learn some tactics from it.

"Last time Chappie fought just the way Schmeling wanted him to,"

Blackburn said. "The time it'll be different. Chappie's going to learn from Armstrong. He's going to set a fast pace right from the start, work inside Schmeling's defense and batter away at his body. He'll start caving in after three or four rounds, then Chappie'll get down to real business and finish him."[9] There was the game plan.

At about this time Louis was making the acquaintanceship of a new sports writer on the scene, one who would become one of the best. Jimmy Cannon got an exclusive with Louis the night before he broke camp as they ate dinner together. Cannon told Louis he saw him winning by knockout in the sixth round. Louis retorted, "It goes in one," he said, and he held up and wagged a single finger to emphasize his point.[10]

It would have been easy enough for Louis to get distracted in his preparations for the Schmeling fight, not only because of the hype surrounding the bout, not only because of the political issues swirling, but because Louis' training camp was nearly overwhelmed by the curious. Never mind the previous type of indulgences Louis had engaged in with golf and women, the sheer numbers of spectators who showed up hot to see him throw a punch at a heavy bag was staggering. One day 9,000 fans flooded the complex.

"Probably the biggest gathering ever to see any boxer work out anywhere," one historian noted. "People gazed upon Louis from trees, fences, roofs and cars."[11] Some of those observers did not gaze at Louis with fondness in their eyes — they wore their beliefs on their sleeves, displaying Nazi swastikas. Louis was told that Schmeling's trainer — and Schmeling — made disparaging remarks about blacks and "went strutting around in a Nazi uniform, especially after public sessions. "The papers said Max was yelling about being a member of a superior race and making some general insults about my race. But Max never talked that shit to me."[12]

Although the fight took place about 75 years ago, the observation that 9,000 fans turning out on a single day for a workout being the largest ever might still hold true. Louis had American fans on his side, rooting for him. But that didn't mean they all thought he was going to win. The division of opinion was dramatic in the newspapers. Some writers felt Louis was a more complete fighter than he had been the first time he fought Schmeling and had turned in no clunkers in his following bouts over the next two years, and so would gain revenge. Others believed that Schmeling had Louis' number and that Louis did not have it within him to adapt, to learn and change. There was a kind of gross underestimation of his ability as an athlete among those skeptics. Those writers looked at Louis and saw all muscle, brawn and natural talent and gave him no credit for brain power. Grantland Rice was one of the offenders who implied that Louis was too stupid to adjust.

It's not clear just how those sports writers could explain away Louis' ability to win the title from James J. Braddock and defend it three times without experiencing growth and maturity.

"He'd won, but I'd looked over those films," Louis said. "For 10 rounds I was going around with my hands down. He should have had me out long before. Now, I know Max looked at those films, too. If it took him all that time to knock me out, he was making some big mistakes also."[13] Sounds a lot like a man who had thought the entire matter through with great care, studied what he had done wrong, and was prepared to correct his mistakes.

Fight day, June 22, 1938, two years after their first bout, finally arrived. Louis indicated he got a good rest the night before, sleeping in until 9 A.M., when he was awakened by a handler. At midday the combatants met in New York City for the weigh-in. Louis and Schmeling nodded at one another as they stepped on the scales, but did not talk. Louis weighed 198¾ pounds and Schmeling weighed 193¾.

As he normally did before New York fights in the Bronx at Yankee Stadium, Louis retreated to an apartment in Harlem. This one belonged to a friend named Freddie Wilson. In the afternoon, Louis, Wilson and Blackburn took a walk and Wilson asked the champ how he was feeling, only to be startled when Louis said, "I'm scared." That was not the response expected. Then Louis elaborated. "I'm scared I might kill Schmeling tonight."[14]

The automobile ride to the stadium was quiet and Louis got to his dressing room plenty early. He was so early that he took a two-hour nap, an action that many other boxers couldn't have contemplated because of nerves. Blackburn was Louis' wake-up call and he began taping the champ's hands an hour before the fight in mid-evening. Mike Jacobs, who like Louis had come from poverty and long believed that Louis was going to make him a millionaire, stopped in for what passed for a pep-talk. "Murder that bum and don't make an asshole out of me," Jacobs said. Louis replied, "Don't worry about a thing. I ain't going back to Ford and you ain't gonna go back to selling lemon drops on the Staten Island Ferry."[15]

Both Louis and Schmeling were wrapped in a cocoon of New York police officers as they made their way to the ring to hear referee Arthur Donovan's final pre-fight instructions. Outside the arena there were anti–Max pickets and the Anti–Nazi League demonstrated. Inside, not even the police escort prevented Schmeling from being pelted by debris such as paper cups and cigarette packs and his ears couldn't drown out the boos or the catcalls.

By that time more people had turned against Schmeling. With the world title at stake and a black man as the foe, this bout had become important to Hitler and his administration. The Nazi regime had sent Arno Helmuth from

Berlin to broadcast from ringside. But Helmuth had been blabbing hysterical comments in the week leading up to the fight, badmouthing New York's "Jew governor" (Herbert Lehman), the fight's "Jew promoter" (Mike Jacobs) and hinting that the officials were going to steal the fight for the U.S. "African Auxiliary," as he called black Americans.[16] Emotions were inflamed even more when it was revealed on the eve of the fight that Hitler had sent Schmeling a good luck telegram.

On a pleasant night with a slight breeze, more than 70,000 fans paid more than $1 million to witness a fight that had been hyped as "The Battle of the Century" and which *The Ring* magazine did name "Fight of the Decade."

It may have been all of that because of the way the world scrutinized the proceedings, but it was also the round of the year, too, because that's all it lasted, one round. When the bell rang to start the fight, it was almost over. Louis did not waste much time or motion setting Schmeling up with wicked jabs that he flicked over and over into the challenger's face. Schmeling barely had time to set himself with Louis constantly in his face pressuring.

Schmeling finally got off one of his patented rights that had so grievously harmed Louis in their first match, but Louis escaped easily. He did land his second try, but it did no damage and instead of reeling backwards, Louis pounced and hit Schmeling with a terrific right to the jaw that sent him flying backwards into the ropes. Schmeling grabbed the ropes to prevent tumbling to the ground and covered up sufficiently so that Louis could not repeat his blow to the head. Instead, Louis immediately focused his attack on the body.

Turning his body halfway to the side while seeking to avoid Louis' ferocity, Schmeling was hit with a brutal punch that caused him to shout out in pain. Later, looking for an excuse, an explanation, or anything to salvage dignity, Schmeling's corner claimed that it was an illegal kidney punch. Louis said it was Schmeling's fault that he turned when the punch was on the way, coming by special delivery. "I just hit him, that's all," Louis said. "I hit him right in the ribs and I guess maybe it was a lucky punch. But man, did he scream. I thought it was a lady at ringside crying. He just screamed, that's all."[17]

Donovan separated Louis from Schmeling briefly, as he still grasped the ropes to prevent collapse. But the few seconds of rest did not help much. Louis charged back in swinging for the head and the finish, and when he struck Schmeling with a huge right hand on the side of the head the challenger pitched sideways flat on the canvas. Schmeling was up at a three count, only to take more punishment and suffer another knockdown.

The fighters had been informed that unlike other venues, New York did not recognize seconds throwing a towel into the ring to concede for their fighter. By this point, a distraught Machon had clearly forgotten that admonition and threw a towel onto the canvas, signaling the end for Schmeling. Donovan scooped up the towel and threw it right back, ignoring Machon altogether as he continued to officiate.

Schmeling jumped right back up and Louis dished out more, scoring with a left hook, followed by a right to the jaw, blasting Schmeling to the ground for the third time in the round. This time he did not get up. The heralded bout was over at 2 minutes, 4 seconds of the first round. It was a savage and thorough beating.

Still at ringside, Louis said, "I waited two years for my revenge and now I got it."[18] True to his own feeling that he was not the real heavyweight champion until he paid back Schmeling, Louis also said, "I'm sure enough champion now."[19]

No one in Germany heard Louis say that on the radio. Before the result was even final the plug was pulled on Helmuth's broadcast. His fight description took an abrupt detour into Richard Wagner music because the Nazi powers that were did not want the nation to hear about the downfall of a hero taking a devastating licking from a black man.

In an era when Americans are bombarded by technological choices, from dozens of cable TV channels, to music, messages, and news reports on their cell phones, it is difficult to image a country where just about everybody and everyone who was not inside Yankee Stadium as a first-hand witness to the fight was sitting in place listening to the scheduled 15-round fight on the radio. It was estimated that at a time when the United States' population was 130 million that 70 million (some say more, but that may have included babes in mother's arms) of them were tuned in to the broadcast.

Just in the way that FDR was a radio president with his fireside chats, Louis was a radio heavyweight champ, with Americans — especially black Americans — glued to the radio whenever he fought. The radio made listening to a Louis fight a community experience, not a solitary one. You listened with your family in the living room. You listened at a neighbor's house if you had no radio. You went to some public place to listen if you either couldn't afford your own radio, or had no other access to one.

On the family peanut farm in Plains, Georgia, the black field hands who worked for Earl Carter asked him if they could come close enough to the house that night to listen to the radio report of the fight and he welcomed them. According to the memory of Jimmy Carter, Earl's son, and the future president of the United States, that night the guests listened to the fight quietly, showing no emotion, politely thanked his father (who had been rooting for Schmeling), made their way across a dirt road and to their own home area—and then erupted in celebration.

"At that point," said Jimmy Carter, "pandemonium broke loose inside that house, as our black neighbors shouted and yelled in celebration of the Louis victory. But all the curious, accepted proprieties of a racially segregated society had been carefully observed."[20]

"Everyone stopped and listened to the fight," said Ferdie Pacheco (later Muhammad Ali's ring doctor) of that particular Louis fight. "Even the street-cars stopped."[21]

If they did indeed stop, they didn't start running again in Harlem anytime soon. Once the decision was in, the coronation of Louis complete, the people of New York City's African American section took over the streets in raucous celebration, singing and dancing, emotions of joy unleashed. Louis once again had struck a blow for their race against The Man. Even under all that pressure, Joe Louis had done it for them. Of course, Louis had done it for him, but the byproduct was doing it for one and all. He had a wide wingspan that could shelter many.

"There was never a Harlem like there was last night," one newspaper on the scene reported after the fight. "If you take a dozen Christmases, a score of New Year's Eves, a bushel of July Fourths and maybe, just maybe, you'd get a faint glimpse of the idea."[22]

While Louis found vindication and was feted not only in Harlem, in black neighborhoods in other major U.S. cities, and throughout the sporting world, Schmeling was taken to Polyclinic Hospital. He remained there for 10 days before being taken by ambulance to the Bremen, the regular ship Schmeling sailed upon between the two countries.

On behalf of Schmeling, some Germans sought to file an official protest with the New York State Athletic Commission that he was stopped by an illegal kidney punch. The German ambassador, Hans Dieckhoff, journeyed from Washington, D.C., to probe the matter directly with Schmeling as he lay in bed. Schmeling discouraged the idea of an appeal. Back home the Nazi Propaganda Ministry played up that angle and also suggested that someone had slipped lead into Louis' gloves. Louis said that he had nowhere else to hit Schmeling based on the way he turned, and even weak and in the hospital, Schmeling agreed with that assessment, saying it was partially his fault because he shifted his body in the manner he had.

Nat Fleischer, *Ring* magazine editor, and a friend to both fighters, chimed in loudly with his thoughts. The headline on his ringside report read "Max Fouled? Bunk!" Fleischer said that Louis proved his absolute superiority in scoring the quick knockout. "It wasn't a matter of luck," he said. "It wasn't any injury suffered by the challenger that brought about his downfall. Nor was it a foul punch that caused his rout. Make no mistake about that."[23]

However, in some quarters that impression lingered, an idea that another writer sought to put to rest in the same issue of *The Ring* magazine, couching the brouhaha under the general heading of the trend for fighters of that period to suddenly whine too much when they were beaten. "Schmeling opened his eyes and started to squawk," said New York newsman Daniel M. Daniel. "He had been fouled. After a while, he decided he hadn't been fouled. Not intentionally. It was an accident. There are thousands of persons in this country and abroad who believe Louis won with a foul kidney punch. Schmeling was not beat by a punch to the kidneys. A wallop to the jaw put him in position to go out. [Schmeling] must have known that any claim of foul he might utter would cast aspersions on the great triumph of his opponent, a clean, gentlemanly fighter."[24]

Louis had done his job mopping up the heavyweight division. His record was 36–1 and he was on a 12-fight winning streak. He was the heavyweight champion of the world with four defenses on his resume. He was the victor in the fight of the century and he had simultaneously defended his own and his country's honor. Everyone agreed he deserved a vacation.

20

Bigger Than Ever

Years after Joe Louis battered Max Schmeling on behalf of all Americans, comedian and social activist Dick Gregory, who was not quite six years old at the time, talked about growing up listening to Louis' exploits on the radio so often it was like a regularly scheduled show.

For black Americans of a certain age, the 1930s and 1940s, when Louis reigned as heavyweight champ represented an awakening in pride. Gregory, originally from St. Louis, offered one of the most telling comments about what Louis' victory over Schmeling meant "It was the first time a black man had become the great white hope," he said.[1]

It was an insightful summary of the moment. But the moment didn't really stop there. Louis remained an active champion, boxing regularly, his fame and reputation growing by the title defense. No one believed that the United States was a fair and just society on racial matters at that time, but by dint of his accomplishments Louis grew steadily in esteem. It might be said that until Louis bested Schmeling he was the most famous black man in the United States. After Louis defeated Schmeling, he was one of the most famous men in the United States. Period.

A 1989 retrospective film about Louis' career reached out to various well-known African Americans, including Gregory, and they gushed about what it was like, how important it was, what a sense of pride they felt, when Louis was the heavyweight champ and what it meant to them each time he defended the crown. It was really something, the poet Maya Angelou said, to realize "some black women's son was the strongest man in the world." When she uttered that sentence on film, Angelou punctuated the comment with a satisfying chuckle.[2]

New York Congressman Charles Rangel called Louis "the epitome of racial pride."[3] And while comedian Bill Cosby felt that was true, there was also a lot of concern for Louis because, what if he lost? What did it mean if

160

he lost? His broad shoulders kept aloft the hopes of millions. He couldn't lose. "You could feel hearts trembling because if Joe Louis loses our whole race would be down," Cosby said. When he won? "Everybody rushed out to the street. They had this release."[4]

Oh, boy, it was something to be Joe Louis back then. He couldn't walk down the street without being mobbed. Crowds followed him when he stretched his long stride alone or with Marva. He always dressed well, couldn't be seen in public without a dazzling suit on. By one estimate, Louis owned 25 pairs of shoes, 30 suits that had cost $100 apiece, and complemented them with brightly colored socks. Once, when he wanted to take leftovers home from his mother's house — he loved her fried chicken — Louis hesitated. It would be unseemly for him to be seen walking down the street carrying some old box or brown paper bag with grease stains seeping through. So Marva wrapped up the chicken in a fancy box and tied a ribbon on it to make it appear Louis was toting home a present.

Smiling Joe Louis. Louis had much to enjoy as the heavyweight champion who was a symbol of power and someone to admire for other American blacks, and the earner of six-figure paydays when he defended his crown (Special Collections, Detroit Public Library).

Louis was making six-figure paydays. He could buy anything he wanted, travel to Hollywood and hang out, go to Las Vegas and gamble, buy nice dresses and jewelry for Marva, give money to his family. He could afford it. He bought himself a black Buick, show horses, 80 Hereford cows, 100 Poland China hogs and a 477-acre farm in Spring Hill, Michigan. It was conspicuous consumption, and author Gerald Astor said it made perfect sense given that Louis was the son of a poor sharecropper.

"The joy of glittering materialism and ostentatious spending was as natural as his table gluttony," Astor wrote.[5] While he didn't drink, Louis enjoyed hanging out with friends in night clubs. Billy Rowe, a black sportswriter who became a friend, said, "When Joe would walk into a place the price of everything went up right away. People would figure he could make the money, that he had the money, why shouldn't he pay it out? And he would invite it. So he would never look at a check, just put his hand in his pocket and pay."[6]

If someone on the street begged for a $5 bill Louis gave him a twenty. No problem. Louis had empathy for the needy and he wanted to be liked. If you hit him just right he'd fund your dreams. Living large was part of being the heavyweight champion of the world. It wasn't sexy or slick to set aside money in a rainy-day account.

On any given day Louis emptied his pockets with gifts to casual acquaintances or panhandlers. Then he would turn to his companion and ask for a few bucks, or drop in on Mike Jacobs' office, and hit him up for a loan much bigger than that. One difference was that Louis never kept track of where his money went and Jacobs did. Louis knew he'd never see his money again. Jacobs expected to be repaid. Louis also lavished his money on women. He had friends who would fix him up with dancers, show girls, and he would disappear for a day at a time with the new babe at the Hotel Theresa. In a general sense Louis was protected in Harlem, except for the high prices he paid for things.

The heavyweight champ couldn't be seen as stingy and by nature Louis was generous anyway. It was never clear if trainer Jack Blackburn or managers John Roxborough and Julian Black, the men who guided his career and truly cared for him, tried to force Louis to save money. Eventually, they all had their own woes that had to be dealt with and Louis out-lasted them all in his long ring career. Unlike many athletes who make foolish big-money deals, are swindled or cheated, Louis ran through his money as if it was water spilling from a spigot that was never turned off. "Nobody cheated him of his money," Marva said later. "He just spent it."[7]

Louis also kept earning it. After some play time post–Schmeling, Louis got back in the gym and began training for his next defense, set for January 25, 1939, at Madison Square Garden against John Henry Lewis. Lewis was the light-heavyweight champion from 1935 to 1939, and like Louis, an African American. He was managed by Gus Greenlee, who was known to his local police department in Pittsburgh for his gambling involvements, but to black sports fans for his long-time commitment and connection to the Negro Leagues baseball operation. Greenlee owned the Pittsburgh Crawfords and the popular Crawford Grill in Pittsburgh while also giving scholarship money to young black teenagers so they could pay for college.

Louis did not really want to fight Lewis and John Roxborough told Mike Jacobs that. Jacobs said Lewis was going around saying he could beat the champ, though, so it might make an OK match. "It will be a lousy fight," Roxborough said. "These two are too friendly for it to be otherwise. Lewis can't hurt Joe and Joe won't hurt John Henry." Roxborough said when Louis was informed that Jacobs was making the match he didn't like it. "I don't wanna fight John Henry," Louis said. "He's my best friend. What's Uncle Mike up to that he wants me to toss punches at my pal?" Louis was appealed to on the grounds that Lewis needed the money.[8]

Lewis was nearing the end of his career and eventually retired with a record of 109 wins, 9 losses and 6 draws. He was losing vision in one eye when he signed to fight Louis, a risky proposition at best, and was really granted the title shot as a favor so he could collect that one more decent payday. Lewis was only a minimal threat to Louis at most, and Louis did not want to hurt his friend. One thing that distinguished the encounter — it was the first time two African Americans fought for the heavyweight championship.

Almost as an act of generosity Louis finished off Lewis in the first round of their scheduled 15-round bout. He said he didn't want to hurt him too badly, but that didn't prevent Louis from knocking Lewis through the ropes on one knockdown and defensively dominating so thoroughly that Lewis never landed a serious blow. The fight was never close and the sports writers asked Louis why he did so much damage to a friend. Louis replied that he didn't, that by wiping out Lewis in a single round it prevented him from taking a beating for 15 rounds. "So you see, I was kind to him," Louis said.[9]

The sports writers had a slightly different definition of kindness. "Maybe there should be a law against letting any of the current heavyweights loose in the same ring with Joe Louis," a New York writer said. "That would be only humane. He should retire until some steel-ribbed, hard-hitting youngster happens along. John Henry is a boxing stylist, one of the best around with speed of foot to back it, but what good are those fistic theories when a guy knows you can't hurt him and proceeds to smack you over? Louis is a fighter, not a fancy man, and when he's hitting he doesn't bunt."[10]

Jack Roper was not such a man with a washboard stomach and the fortitude to match. Louis made him the victim in his sixth defense of the title on April 17 of 1939, keeping to a busy schedule. Roper, like Lewis, was an active fighter who put together a lifetime mark of 63-43-10. The bout was fought in Los Angeles, providing Louis with a fresh audience, and 35,000 residents were intrigued enough to show up at Wrigley Field. It was the first time in a decade that a heavyweight had defended in California.

Roper, 36, was about as well known as a studio electrician as he was a heavyweight contender, and Louis wasted no time ridding the stage of him, though that came after Roper had his one second of glory with a sweeping left hook that connected with Louis' jaw. Roper lasted just 2 minutes, 20 seconds with the champ, who shook the challenger to the core with a perfect right to the jaw. Roper dropped and didn't get up by a 10 count.

"I was conscious as I went down," Roper said after the fight, "but my legs seemed paralyzed, and after I hit the floor I tried to get up, but my muscles just wouldn't work. It took a champion to knock me out for the first time since I started fighting in 1923. I've lost fights by technical knockouts, but never on the floor. But I landed one left hook that I know he felt it."[11] Maybe so, but Roper was asked less about his one serious blow than to sum up generally what happened. "I zigged when I should have zagged," he said.[12]

There seemed to be a new, better-than-ever model of Joe Louis on the loose in the ring since he disposed of Schmeling. Part of it was that he was fighting guys who weren't as good as he was, or even in his class (though part of that was that there were not many guys in his class). Since the Tommy Farr fight, which went the distance, Louis had been on a scorched earth swing through his opponents. Roper represented his third straight first-round KO. Fans love a knockout king, but they also like to get their money's worth and Louis was making it tough on them. Fans had to learn they better come early for the under-card and not get caught going out for popcorn before a Louis fight or they wouldn't make it back to their seats in time to see the main event.

It had been nearly two years since Louis won the heavyweight crown and he already had six defenses on his record. He was 38–1 and was not yet 25. It appeared Louis was in for a long reign.

By triumphing over Schmeling and by defending his title often, Louis kept his name in the public eye. If at one time a heavily-muscled black man with fists of thunder would have seemed menacing to American whites of a certain stripe, Louis was now a familiar face on the national scene. If you thought of boxing, you thought of Joe Louis. It was that simple. He was the best and everyone knew it.

Joe Louis was the most famous black in the United States during his heyday, but after 1936 when he won four Olympic gold medals, Jesse Owens (right) rivaled him for attention. The two men became close friends for the rest of their lives (Special Collections, Detroit Public Library).

That status made Louis an almost surreal celebrity in African American eyes, though for the first time, concurrent with Louis' capture of the title, there was a second black athlete that rose from obscurity and poverty to become almost as famous. Jesse Owens was the most famous track man in the country, winner of four gold medals at the 1936 Olympics, and another black man who had taught Adolf Hitler a lesson that a man's superiority did not relate to the color of his skin.

Louis and Owens became close friends, a lifelong friendship. They shared confidences and they dined out with their wives. They were of similar temperament. They both recognized the injustices visited upon American blacks and the prejudices that prevailed and did harm to their countrymen. They had much in common. Both were born in Alabama. Both had fathers that were sharecroppers who moved the family north for better opportunity. Both were the grandsons of slaves.

While Louis was counseled not to smile too much when he beat up white men, Owens smiled broadly when he out-ran them. Also, Owens attended college, at Ohio State, while Louis dropped out of school as a teenager.

Owens' spectacular effort in winning four gold medals in Berlin in the Summer Games of 1936 — in the 100 meters, 200 meters, long jump and relay — provided him with fame throughout the United States, but in the 1930s, and for much longer, track and field was a purely amateur sport. Unlike Louis, who could make hundreds of thousands of dollars with his fists every time he signed a contract, Owens couldn't make a penny with his feet if he wished to continue competing in track.

Relinquishing his amateurism soon after the Olympics because he had to make a living, Owens was pushed out of his sport too soon. He thought his name would be as golden as his awards, and while it was in some circles, those were not financially beneficial ones. Owens was working at a gas station in Cleveland the year before he won Olympic gold and his prospects weren't much better the year after.

Owens was already a recognized star because in a single day at the Big Ten championships of 1935 he set three world records and tied another. When Joe Louis came to Ohio the two men met for the first time later that year at a hotel where Louis was staying. The meeting was originally a little awkward because Louis was already a big star and Owens had admired him from afar, much like one of the many thousands of other Joe Louis fans.

When they settled down to talk in Cleveland, though, they realized they had much in common and Louis' demeanor calmed Owens. When Louis and Owens went out to eat at a lunch counter their presence attracted such a mob of fans seeking autographs from both of them that the local police thought they needed backup to control a riot. The men began spending time together, but Louis had money to spend, while Owens was nearly always broke.

Antiquated Amateur Athletic Union rules that remained in effect for several more decades pretty much ensured that any athlete not being supported by a college scholarship had to be either independently rich or live on a shoestring. That summer, Owens was charged with violating amateurism rules for being paid $159 as an Ohio State legislative page, more than the going rate, and he was temporarily suspended by the AAU.

Owens was a naturally upbeat person. Rather than complain about living in a segregated society he was sure that things would change soon. He had faith in ignorant whites to adapt and grow and mature. "When white folks see that we dance as well as they, when they see that we eat and drink the same things, and laugh and cry over the same things, they begin to realize we are human beings," Owens said. "All this bleating about downtrodden doesn't do any good."[13]

In 1935, when Louis and Owens were first getting to know one another, Louis was far better known. They had both attracted the autograph seekers that first time because they were in Cleveland, Owens' stronghold, but when they got together elsewhere Louis garnered most of the attention. After Owens' gold-medal haul in 1936 their celebrity was more on par.

It was later, when his accomplishments and good name weren't worthy enough to land him a good job, that Owens had to fight off bitterness. Louis, meanwhile, merely had to fight off every contender put in front of him. There was no reason to think that his dominating knockout streak would end any time soon when it was announced that a New Jersey bar owner with a bulging belly named Tony Galento would be his next foe.

21

Two-Ton Tony and
Tons of Others

By the time Joe Louis finished off John Henry Lewis some sports writers were beginning to call his frequent defenses of the heavyweight title "The Bum of the Month Club." It was an unkind analysis of boxers willing to put their lives and reputations on the line against Louis. If they were not a collection of famed fighters, but who was available and who might be respectable, Two Ton Tony Galento fit right in the mix.

To some Galento seemed like a cartoon character come to life. He stood 5-foot-8 and weighed about 235 pounds. Instead of a sculpted physique, he had a round one. Rather than being respectful of Louis and his accomplishments, Galento belittled them, and he boasted as loudly as one could without a megaphone that he could whip Louis' butt.

He was a New Jersey bar owner and more looked the part of that role in life than heavyweight contender. Galento made people laugh with his braggadocio and in some ways he represented the Every Man on the street, a working stiff who also knocked other guys stiff when they met him in the ring. His brawling style was suitable to being a bouncer at his own bar. He did not fight elegantly as Louis sometimes did. Writer A.J. Liebling called boxing "the Sweet Science." As practiced by Louis, it was. As practiced by Galento it might as well have been a different sport. It was easy to envision Galento as being a movie tough, a bodyguard protecting some underworld kingpin.

Galento was not a shy man and he was willing to promote himself in just about any way possible. He once fought a 550-pound bear and also a kangaroo, and he wrestled an octopus. Some wags figured wrestling an eight-arm octopus was what it was going to be like when Galento fought Louis. It would seem as if Louis was throwing punches with eight arms when Galento was in the ring with him.

Although the idea came to him long before Fourth of July eating contests became a staple of America's birthday celebration on Coney Island, Galento once ate 52 hot dogs at a sitting. Sitting was where he should have stayed after indulging, but he ridiculously climbed into the ring to box. It was said Galento's belly, ample under any circumstances, bulged out in extra large fashion that night.

Galento was six bouts from the end of his 112-fight career (80 wins) when he signed to fight Louis for the heavyweight crown on June 28, 1939. Just days before the fight was set at Yankee Stadium a first-person story written by Galento appeared in *Liberty* magazine. In it he predicted he would clobber Louis and lift the title. Mike Jacobs had to love Galento because he was great box office. He stirred things up and got fans thinking. First he made them laugh. Then he made them fall in love with him. And then he convinced a few of them that he might actually win. He was great theater and whether you really thought he had a puncher's chance against Louis or not, it was worth the price of a ticket to go see what happened.

In the magazine article Galento did not waste words or space getting to the point. The story led with this sentence: "I will knock out Joe Louis and become the next heavyweight champion of the world." The headline was less subtle. "I Will Mash Joe Louis," it read. Going into detail, Galento predicted he would knock Louis down early in the fight and finish him off within five rounds. He even predicted the precise punch and its landing spot — a right cross to the jaw.[1]

Galento was built like a jeep and he did pack a huge wallop in his fists. That power, he said, is what was going to provide the advantage now that he had the chance he had long coveted to gain the title. "Perhaps you think I am bragging (heavens no!)," Galento said, "trying to annoy Joe as I had to do to get this match, or just talking for publicity. If so, you are mistaken. I've waited a long time to get Louis. I've studied him ever since he first came up, and I know I can beat him. I can punch harder than Joe. I can take it — Louis cannot. I have never been knocked off my feet in more than 10 years of fighting."[2]

Not everyone on the fight scene was taking Galento seriously and he was well aware of that. He read the newspapers and remembered what writers wrote, such as the ones that referred to him as "a fat, beer-soaked clown." Not Galento's favorite prose. "I am not a clown and though I like beer, I have cut down on it and have trained very seriously for this fight."[3]

Over the years Galento did indulge in beer. He told people he trained on spaghetti and meatballs and did his road work at night because he fought at night. His most memorable quote stemming from the Louis match was, "I'll moider the bum."[4] Galento uttered the phrase so often it caught on with the public. He was even in newsreels, posing with a beer barrel, saying "I'll moider the bum." He actually had been saying it for years before fights, but his audience had expanded exponentially for this bout and it was fresh to the newcomers.

Later in the life Galento actually did play the type of thug he resembled in the movie On the Waterfront. Everyone agreed it was perfect casting. Galento just had a better sense of humor than those types of guys. If his body structure hadn't more resembled a bowling ball with muscles Galento likely would have welcomed playing Tarzan. He loved the loincloth-wearing jungle character and often mimicked the Tarzan yell of the movies.

Galento quit school at age 10 and made some money by carrying ice. He was once late for a bout because he had delivered about two tons of ice. So the nickname "Two Ton" came not from his weight, but from his day job. "I had two tons of ice to deliver on my way here," Galento reported to his manager.[5]

About the 52 hot dogs. Galento won a bet, raced to the arena for a fight, but when he tried to fit into his usual pair of boxing trunks the waistband was too tight. It was seamlessly adjusted and Galento won the bout on a third-round knockout. The guy was a laugh riot, an American original. For the most part people enjoyed being around Tony Galento because he was a card.

Although Galento's general pre-fight brashness was not too offensive, he did cross the line by making late-night phone calls to Louis at his Pompton Lakes, New Jersey, training camp. Why on earth the champ bothered to come to the phone makes little sense, but it was reported later that Galento did not use the occasions to become phone pals. Instead, he insulted Louis, called him names, made racial slurs, and even talked dirty about Marva, Louis' wife. If Louis indeed came to the phone more than once it had to be to let Galento provide him with additional motivation, though Louis seemed to think of Galento as just some weirdo he was assigned to fight. "There's no harm in him," Louis said. "He's just full of wind, like the barber's cat."[6] As unlikely as it seemed, the two men became friends later in life after Galento apologized for those phone calls, and Louis even sometimes visited Galento at the Orange, New Jersey saloon. But that was sometime later.

Galento just didn't look like a professional fighter. His squat build and balding head and otherwise hairy body didn't square with the image of a sleek boxer. His looks led Louis to describe him as "That funny little fat guy."[7] Maybe that wasn't the most complimentary of comments, but it was pretty accurate if you counted funny as meaning hah-hah funny.

Galento built himself up sufficiently that 35,000 ticket buyers believed he had a puncher's chance against Louis, unless they all turned out at Yankee

Stadium to watch Louis "moider the bum." Not even during the ring introductions and instructions before the first bell did Galento cease his relentless chatter. Louis was known for his stone face in the ring and Galento wanted to upset him and psych him out. In the ring he told Louis what he was going to do to his wife after the fight.

Galento actually got off to a good start. He nailed Louis with a righty-lefty combination that knocked him off balance. Galento fought in a crouch, making him difficult to reach, though he bore straight in on Louis. Galento was no ballerina in the ring, either, so he did not move side to side well.

Known as a bleeder, or a fighter who was susceptible to being cut, Galento's face became Louis' target board in the second round. Sure enough Galento was bleeding from cuts before the end of the second three-minute stanza. At one point Louis nearly had Galento out. But Galento was not easy to get rid of, and although he was taking considerable punishment, he fought back and he caught Louis flush in the face with a left hook and dropped him to the canvas. It was the champ, not the challenger, who was on the ground.

Galento's power was on display to the astonished world then and he had backed up much of his big talk. But he could not follow up, even though Louis was groggy and relying on his instincts, as well as possibly his anger. Louis fended off Galento's charges and quickly regained control. Galento went to his corner elated and in the fourth round abandoned any appearance of strategy. He went after Louis hard, but the champ had recovered, and using superior hand speed and movement, he once again began to pick apart Galento.

Galento had his chance and missed it. Louis had the upper hand — both hands — and subsequently tore him apart, ripping into the challenger with lefts and rights that bloodied and dazed him. Referee Arthur Donovan stopped the fight before the fourth round's three minutes were up.

It was an embarrassing moment for Louis when he was dumped on his butt, and a close call, as well, but he churned up Galento's face as if it was a hunk of meat. The United Press lead on its fight story read, "Tony Galento, as a game a guy as ever bled for a lost cause, chewed the bitter fruit of defeat today and passed his plate back for another helping of the same dish."[8]

Still, Donovan said afterwards that Louis, in his estimation, had been affected by Galento's big shot. "When Galento knocked Louis down, I could see that the champion was badly hurt," Donovan said, "even though he jumped to his feet without a count. If Tony could have landed another left hook, he would have won the title."[9]

One mark of a champion, however, is his ability to react to adversity, to take the punishment (which Galento had said he couldn't) and rebound from it. And the difference between Louis' and Galento's skill as fighters was that Louis had the killer instinct and the hand speed to follow up and finish off a man in trouble, while Galento couldn't catch up to Louis.

Sitting for a long time in his dressing room contemplating what happened, Galento was battered and bruised, but not mentally beaten. He complained to trainer Whitey Brimstein that his corner men didn't let him fight his fight and added, "I would've knocked that mug cold!"[10] Brimstein may or may not have reminded Galento that no one had been stopping him from doing that except the mug, Joe Louis. Whatever he really believed, Galento dined out for decades on the fact that he had once knocked the great Joe Louis down in a fight for the title.

Louis admitted that Galento hit him hard and knocked him off balance and that his eyes glazed over. He also said he found it difficult to believe Galento survived the huge smash that Louis struck him with in the second that lifted him off the floor and tossed him in the air.

"I won, but it was a funny kind of fight," Louis said. "A lot of people were pulling for Tony. He had a special appeal to a lot of white people. I knew people liked me and were cheering for me, but at the same time, how much did they want to let a black man get ahead?"[11]

Louis stayed ahead. He kept on defending the title, kept up a busy pace, taking on anyone Mike Jacobs suggested he fight. The next opponent was Bob Pastor, for a second time, in Detroit. Louis' trademark was always improving his performance when he met a man for the second time and this was also true with Pastor. About two months after Louis demolished Galento, he stopped Pastor in 11 rounds in an event that oddly was scheduled for 20 rounds.

In their first match in January of 1937 Pastor had run from Louis as if he was competing in the Olympic 100-meter dash, not a fight. This time Pastor seemingly had lost some speed. Louis knocked him down five times in the first two rounds before Pastor managed to stay out of reach for a while. When the end came in the 11th, Pastor was so dazed by Louis' punches that he did not hear referee Sam Hennessey count him out. "I knew I was in there for a 20-round fight," Louis said. "I wasn't in any hurry after I hit him so much there at the start."[12]

The next bout, against Arturo Godoy of Chile, was not a snap, however. Jacobs had to find some fresh faces for Louis to punch. Scheduled for February 9, 1940, Louis was carried the distance for the first time since the Tommy Farr contest in 1937. Godoy was a 10–1 underdog, but he did not go away easily. The fight went the 15-round distance and Louis retained the title at Madison Square Garden on a split decision. The result occasioned some boos and complaints from those who felt Godoy did enough to take the heavyweight title from the champ. Most peculiarly, at one point before the results were reported, Godoy leaned over and kissed the startled Louis on the forehead. Godoy was lucky Louis didn't knock him cold then.

The official viewers were very split. Referee Arthur Donovan saw the fight 10 rounds to 5 for Louis. One judge saw it 10–4, with one even, for Louis. But another judge had it 10–5 for Godoy. It was an unusual disparity. The Associated Press card had it 10-4-1 for Louis, as well.

More discerning observers believed that Godoy spent too much time keeping his distance from Louis in order to avoid being smacked than engaging in the type of combat a challenger must display to take a champ's crown. Strangely, in the 14th round, Godoy came out of his corner mimicking a gorilla by dropping his arms to his sides and dancing around briefly before seemingly committing to crawling around for a round.

A day later Louis indicated it was Godoy's style that protected him, bending into a crouch and seemingly focusing much more on defense than offense. Godoy's crouch was compared to Galento's. "Yeah, but Galento fought," Louis said. "He stood up and he fought."[13]

The result was close enough and controversial enough that it was inevitable Louis and Godoy would meet in a rematch. First, Louis took a breather by overpowering Iowan Johnny Paychek in another defense. Paychek may have had a cool name, but there were some who questioned whether he earned his paycheck when Louis pulverized him on March 29, 1940, at Madison Square Garden. Louis knocked Paychek down three times in the first round and ended the fight in the second.

One writer said Paychek landed only one punch on Louis and summed up the night with this: "Joe Louis sang Johnny Paychek sound to sleep with five punches tonight without even mussing his hair ... knocked him stiffer than a frozen frankfurter in 44 seconds of the second heat to dance out of the ring with his title as safe as money in the bank."[14]

Louis' record stood at 42–1 as he prepared for the second time around against Godoy. Godoy, who was the South American heavyweight champion and looking to add more geography to his title, brazenly followed in the footsteps of Galento by also penning a prediction story that was headlined, "How I Mean to Beat Joe Louis."

In the piece Godoy said he was going to knock Louis "slap happy" and belittled his punching power because in the fifth round of their first contest Louis belted him on the chin and it didn't hurt very much. "It was the most shocking punch Louis ever landed, for it shocked two people, him and me!" Godoy wrote. "It was shocking to me that the punch, landing as it did with all that Louis could possibly put into it, merely jarred me and that was all! I wasn't even dazed!"[15]

Well, if Godoy wanted to be dazed, Louis obliged him the second time out. Again scheduled for the championship distance of 15 rounds, Louis made sure the result was not left to judges this time. He solved Godoy's offbeat defense, penetrating with blows from both hands that ripped into the challenger's face and drew streams of blood. By the time referee Billy Cavanaugh stopped the contest in the eighth round Godoy could not see because his eyes were swollen shut. He was better off that way, not being able to look in the mirror, because Louis carved cuts into him that were filled with rivers of blood.

Whether it was a bum of the month club or not, Louis did conduct a national tour when he put the title at risk. Name that city and he was liable to show up to punch out some unfortunate pretender who thought he was a

One of the staples of any boxer's training his hitting the speed bag, the leather bag that dangles from a hook and rhythmically responds to a puncher's quick bursts. Joe Louis could make the speed bag sing (courtesy Charles H. Wright Museum of African-American History).

contender. In December of 1940, the victim was Al McCoy, at the Boston Garden. McCoy lasted into the fifth round. The fight ended with McCoy sitting on his stool for the start of the sixth, talked into sitting down by his seconds rather than taking more punishment, which he argued for. McCoy, who weighed 21 pounds less than Louis, worked hard to stay out of his way. "It was a lousy fight," Louis said of his showing.[16]

Louis attributed his lack of sharpness to being on vacation and not defending the title for six months. So he signed to meet Red Burman six weeks later in Madison Square Garden. Burman, who was from Baltimore, compiled a 78-22-2 record in his career, but the night he met Louis for the title was not one of his best. He probably wished Louis was still on vacation.

By the fifth round, when Louis ended matters, he had been busting Burman regularly. The wallop that ended the fight at 2 minutes, 49 seconds of the round was actually a body punch, a sizzling right hook to the belly that keeled Burman over and was so forceful he could not rise from the canvas. "I had to hit him the hardest I ever hit a man," Louis said. "That's a good, tough boy."[17]

Mike Jacobs kept lining up the opponents and whether by knockout or superior boxing, (mostly by knockout) Louis took them out. Next came Gus Dorazio, victimized in the second round of the scheduled 15-rounder in Philadelphia. Abe Simon went down next in the 13th round of a scheduled 20-round bout in Detroit. Tony Musto fell in the ninth round in St. Louis. The sports world had become so used to Louis being the heavyweight champion, and seemingly untouchable in the role, that when the Musto fight was announced, one newspaper ran this headline, "Musto will be Bomber's Next Victim in April."[18] He was. Then Louis went on to meet a more impressive opponent.

Louis was 48–1 when he encountered his next foe on May 23, 1941, at Griffith Stadium, home of the Washington Senators, in the District of Columbia. The opponent was Buddy Baer, younger brother of Max. Baer stood 6-foot-6½ and compiled a lifetime record of 51–7. He packed TNT in his fists and among his victories he counted a knockout over Tony Galento, which as Louis knew was not something easy to accomplish.

While Baer had the tools to create mayhem, Louis took him apart in the ring. Baer, an 8–1 underdog, did not come out for the start of the seventh round in a fight that ended controversially from Baer's perspective. Baer landed the fight's first punch in the first round and then shocked the 23,000-plus fans on hand by knocking Louis clean out of the ring. Louis landed in press row, but was up quickly and back in the ring, snarling his determination to avenge the dramatic knockdown.

"As I saw him coming back into the ring, I said, 'My God, what have I done?'" Baer said much later.[19] Yet the hard-hitting Baer opened a cut over Louis' left eye, too. The combination of those two developments clearly made Louis aware that his title was at risk regardless of what the odds said.

As he had done several times in his career, Louis bounced back from trouble. Louis became the master of the exchanges and he was whaling away almost unimpeded at the end of the sixth round. Just before the round ended Louis smashed Baer in the jaw with a right that knocked the challenger down. He was literally saved by the bell, but not for long, since he never rose higher than a sitting position on his stool. Baer's seconds protested the result, alleging that Louis hit Baer after the bell rang. Referee Arthur Donovan denied the claim and then later wrote a newspaper article emphasizing his decision.

After the fight sports writers asked Louis if the sight of his own blood had angered him and he answered in a droll way, "Well, it didn't do Buddy any good."[20]

After the Baer victory, Louis had defended the heavyweight championship 17 times and had owned the crown for four years. He had grown on the job, too, learning to converse and joke around a little with sports writers, as opposed to the beginning of his pro career when he was too shy to do much besides mumble answers.

Louis had followed the rules of behavior issued by co-managers John Roxborough and Julian Black and emphasized by trainer Jack Blackburn, and as a result he was never perceived as the second coming of Jack Johnson. Where Johnson was hated, Louis was appreciated by most white Americans.

Johnson had his detractors even in the black community when he was the champ, cavorting with white women and angering whites with his gloating. Not Louis. He was beloved in the black community. He was a legend. When Louis fought, and he fought often, the event halted most daily, routine tasks in black neighborhoods, from Harlem to Chicago's South Side, to Detroit and St. Louis. Nothing was more important than listening to Louis' bouts as he defended his title and he defended the black race, and so millions and millions, boxing fans or not, sports fans or not, tuned in on the radio.

Eddie Macon, who became a pro football player, said his father had a ritual when Louis fought, taking him to the corner grocery store in Stockton, California, where he grew up. The man who owned the store put a radio in his upstairs window and played it loudly so those gathered below could hear. "The first time I went," Macon said, "Max Schmeling knocked out Joe Louis and the black community was sick for a year. Then, when Louis won the rematch, we celebrated because we had a champion again."[21]

It was a similar story for Eddie Bell, another future pro football player, who grew up in Philadelphia. It didn't matter where you lived in the nation, if you were black, Joe Louis belonged to you. He was like everyone's big brother. "When Joe Louis fought," Bell said, "that was one time we could stay up late, to listen to the fights. And when he won we ran out into the streets and cheered."[22]

All Louis had to do was walk down the street to see how much he was revered. And all he had to do was open his mail and read what fans said about him to know that he was a symbol not only to members of his race, but to everyone in the country. Heck, all he had to do was turn on the radio during the day, or just before bed, and he was liable to hear a song being sung about him and his successes.

When he was a boy, the man who became Malcolm X and a leader of the Black Muslim movement in America in the 1960s wanted to be a boxer just like Joe Louis. "Every Negro boy old enough to walk wanted to be the next Brown Bomber," he said.[23]

Why not? Joe Louis was invincible. Joe Louis was every black person's savior. Widely reported over the years, though questionable in reality, a story was often told that a North Carolina black man convicted of murder and on his way to his execution cried out, "Save me, Joe Louis!" Joe Louis, black people felt, could do anything. An African American who could get away with beating up white men and get rich doing it must have magical powers when the rest of black America was mistreated and had almost no real rights at all.

22

The Tough Guy
from Pittsburgh

When Joe Louis' heavyweight title defense against Billy Conn was announced to the world, some felt they were the ones being victimized by a con. Conn was the light-heavyweight champion and the division's limit was 175 pounds. Louis fought at about 200 pounds.

As if it wasn't a daunting enough task to take on Louis, the dominating heavyweight king, Conn, it was envisioned, might be giving away 25 pounds in the ring, too. But Conn was after the Big Boy title and in May of 1941 he surrendered the light-heavy crown in order to take on Louis on June 18, the next month.

By that time Louis had swept past just about any worthy heavyweight contender at least once and Conn seemed as credible an opponent as anyone out there who was of genuine heavyweight size. Conn was popular, had a public following, and was a respected fighter.

Although Conn was a world champion, he recognized that there was always going to be a difference in public perception between the light-heavyweight crown and the heavyweight crown.

The heavyweight title was the big enchilada, the prize that brought greater fame and respect, and was, if used correctly, a gateway to riches, not only in title bouts, but through boxing exhibitions and by making appearances.

If you walked down the street as heavyweight champ everyone would recognize you almost no matter where you went. When Conn walked down the street in his hometown of Pittsburgh he was feted like the king of the world, but in New York, Chicago, Detroit, not so much. In some ways one could compare being heavyweight champ to being the World Series winner and the light-heavyweight champ to being the champion of AAA baseball. It wasn't fair, but the gap was there.

Conn was Irish to the core and Pittsburgh to his toes. His nickname was "The Pittsburgh Kid" and he was 23 when he agreed to meet Louis in the ring. Louis was 27 and had gained an aura of invincibility by seizing the crown from James J. Braddock and demolishing Max Schmeling in the geopolitical war otherwise known as their rematch. Then he had built on his reputation by fighting often and eliminating all other pretenders to the throne. It might be said that Louis had become the New York Yankees of the ring. Everyone plotted his demise, but he was tough enough, resourceful enough and good enough to fend off all challengers.

While Conn stood 6-foot-1½, same as Louis, he was naturally a smaller man. His reach was shorter, his chest smaller, his biceps smaller and his weight, no matter how much of his beloved wife Mary Louise's cooking he devoured, was not going to grow much beyond that light-heavyweight cap. He had a passionate following, especially among his Irish brethren, and to them he might as well have been a leprechaun, a living four-leaf clover. The loyal rooters of Billy Conn favored green in their wardrobes right down to a green bowler for many of them. He was their guy and he represented the old country which their parents had left behind to come to the U.S. Conn made them proud when he claimed one world title. Now he was after the big one and they couldn't think of anything more exciting in their world, even a St. Patrick's Day parade in Manhattan. Heck, if Billy won, they'd throw their own parade.

Conn's father, William, was a policeman at first, but became a steamfitter and the work was steady. He was a hot tempered man who engaged in fisticuffs regularly — not in sanctioned bouts. William made sure his three sons learned the art of self-defense, but none of them took to it quite as passionately as Billy. Professional boxing beckoned and he turned pro before he was 17 years old in 1934. He made 50 cents for his debut, but thought he was supposed to make $2.50, so he felt cheated. He lost the fight, too.

In 1935, still a novice, Conn had his first encounter with Joe Louis. Not that Louis would remember him. Conn was hired to hold Louis' spit bucket in his corner during a Detroit fight. It was not glamorous work, but the ringside view paid off with $20 at the urging of Louis.

For the first two years of his career Conn stayed active in six-rounders primarily, winning most of his fights, but occasionally losing. In 1936 he won a tough split decision from Fritzie Zivic and that put a name on his list of conquests. "A young punk who moves like a greyhound and jabs better than Barney Ross," Zivic said.[1]

Conn could box and he had speed. He was not especially known for packing dynamite in his fists. He routinely fought 10, 12, even 15-rounders that went to the judges. His record is littered with decisions, split decisions and majority decisions from late 1936 on. Conn won a lot of bouts on points, whereas Louis was a one-man wrecking crew, knocking down big men and watching referees stand over them and count them out.

The Pittsburgh Kid also acquired a reputation as a fighter who could take a punch. Solly Krieger battled Conn three times between 1937 and 1939 and lost three 12-round decisions. Krieger believed he dished out sufficient punishment to topple Conn, but he couldn't do it. At one point Krieger predicted that within a few years "I wouldn't be surprised if he lifted Joe Louis' heavyweight crown."[2]

In January and February of 1939, Conn met Fred Apostoli and bested him twice, going the distance both times and winning unanimous decisions. They were big, attention-getting wins, wars, too, and at times Conn was in trouble and had to fight his way out of danger to impose his will and grab the victory. The action-packed contests added to Conn's allure with the fans. The New York newspapermen who liked to think of themselves as kingmakers in the sport took to Conn and praised him. They labeled him an emerging star.

The first fight was close enough that many believed if it had been scheduled for longer than 10 rounds, Apostoli would have won. The second match was set for 15 rounds. Early in the second bout Apostoli and Conn butted heads and Conn began bleeding profusely. He blamed Apostoli for the contact and protested to the referee, who ignored him. Then Conn was thumbed in the eye and became enraged.

"Listen, you dago bastard, keep your thumb out of my eye," Conn yelled. "Listen, you Irish sonofabitch, quit beefin' and come on and fight," Apostoli responded.[3] A lot of blood was spilled as the fight went on with some back and forth, but with Conn gradually taking over.

Compared to the cheap payday from his pro debut, Conn was building up his bank account. Not with the shares of the gate that Louis could grasp, but for the second Apostoli fight Conn was paid more than $10,000. To him that was a very big deal and he said, "I had heard there was that much money in the world, but I was always puzzled just how to get it. Now I know."[4]

It was not long after defeating Apostoli twice that Conn gained the chance to fight for the light-heavyweight title against Melio Bettina on July 13, 1939. Some governing authorities recognized Bettina, from Beacon, New York, as the champ. Others considered the title vacant. The bout attracted more than 15,000 fans to Madison Square Garden and Conn captured a unanimous decision by scores of 10–5, 8–7 and 9–6 in an extremely hot environment. Conn had won a world championship.

Conn reeled off nine more wins in a row before signing to face Louis. Almost from the moment he won the light-heavyweight crown he was asked when he was going to fight Louis. Conn had been a middleweight, at the 160-pound level, and excelled at 175. Did he really have the body of a heavyweight? The world was about to find out.

There was no evidence that Conn had any fear of Louis and his vaunted punching power. More than a year before he agreed to meet Louis, he made brash comments about how he might fare against him. Conn said that some fighter was going to come along and make a million dollars beating Louis and he figured he was the guy to do it.

As the fight date approached Louis admitted feeling discomfort about the likely weight disparity between the two men. He wanted to fight a man who looked like and weighed in as a heavyweight. He had visions of weighing in at 202 pounds with Conn at 172 or less, which would have been a huge weight spread. "This would make me feel like I was a bully taking advantage of a smaller man," Louis said.[5]

A theme the sports writers built up and focused on was how quick Conn was with his hands and on his feet. Louis was frequently asked if he would be able to catch the smaller man to punch him. Louis uttered one of the most famous lines in boxing history, and indeed, in all sports history, to analyze the situation: "He can run, but he can't hide."[6]

The utterance was an example of Louis' more polished articulation, a phrase that everyone remembered and repeated. More than 70 years later it is still in use, something that has become a cliché of sorts because it has been said so many times. But Louis was the originator.

Conn had come a long way from his earliest days as a high school dropout who hooked his future to trainer Johnny Ray, a man who came to be like a second father to him. Ray was one of those training wizards who understood the intricacies of the Sweet Science and could teach them. He had one major flaw — he drank way too much. Nothing Conn said could disabuse him of abusing the bottle, but Ray knew the fight game, loved Conn like a son and always protected his interests. Conn never committed to any boxing development or offer without Ray's blessing.

The fighter, who was no abstainer either, recognized Ray's fault, but lived with it and trusted him implicitly. If anyone else criticized Ray's drinking, Conn had a ready response: "Johnny Ray knew more about boxing drunk than anybody else did sober."

Conn had bigger personal problems than Ray's sobriety as he prepared to battle Louis. Conn had tested his mettle against bigger men in recent months and beaten Bob Pastor, Al McCoy and Lee Savold. He showed he could fit in with the heavyweights. Of course, those guys didn't compare to Louis, but it was legitimate preparation. As the days dwindled to the show-down with Louis, Conn's mother, Maggie, with whom he was very close, was hospitalized and dying of cancer. He visited her as often as he could and in his final bedside chat before the bout the scene that emerged was as melodramatic as anything Hollywood put on the screen. The sad truth was this was real life. Conn said, "I gotta go now, but the next time you see me, I'll be the heavyweight champion of the world." To which Maggie Conn replied, "No son, the next time I see you I'll be in Paradise."[7]

Louis was the most active champion ever. The owner of the heavyweight crown for more than four years at that point, Louis was probably overworked. The theory of his management team that the public would not accept an African American champion who didn't regularly defend his title may have been true, but promoter Mike Jacobs likely took things too far. Conn marked Louis' 18th title defense.

Worse for Louis was that once he got it in his head that he was going to look gargantuan next to Conn, he over-trained, trying to shed a few extra pounds. The reality was that Louis should not have let any such idea bother him and just figure it was Conn's problem if he was too small to withstand Louis' blows. But rather than rest the day before the fight, Louis said he trained as usual and he ticked off trainer Jack Blackburn by doing so.

"Chappie was mad as hell," Louis said. "I dieted and drank as little water as possible. I made it to the weigh-in without any breakfast. I felt like shit. I had no pep, and as soon as I got to Edgecombe Avenue my chef, Bill Bottoms, had a good meal ready for me. Steak, black-eyed peas, and salad. He knew I needed pumping up."[8]

The official weights for the bout later than night at the Polo Grounds before nearly 55,000 fans read 199½ for Louis and 174 for Conn. It is often said in boxing and other sports that a good big man will overpower a good little man, but nothing is 100 percent certain once competition begins.

Louis was a 3–1 favorite, somewhat short odds compared to recent title bouts because this fight promised to be a better match than any of Louis' other defenses of the last year or more. Conn's Irish supporters did not let him down. They showed up in force and were loud. He was buttressed by trainloads of his Pittsburgh backers, come to cheer for their own.

While virtually nobody engages in making sports predictions a couple of years in advance because it makes little sense and is of little interest, sports writer Jack Miley, the one who dubbed Louis' tour of the heavyweight division "The Bum of the Month Club," did pen a remarkable comment in 1939, two years before the Louis-Conn bout. He was so enamored of Conn's skills that he felt he would become the heavyweight champ one day and that he would take the crown from Louis, not some other foe who appeared. "By 1941, Louis will be even more jaded from fighting all the bums," Miley wrote. "And Conn will astound with his fearlessness, his speed. Heigh-ho, it is written in the cards, mates."[9]

Miley outshone Nostradamus in his ability to look into the future because what he foresaw was pretty much what transpired. Indeed, Conn did not fear Louis. Pretty much nothing scared Conn. From the start of the scheduled 15-rounder Conn employed his speed to try to stay clear of Louis' big overhand right and powerful left hook. His hand speed enabled him to infiltrate Louis' defense with some short stuff. The first three minutes represented a feeling-out round, but Louis landed the more telling blows. At one point Louis clipped Conn on the head and while he did go down to the canvas, referee Eddie Josephs did not rule a knockdown.

Conn did a fair amount of probing in the second round and learned he could reach Louis with left hands. He scored with those punches, but Louis scored with bigger blows.

Action in the third round was more wide open. Conn took more chances and landed better punches than he had and than Louis did. The crowd was energized as the duo traded exchanges in tight to the head and body. Conn knocked Louis into the ropes near the end of the stanza. It was more of the same for Conn in the fourth. He managed to reach Louis' mid-section and connected to Louis' jaw, as well. The champion missed wildly on several occasions, testament to Conn's quickness.

By the fifth, Louis drew blood from a cut on Conn's face and he added a second slash in the sixth. While Conn seemed in no way hesitant, the bigger man did well in these two rounds. Yet momentum began to shift in the seventh round. Conn kept penetrating and hitting Louis in the belly and periodically on the jaw. Louis' rhythm seemed shaken and while ordinarily a very accurate puncher he missed frequently.

By the eighth, the spectators recognized something unusual was afoot. The light-heavyweight champ seemed capable of dethroning the heavyweight champion. Conn moved in and struck with big shots to the head. Repeatedly, his left hand found Louis' face and chin. Through the ninth, Conn continued to get the best of the exchanges as what began as a murmur in the crowd spread to a roar. The action was plentiful and the on-stage drama played out in a way few expected. The Irishman from Pittsburgh was shoving around the Brown Bomber.

Louis rallied in the 10th, blasting Conn with both fists. But Conn was strong enough to trade with the champ and fit enough to take Louis' hardest hits and remain standing. More tellingly, he didn't go down, set the tempo and forced Louis to submit to his game plan. Rounds 11 and 12 were critical. It might be argued that the bout was even after the first 10, but in those two late rounds rather than wilt, Conn continued to pile up points.

By the middle rounds, Conn had engaged in a different type of exchange with Louis, boldly saying, "You've got a fight on your hands tonight, Joe." And Louis answered, "I know it."[10]

Left, right, left, right, Conn landed big punches to Louis' head and body and kept him offguard in the 11th. In the 12th, there was more fury, more back-and-forth, but Conn seemed to get the best of trading. The general belief going into the 13th round was that Conn led on the scorecards and if he could fight a smart fight for the remaining few rounds, he would score the upset and become the new heavyweight champion.

To this point, Conn had executed a brilliant game plan. He boxed the way he wanted to, kept Louis off of him, avoided most of Louis' power punches and stayed nimble. The one thing Conn wished to avoid was going toe-to-toe and slugging it out. Almost no one in the universe would have suggested such an idea, and after a dozen rounds those in the know sagely observed how wise Conn had been not to mix it up with the champ more than necessary. Bravo, exclaimed the strategists. This was the way to grab the title.

Reposing in his corner during the 60 seconds between the 12th and 13th round, Conn and Johnny Ray conducted a conversation that alarmed the trainer. Conn said, "This is easy, I can take this son of a bitch out this round." That was the ever-cocky Conn speaking with his gut feeling. Ray saw things differently. Why alter what was working? "No, no, Billy, stick and run," Ray said. "You got the fight won. Stay away kiddo. Just stick and run."[11] It was sound advice, but Conn was known for his stubbornness. Not even Ray knew if it was just Conn talk, or if going after the exhausted Louis for the kill was his true intention.

To the crowd, although bleeding from some cuts, Conn looked pretty fresh. Louis, who was usually a very composed, efficient athlete, seemed out of synch and weary. If Conn or Ray had shared Conn's idea on the loudspeaker, a fair amount of fans would have vociferously endorsed the idea. A smaller percentage, less emotional, more analytical, would have recommended against such a notion on the grounds of recklessness. You don't tug on superman's cape.

In the champ's corner, neither Louis nor Blackburn was the kind of man to panic. But they were aware of reality and they seemed pretty sure Louis was in need of a knockout to retain his title. Louis was not blind to the night's developments. "Billy Conn was like a mosquito," Louis said. "He'd sting and move. I kept after him, though, but I couldn't catch him. Conn was just too fast, too much speed for me. First two rounds I gave it to him. Thought I had him and the fight would be over soon. But that tough Irishman stood up to my fists."[12]

Louis admitted he was very fatigued between the eighth and 12th rounds when Conn piled up points. But Ray would have been surprised to hear that Louis always believed Conn was going to come after him at some point and stand in and throw haymakers. He just sensed it and Louis said that after studying Conn for 12 rounds he hoped he would do just that, and he felt he had the answer for Conn's thrusts in his own arsenal.

"I had been studying him all night and I knew if he started to throw the long left hook, I had him," Louis said. "At the end of the 12th, Chappie said, 'You're losing on points. You got to knock him out.'"[13]

Anyone with an all-seeing eye and ear who was able to listen in on both corners might have sensed what was coming in what became one of the most dramatic rounds in boxing history, but no one had that capability.

If Ray owned elastic arms he would have reached halfway across the ring and grabbed Conn the moment he settled himself into an upright stance in the center of the battlefield, prepared to goad Louis and finish him off. Louis was game and inwardly overjoyed that the dancer had become a stationary target. Conn began throwing bombs and landed some. They were big enough punches to slow Louis.

The inside exchanges went on for a bit and then Louis spied his opening. In an instant, with the killer instinct that it takes to be the heavyweight champion of the world, Louis snaked out a stunning right hand over Conn's outstretched left and sent the challenger reeling into the ropes with wobbly legs. It took 12 rounds for Conn to construct the building blocks of his invincibility in his mind and about five seconds for it to ooze away, just like his dream. Louis pounced and unable to protect himself, Conn absorbed, 10, 15, 20 straight blows, rights and lefts. Then he tumbled to the canvas on his back. Conn made it no closer to regaining his feet than sitting on his butt. It was over. Joe Louis was still champion of the world, winner by knockout with two seconds left in the 13th.

The esteemed Nat Fleischer at *The Ring* magazine said it was Conn's cockiness that did him in. "It was an uphill battle in which Billy came along at an amazing rate of speed to take the play away from the champion," according to Fleischer, "and had he been able to continue to the end of the 15th, the odds were in his favor that he would have annexed the title. He was too game for his own good."[14]

In the privacy of his dressing room, in the presence only of his seconds,

Conn cried freely, mourning the close call, devastated by a loss he thought he should have won. When sports writers reached him Conn was more of his jocular, outgoing self, the man they were used to seeing in public. When they asked how the fight got away from him, he said, "I'll bet it's the first time a fella ever lost a fight because he had too much guts. I thought I had him and I simply couldn't do anything else but go out after him. What's the sense of being Irish if you can't be dumb?"[15]

Conn had fought bravely, indeed shown guts and talent, and people appreciated that he had made the toughest man in the universe look human. He did not win the big prize, but Conn did something more difficult by making the fight game view him with the utmost respect and by contributing to history as the near-victor in one of the sport's classic bouts. To some it was a reenactment of the famous Biblical bout, David versus Goliath. Although Goliath did win this match-up, the courage of the underdog stood out.

For Louis, Conn represented perhaps his most difficult of the 18 successful defenses since winning the title. He made mistakes, both in preparation and in the ring, but when his opponent made the biggest mistake of all, he capitalized and once again proved that he was a dominant champion who could even win on an off night. No, Louis wasn't just fighting so-called bums. If fans didn't recognize it before the fight, they realized afterwards that Conn was one of the best opponents Louis could have faced. "Beating good men is what makes you the best," Louis said.[16]

The fight was good business the first time (Louis was paid $153,000), it was aesthetically pleasing, and the talk of the nation, so there was no reason anyone could see not to have a rematch soon. Pretty soon a reason did surface. It was not long before a different sort of confrontation focused minds and attention. World War II — already raging in Europe with Germany seemingly bent on complete geographic domination of the continent, and in Asia, where Japan appeared to be carrying out a similar plan — did, within months, engulf the United States.

It would be a long time before Joe Louis and Billy Conn met in a boxing ring again. There were other battles to fight.

23

You're in the Army Now

For a change, Joe Louis, Billy Conn, the boxing public, and boxing officials were in agreement about the next move for the heavyweight championship.
The Louis-Conn bout just whetted appetites for more. Everyone wanted to
see a rematch and the principals seemed ready, willing, and able to do it all
again, too. And still, something interfered to prevent an immediate rematch.

From the moment he laid eyes on her, Conn was infatuated with Mary
Louise Smith. She was only a teen and her father was the wealthy Pittsburgh
businessman Jimmy Smith, known as "Greenfield Jimmy." While Greenfield
Jimmy was an admirer of Billy Conn the fighter, that didn't mean he wanted
his daughter involved with a pug. For quite some time he didn't have to worry
about that because Mary Louise was only friendly with Conn. But as time
passed their relationship blossomed and they began thinking of one another
in a different way, as in the boy-girl type thing.

There never was going to be a thaw on that front as far as Greenfield
Jimmy was concerned. But the guy and doll were committed, even if they
preferred his approval. They married without it, but it didn't remove the sneer
from Greenfield Jimmy's face any time he was in the same room as Conn.

When the couple had a baby boy they were certain Greenfield Jimmy
would attend his christening, especially since this was his first grandchild. A
mutual friend between Conn and Greenfield Jimmy suggested it was time to
make peace and that Conn's father-in-law was prepared to holster the blade
if Conn went to his home. To suggest that things took a sour turn would be
serious understatement. An argument broke out in the kitchen, punches were
exchanged, and Conn fared about the same as he had against Louis.

Conn broke his hand, had to be treated at a hospital, and blew a $125,000
payday because the rematch with Louis was off. New York tabloids went crazy
over the incident as only they can with type size about equal to the height of
the Empire State Building. The scribes were more sympathetic to Conn when

he was defeated by Louis than when he was ordered to keep his left hand in a cast for six weeks after the apparent defeat by Greenfield Jimmy. "I guess the only place he wanted to bury the hatchet was in my skull," said Conn after breaking his silence over the matter when sports writers finally caught up to the story.[1]

Conn's trainer, Johnny Ray, was incensed at Greenfield Jimmy. He blamed Conn's father-in-law for upsetting him before the first Louis bout, disrupting his sleep, and therefore being at fault for the loss. That was questionable. But his lament this time rang all too true. "I didn't even get a percentage from that Smith scrap," Ray said of what was labeled "The Battle of the Pantry" by some newspapers.[2]

As a result, for the time being, at least, Billy Conn exited from Joe Louis' life. There was always someone else to fight, even if fans weren't as excited about the options. There was nothing to be done, however. Neither Louis nor Conn was ducking out and politics didn't interfere, only circumstances beyond their control. An early version of *Family Feud* had wiped out the potential big gate and Conn's big chance.

Instead of the big money rematch with Conn, Louis signed to put the title on the line next against Lou Nova at the Polo Grounds on September 29, 1941. In the context of the times, long before such things were fashionable, even in California where Nova hailed from, he seemed off-beat and a little peculiar to the average American. Nova practiced yoga and said he possessed a "cosmic punch" that would help him KO Louis. A self-proclaimed Man of Destiny, Nova said the cosmic punch stemmed from his "seventh vertebra, the center of balance."[3] The general response was, If you say so, Lou.

Louis was pretty much a grounded guy and he didn't think much of Nova's outer space lingo, or the secret weapon it supposedly described. "He can cosmic punch me all he wants," Louis said, "but he better do it fast because the good, old, left-right combination punch is gonna be hard for him to handle."[4] Louis didn't have fancy names for his blows, but they had served him fine so far.

Well, it was different, but neither yoga nor yogurt would have saved Nova. Louis smoked him like lox. The champ stopped the challenger in the sixth round of the scheduled 15 for his 19th title defense. He also made $200,000 in raising his record to 51–1.

Before even the very active Louis could fight again, the world pretty much went to hell. On December 7, 1941, the day that will live in infamy in U.S. history, the Japanese mounted a sneak attack on Pearl Harbor in Hawaii on a sleepy morning. The assault that horrified and infuriated Americans catapulted the country into World War II.

Although President Franklin D. Roosevelt and done his best to prepare the nation for war, there were isolationists of influence who had thwarted some of his budgetary requests that would have helped build the Armed Forces, and many in Congress had worn blinders in the belief America could steer clear of the march of the Nazis in Europe and the aggression of the Japanese in Asia. That was not to be, and as the year turned to 1942 the United States was fully engaged in the terrible two-front conflict that dragged on until 1945.

Louis had his next defense, a rematch of a previous win, against Buddy Baer, the brother of previously conquered Max, on January 9, 1942. The big picture had changed, and although Conn was healing, the nation was preoccupied with its own defense, not the defense of the heavyweight title. No one realized that the next stage of Joe Louis' life was dawning and that he would emerge from World War II as an American hero, although not in the same manner as winners of the Purple Heart or Congressional Medal of Honor did.

Louis was of draft age and shape and there was every chance he was going to be called up not long into the conflict. Louis was asked about his military plans. "I'm anxious to do anything the government wants me to do," Louis said. When he met with soldiers, even before his own path was set, he said, "We all have to do our bit."[5]

Decades later, much would be made of the contrasting positions taken by two very different heavyweight champions, Joe Louis during World War II, and Muhammad Ali during the Vietnam War. Louis was a self-described patriot who supported his country's stance on everything to do with the war, even if he was aware of the level of discrimination that remained within the ranks of the Army and Navy. Ali became a conscientious objector, saying he had no quarrel with the Vietcong, and that it was against his religion to go to war. Conservative opinion would cite one man as right and the other as wrong. The reality was that Louis and Ali lived in different times and their wars were pretty much apples and oranges, as well.

Even conscientious objectors during World War II basically agreed with the cause of fighting for democracy in the face of Fascism and fanaticism. Public opinion was completely splintered about whether Vietnam was a just war.

Louis was the right man in the right role for his times. He was very much a believer that the United States was the best country in the world, even though he was very conscious of its flaws, especially with regard to fellow blacks.

After finishing off Nova, and with a Conn rematch on the back burner, the next time Louis defended the crown against Baer, he was not only fighting for himself, he was literally fighting for the country. In a gesture that stunned the cynical press, Louis announced that when he battled Baer he was going to donate his entire purse to the U.S. Navy Relief Society. In essence, he was going to risk his title for free. That was unheard of and unprecedented.

Suddenly, Louis won a legion of new fans impressed with his offer. In a famous comment offered in the *New York Daily News*, sportswriter Jimmy Powers wrote, "The more I think of it, the greater guy I see in this Joe Louis."[6]

Baer had shown potential throughout his career, but probably wasn't the equal of his brother Max in the ring. This Baer served as a Louis tune-up before the Conn fight and lost by disqualification in the seventh round. "I guess I took about every punch Louis had in our first fight," Baer said. "I feel much stronger now and there's nothing bothering me. I expect to hit Joe just as hard and often as I can and one of us is going to get knocked out. This time it'll be Louis."[7]

Louis dismantled him inside a round, and in *The Ring* Nat Fleischer called Louis' performance one of his greatest, even though Baer outweighed him by 50 pounds and stood five inches taller. "Not even in the second fight with Max Schmeling ... did the Detroit Destroyer show as much as he did against Buddy. Joe had everything. He was magnificent. He was a whirlwind on attack, a master on the defense, a terror with his devastating punches. Whang! Bang! Zoom! The punches came flying from all angles at a mile a minute rate only two seconds after the bell had sent the rival gladiators on their way and before poor Buddy could catch his breath."[8]

A few days after the bout, Louis, John Roxborough, Julian Black and Mike Jacobs made a public show of donating $89,092 from their earnings to the Navy Relief Society. Not only was this unique in heavyweight boxing annals, it was a courageous decision on Louis' part for two other reasons. The first was that the Navy was known for its discrimination against blacks. Even in war-time African Americans were given only the lowliest of jobs aboard ship and some black leaders protested Louis' choice of charity in this instance. He considered the U.S. military to be the greater cause at the time. The other reason this was a particularly generous move on Louis' part was that he was in debt and needed every dollar he could get. While Louis was one of the biggest wage earners in the country, he was also just about the biggest spendthrift. He had already begun a cycle that would dominate the following decades of his life once the Internal Revenue Service jumped upon him for back taxes. The man who grandly dispensed $100 bills to the needy was in reality one of them in a complex way.

It was before the Baer fight that trainer Jack Blackburn began showing signs of physical weakness. His health began to decline. Blackburn had lived hard, not only as a fighter, but serving time in jail, and his fondness and apparent addiction to alcohol was no secret to his favorite pupil. Moments before the Baer bout, Chappie told Louis as they were about to climb the few stairs to their corner, "My heart's bad. I don't think I can climb those stairs." Concerned as he was, Louis had a ready answer. "You don't have to climb them but once Chappie."[9] Right he was. Louis felled Baer within the first round. It was much easier for Blackburn to climb down the stairs.

Baer lasted 2 minutes, 56 seconds before biting the canvas, pretty much what the spectators at Madison Square Garden paid to see. By the time Louis signed for another defense of the title, his 21st, March 27, 1942, again at the Garden, he was in the Army.

In-between his KO of Baer and the delivery of the donation to Navy Relief, Louis enlisted at Camp Upton on Long Island. His arrival was orchestrated for the press and he was officially going from making six figures per fight to the rock bottom Army private's salary of $21 a month.

Although Louis showing up for induction into the Army was big news, there was nothing much out of the ordinary about his sign-up and processing, and that precisely was the point. Louis joined up to be treated the same as everyone else. Thinking like that was pretty much unrealistic, however, because he was one of the most famous men in America and definitely the most famous black man in the country, Jesse Owens notwithstanding.

A different type of person might have tried to elude service altogether, or seek out a rank seemingly befitting his status. Indeed, Louis was offered the chance to become an officer, but declined, choosing to enter the Army as an enlisted man. It was consistent with his character and true to his nature. He didn't want to take on a responsibility he didn't feel qualified for and his instincts of going into the Army as a private and choosing not to enjoy special treatment in training appealed to his followers.

Joe Louis was Joe Louis, easily recognizable, of elevated stature. Not so the estimated one million other black Americans who served in uniform during World War II. They were not treated as well, either by the military or the general public. Many had their wills tested and enthusiasm for service tested because of discrimination. They were defending a country that did not treat them as equals, putting their lives on the line for the freedom offered by the United States. Yet even in uniform on military bases they were treated shabbily, especially those situated below the Mason–Dixon Line.

Although Louis did not covet rank, the Army was not so obtuse as to shunt him aside and bury his celebrity. He became a morale officer, in the coming years deployed throughout the world to visit with troops at different fronts, to buck up spirits. It was an enlightened and wise use of Louis' talents.

Just how the Army was going to use Louis was not yet set in cement when he was training for Baer, but he did make an appearance at a Navy Relief fund-raising dinner. Before the event a friend urged Louis to jot down a few ideas in case he was called upon to speak. Louis naively said no one was going to ask him to talk. Wrong. Louis was asked to say a few words. He uttered only a few words off the cuff, but they proved to be memorable.

The United States, Louis said, was going to win the war. "We can't lose because we're on God's side," he said. The friend initially told Louis he got it backwards, that he should have said, "We can't lose because God's on our side." The guy teased Louis, saying he was a dummy. However, Louis' phrasing made people think. The public decided it very much liked the way Louis put things. The comment got widespread attention, to such a degree that some newspaper people began saying Louis had named the war. "Who's the dummy now?" Louis replied to his friend.[10]

The first blush of reaction was one thing, but the groundswell of belief and enthusiasm touched off by Louis' comment mushroomed. Carl Byoir, who is regarded as one of the early developers of the art of public relations, was so inspired by Louis that he wrote a poem about the heavyweight champ's comment.

It was a lengthy poem and read in part: "And you have named the war. This is God's War."[11]

After knocking out Buddy Baer, Louis committed to meeting Abe Simon for a second time. He had already bested Simon once, in 1941 in Detroit, but this bout was also for a worthy cause. When Louis stopped Simon in six rounds he donated $64,980 to the Army Emergency Relief Fund. It was hard not to be a Joe Louis fan when he was giving so much and risking so much for so little in return. Louis had always been excessively criticized by sports writers of the Deep South. Even if they could not find it within themselves to praise Louis and like him, now they did refrain from prose that belittled him. Even former critics, who had not believed in Louis in his early years in the fight game and who dismissed him with stereotypical descriptions, applying one of the cuckoo nicknames or just too quickly misjudged his intelligence, came around. Not only was Louis apparently invincible in the ring, in the midst of the longest run of all time as heavyweight champion, he stood for something.

Paul Gallico, later known as a novelist but then a New York sports writer, had been one of those early-to-judge scribes on Louis' case. He began writing favorably about Louis, suggesting that Louis the man had come a long way. "Somewhere on the long, hard row from rags to riches, Joe Louis found his soul," Gallico wrote.[12] More likely, Louis had been well aware of his soul all along, but writers like Gallico had just discovered that he had a soul.

As tough as Louis was with his fists, and as stout of heart as he was, the Army realized that when it came to shooting off rifles and the like, he was not very different from any other man. Joe Louis had a reputation. He was admired by millions. He was famous. He wielded influence. The Army decided that Louis could best serve his country not by fighting in the front lines, but as someone who could boost morale on the home front and on those front lines. His one-liner sealed it. After Louis' little speech, the Army manufactured posters that featured a picture of Louis wearing a helmet and wielding a bayonet and including the words, "Pvt. Joe Louis says — 'We're going to do our part ... and we'll win because we're on God's side.'"[13]

Although Louis was willing to continue training and fighting as the heavyweight champ and plans were formulated for another Conn bout, the Army stepped in and said no more. After the Simon fight, with Louis' record standing at 53–1, his boxing career was on hold. The heavyweight championship was frozen, as well. It was deemed that Louis was more valuable for the war effort in other ways than punching out other Americans. Ironically, in 1938, long before war broke out, when the appeasers of Hitler were still arguing that all he wished to do was rebuild Germany, Louis had had an audience with FDR. Over the years the essence of that conversation that has survived went like this: "Lean over Joe, so I can feel your muscles," the president said. "Joe, we need muscles like yours to beat Germany."[14] At that point in his life a few years before the war the only German Louis was interested in beating was Max Schmeling.

Interestingly, in 1940, Louis publicly and outspokenly supported Wendell Wilkie, the Republican candidate for president opposing Roosevelt. Louis even campaigned. It was a rarity for Louis to take any kind of public political stance. But he said he was doing so because he believed a Wilkie administration would offer a better shake to African Americans. Although Wilkie was thrashed by FDR as thoroughly as Louis manhandled most of his opponents, Louis and the Republican candidate remained friends.

While attitudes were changing in the United States towards blacks at the outbreak of World War II, the Armed Forces were still segregated and in high places there was definitely an awareness that issues might arise. The Army appointed Truman Gibson, a friend and attorney for Louis at various times in their lives, inside the War Department as a Washington, D.C.–based liaison to the blacks in the service. The phrase did not exist at the time, but Louis had Gibson on speed-dial of a sort. Louis had carte blanche to pick up any phone, anywhere he was, on a base, overseas, and if he saw things that seemed discriminatory to report them. He expected, with good reason, to get a swift response.

Louis had not chosen to take a higher rank to benefit himself in the Army, but again, consistent with his nature, behind the scenes during the war he was a very active advocate. Louis may not have been a man who called for demonstrations, or who screamed from rooftops, but he recognized injustice when he saw it and made it his mission to fix problems through his connections. Sometimes he found problems. Sometimes the problems found him.

Even before Louis joined the Army and assumed his special role, he had become an advocate for black Americans in certain ways. By the mid–1930s, he was a member of the National Association for the Advancement of Colored People (NAACP). He supported the Detroit Urban League. He urged fight promoters, mostly Mike Jacobs, to price tickets to his bouts inexpensively enough so that his black fans who were not of means could afford them. Even Joe Louis ran into some difficulties in the South when he wanted to eat in certain restaurants and was turned away. He knew discrimination was still very much out there in the American heartland. He couldn't fix everything, but if he encountered a problem in the Army he did have a shot at providing an answer.

Once scheduled to fight an exhibition for a group of soldiers, Louis realized that all of the best seats were going to white men and that blacks had to sit in the back. He refused to go on unless the situation was remedied. While stationed at Fort Riley in Kansas, Louis became aware that many seemingly qualified African American soldiers were being denied the chance to attend Officer Candidate School. One of them was Jackie Robinson, later the man who broke baseball's color barrier with the Brooklyn Dodgers. Louis reported the situation to Gibson and those men were accepted into the program. That was not the only time Louis assisted Robinson and their friendship grew.

On another occasion Louis informed Gibson that this United States outpost not only had separate buses for black and white soldiers on the base, but even separate bus stations. Word got back to Fort Riley that was a no-no. At another base in Alabama, Louis, who was with Sugar Ray Robinson, the future middleweight champion of the world, sat down on a "whites-only" bench. Robinson met Louis for the first time some years before when Louis was fighting in Detroit. He ingratiated himself with the older man by carrying his bag around. This time they became ensnared in a conflict with military policemen over the seating. Once again it took a phone call to Washington to smooth things over.

Sailors called Louis a nigger, and an officer, in his presence, derided a black jeep driver for being late by summing up that all "niggers" were perpetually late. Louis got the officer removed from his assignment. On a startling occasion, MPs arrested Louis for making a phone call from a whites-only pay phone. When the situation could be handled without Gibson's intervention, Louis took control on his own by complaining to the base's commanding officer. Other times Gibson intervened.

Yes, Louis' country needed him in the service as a morale builder, but everywhere he went, it seemed, his people, black Americans, needed him even more. What was most impressive was how he continuously rose to the occasion. He was no longer the shy teenager from Alabama and Detroit starting out in the world. He was a mature man, one of the most distinguished sporting figures anywhere. He had become more assertive in places outside of the boxing ring.

Louis had reached an exalted place in American society. He was a black man who could speak for blacks when he chose to and he was a black man who could speak for the country when necessary. He had not single-handedly cured discrimination, but perhaps it could be said that he narrowed chasms of misunderstandings into more manageable ditch-width misunderstandings. It took broad enough shoulders to accomplish even that.

Much later, Joe Louis Barrow, Jr., Louis' son, who mostly grew up with his mother Marva, and was not a fan of prize-fighting, wrote a book about his famous dad and examined his role in the Civil Rights movement during his time in the Army and afterwards. Barrow indicated his father probably called Gibson once a week with complaints during his service time. And after the war years, and in his own later years, Louis did not depart from character and turn into a fiery orator or a street demonstrator, but continued to deal with discrimination when he confronted it.

"Louis was well aware that many blacks thought he didn't do all he could for the Civil Rights movement," Barrow said. "But he also knew his limitations. 'Some folks shout, some holler, some march and some don't,' he explained without animosity toward those who belittled him. 'They do it their way; I do it mine. I got nothing to be ashamed of. I stand for right and work for it hard because I know what it means not to have the rights what God give us.'"[15]

The Army deployed Louis non-stop for perhaps 100,000 miles during his service. He was supposed to be fighting enemies like the Germans and the Japanese by speaking out against tyranny and for democracy as he visited with between four million and five million troops in a wide array of countries, including bases all over the U.S., plus Alaska. Less visibly to the average American, he also fought against bigotry. As part of his work entertaining the troops, Louis boxed between 70 and 100 exhibitions during his service years, while also rising to the rank of sergeant. "He was a real trouper and soldier," said Nat Fleischer, "a morale builder and lifter of the highest order."[16]

Throughout it all he made friends just by being Joe Louis, displaying the personality that came naturally to him, even as he was idolized by many of those he spent time with. "You don't know what war is until you visit one of the hospitals with tough cases such as I saw in Naples," Louis said, "and then you just can't do enough for those boys who went through hell."[17]

24

A Young Man
Named Robinson

The elevation of Joe Louis into American hero status across ethnic boundaries was solidified during World War II. Willingly, accommodatingly, helpfully, Louis enlisted in the U.S. Army, raised money for the cause and traveled thousands upon thousands of miles to boost troop morale. After more than a decade as a popular sporting figure known to everyone in the land for his fisticuffs, Louis was no longer quite as reticent in public, and he was in more of an activist mode.

Never one to make waves in the spotlight, whenever Louis saw injustice as it was applied to African Americans, he aggressively sought a fix. Another type of man might have worked to turn the bright lights of the media on his accomplishments or causes, but Louis always worked through channels to get things done.

After years of prize fighting, after years of holding the prestigious heavyweight title, and after defending America's honor in the ring when called upon as a symbol against Fascist Italy and Nazi Germany, Louis had earned a certain amount of political capital. He was not a political man, but he had gained wisdom in the way things worked. Just by being Joe Louis he had developed a huge following, a devoted following, and as importantly as anything else, a large cadre of true believers.

Louis was known as a straight shooter, as an honest man, as a patriot. In a time period when parents still told their children that all they had was their good name, Louis had his good name. In a sometimes unseemly profession, no scent of scandal had attached itself to Joe Louis. When needed to rise to the occasion in the ring, he had done so. When called upon to help his country in the best and most useful ways that he could, he was front and center, a volunteer, not someone dragged into doing his duty.

What an extraordinary accomplishment that was to gain the confidence of the nation. When Louis arrived on the boxing scene he was told by his own handlers that he might not be able to ever fight for the heavyweight title because of the color of his skin. Emerging as the most famous black man in the United States, and perhaps the world, Louis was a transitional figure.

Through his sporting accomplishments and his basic decency, Louis became the hero of African Americans. But he bridged the racial divide in American society more seamlessly and more thoroughly than any black American had done before. There were always going to be ignorant bigots, but Louis was accepted by mainstream America in a way that no other black man had been. He was admired for what he accomplished in his specialty, but against all odds Louis was admired for what he said and did outside of the ring, as well.

The first two actions Louis took after the Japanese bombed Pearl Harbor and World War II engulfed the United States, earned him universal praise. Immediately he volunteered to fight a fund-raising bout for the Navy Relief Society. He offered to donate 100 percent of his purse. Then Louis enlisted in the Army as a private. Other famous American figures went into the service as officers. Louis accepted the rank of the humble private, the lowest rank in the hierarchy.

While in the Army Louis gained the acquaintance of the black athlete who would succeed him as the most influential in America. Jackie Robinson, who in 1947 would join the Brooklyn Dodgers and become the first black Major League baseball player since the 19th century, was temperamentally the opposite of Louis. Robinson sizzled beneath the surface. His method of righting wrongs was to use either his stinging tongue or his fists. The fiery Robinson accepted no slights. Robinson's refusal to acquiesce to the racism in the U.S. Army nearly got him court-martialed and imprisoned due to an incident with a driver when he refused to move to the back of a military bus.

Robinson had attended UCLA, where he was a multi-sport star. But that did nothing for him in the Army. He stated his application to Officer Candidate School languish for months at Fort Riley, Kansas. It was Louis who jump-started the process to get black men promoted through his contact with Truman Gibson, an advisor to the War Department. Gibson's job was to act as a go-between who could smooth relations between the Army and its disgruntled black troops. Gibson asked Louis to be his eyes and ears and all it took was a phone call from Louis to Washington to get things going. Louis possessed atypical clout for a private.

Robinson had completed basic training at Fort Riley, and even excelled as a marksman. But he was one of many black soldiers who were being held back from attempts to become officers. When Louis showed up at Fort Riley,

Robinson had already been on the base for some time. They found one another and in their spare time began playing rounds of golf.

"Almost the first person I met at Fort Riley was a guy named Jackie Robinson," Louis recalled years later. "He was a helluva guy. He was just like he turned out to be on the baseball field. He wouldn't take [crap] from anybody or anything. I remember him saying he was just as good as anybody else. Mind you, he would never say better than anyone else, but just as good — white, black, or green. If there would be anybody I'd have liked to be like in this world, I'd have to say it would be Jackie Robinson. And Jackie showed me a lot of respect. He told me I was his idol."[1]

Louis always came off as someone who was happy in his own skin, so it was interesting to hear his comment about wanting to be like Robinson. What he no doubt meant was the ability to be more forceful and outspoken. That was not his way and he knew it. Louis never tried to pretend to be something he was not, but it is fascinating that at least this once he lamented not being a different type of person.

At the time Robinson was playing for the base's football team, but he was shut out of competing for the baseball team. Louis' intervention with the base commanding officer remedied that. "There was a lot of racism in the service.... That made me real mad. I knew I had influence,"[2] Louis said.

During one of these golf sessions Robinson told Louis about the more pressing problem he and 19 others (all of whom had attended college) faced regarding the officer training school. Louis phoned Gibson and Gibson came to Kansas to investigate. Gibson ended the months-long delay that sent the group, including Robinson, into Officer Candidate School.

Gibson later spoke of a more hushed-up incident. He said that during officer training a white officer called another individual "a stupid nigger son of a bitch." Although the disparaging remark was not directed at him, Robinson jumped in. A brief exchange of obscenities resulted in Robinson beating up the man. Gibson said that Louis' presentation of "very expensive gifts," in other words, a bribe, is the only thing that allowed Robinson to finish officer training school.[3] Louis' efforts began his friendship with Robinson. Robinson, thanks to Louis' intervention, came out of the training as a second lieutenant.

The most publicized incident that plagued Robinson during his Army career took place at Fort Hood in Texas. He sat down on a bus next to a woman whom he described as the wife of another black officer that he knew. The woman was black, but light-skinned and was mistaken for Caucasian. The bus driver stopped the vehicle and ordered Robinson to the back of the bus. Robinson wouldn't move and a heated argument followed.

The driver continued the route, but upon arrival at the depot, he summoned MPs, who arrested Robinson. Robinson was referred to as "that nigger lieutenant"[4] and he ferociously shouted back not to call him that and give him the respect due an officer. That defused nothing. Robinson faced three charges at a court-martial. However, between the time Robinson was arrested and he faced the military court, Louis had swung into action. He contacted Gibson and somehow the story was picked up and highly publicized in the black press across the country. The NAACP got involved and charged that Robinson was being set up.

Certain allegations were dropped, a court proceeding took place, but with watered down issues being considered. In the end Robinson was simply able to leave the Army. Although there is no doubt that the Louis-Gibson pipeline was influential in easing the pressure on Robinson, it was not something overly publicized at the time. Nor did Louis want it to be.

In the first half of the 1940s, compared to Joe Louis, Jackie Robinson was an unknown. He had been a star college athlete at UCLA and he had played some baseball — not everyone even thought it was his best sport. After World War II ended, when Dodgers general manager Branch Rickey embarked on his search for what he considered the perfect candidate to break Major League baseball's color barrier and settled on Robinson, then with the Kansas City Monarchs of the Negro Leagues, for the role, Robinson exploded into Americans' consciousness.

Eventually, Robinson's fame and the credit given him as a barrier breaker enabled him to eclipse Louis on the national scene. His baseball star was ascendant as Louis' boxing stardom was on the downswing. Both men were pioneers. Both men used sport as their vehicle. Louis came first and helped pave the way for Robinson. But he was a name in an individual sport, which over time declined in popularity. Robinson helped integrate a team sport and one that remains in the forefront of sports fans' rooting interests today.

Baseball was indisputably the most popular sport in the United States in 1942 and one Robinson biographer noted, "Robinson was being compared to Frederick Douglass, George Washington Carver, and Joe Louis, with some writers concluding that this man would do more for his people than any of the others."[6]

Some years later, author James Baldwin, who was also an African American, wrote of Robinson's Major League baseball debut, "Back in the Thirties and Forties Joe Louis was the only hero that we ever had. When he won a fight everybody in Harlem was up in heaven. On that April day the large contingent of blacks in the crowd of nearly 40,000 had another hero to be 'up in heaven' about, another hero to stand beside Joe Louis."[5]

From the vantage point of the 2000s, it is difficult for younger people to envision how thoroughly African Americans were outcast from daily life in the first half of the 20th century. That included newspaper and radio coverage. Historians looking back at the 1930s suggest that even before Louis became heavyweight champion, making his name known worldwide, and by merely becoming a contender, he had increased his visibility a million-fold. "He immediately became the most prominent black in America. Louis took Harlem by storm."[7]

Rickey had thoroughly scouted Robinson and he knew the nature of his player's volatile temper. In exchange for the chance to integrate the big leagues, Rickey made Robinson promise that he had to turn the other cheek to the inevitable insults that would accompany his breakthrough for a two-year period. Robinson agreed.

Beyond that Rickey invited Louis, Bill "Bojangles" Robinson, and Paul Robeson, prominent African Americans in the world of sport and entertainment, to talk with Robinson about what his ascension would mean and how closely scrutinized his behavior would be by white America. "We didn't need to say anything to Jackie," Louis said. "He'd been in the Army. He knew just what to look for. He knew he'd have to be strong and take the [crap], or he'd close the door for black people in baseball for Lord knows how many more years."[8]

There was an irony in this. Louis was coaching Robinson on how to succeed himself as America's most iconic black athlete. When Louis rose to prominence — and for several years after — many times he was barely even described in human terms. He was always an animalistic figure in the ring and newspaper cartoons exaggerated his features and demeanor.

Now Louis was the role model for Robinson. Louis had not only tamed the heavyweight division, he had tamed the sports reporters. Whereas once most of the writers viewed him as a caricature, now they admired him as a man. He had been around at the top of the sport for so long he out-lasted some of them and changed the minds of others.

Baseball ranked much higher in the public estimation than boxing. It was called the National Pastime and for years sports writers in the black press, working for such outfits as the *Pittsburgh Courier* or the *Chicago Defender*, had lobbied the sport to open access to African American players. It had been a long struggle and Robinson was one man who recognized that without Joe Louis' help (in the Army and beyond) that he might never have been able to fulfill his own destiny.

"I have said many times before that I only hope I can do half as much for my people as he has done," Robinson wrote. "He's been an inspiration to us all. Joe has made it easy for me and the other fellows in baseball. I imagine that Mr. Rickey said to himself when considering the idea, 'Joe Louis has proven that a Negro can take honors and remain dignified.'"[9]

Sam Lacy, one of the best-read and best sports writers toiling in the black press for the *Baltimore Afro-American*, once assessed the dual impact of Louis and Robinson from the perspective of a parent. He said he hoped his son would blend the traits of the two trailblazers. "I'd want him to combine the wisdom of Joe Louis with the courage of Jackie Robinson," said Lacy. "I'd hope for him to have Jackie's ability to hold his head high in adversity, the willingness to withstand the butts and digs and meanness of those who envy him."[10]

Robinson, who had much to be thankful of directly due to Louis during their overlapping time in the Army, paid homage to him for the fighter's impact on the American scene that Robinson encountered after World War II. "I'm sure if it wasn't for Joe Louis the color line in baseball would not have been broken for another 10 years," Robinson said.[11]

Louis had not retired from boxing when he joined the Army. He was on hiatus. By the time he was discharged and a real fight was arranged, it was more than two and a half years since Louis met Simon in the benefit bout, and the heavyweight champ had not been in serious training since. Likewise, the heavyweight championship was in suspended animation while Louis served his country.

At age 30, Louis was ready to return to his primary business. Waiting for his second chance was Billy Conn, a rematch made in heaven that took five years to make. Besides a war and Louis' role in it for the Army, the champ had become a father, he had become a friend to Robinson, who in some ways very soon would come to represent a kind of passing of the torch for African Americans, and those both close to Louis and only connected to him from the sport would undergo dramatic changes, too.

25

After the War

Joe Louis emerged from World War II with elevated standing on the American scene. Before the war he was a prominent sports figure. After the war he was a prominent man. As the heavyweight champion of the world Louis was already one of the best-known sports figures anywhere. But for the most part, he was still seen merely as a boxer. After the war he was recognized as an American hero.

A man who excelled in a profession where he was routinely praised for his killer instinct gained exalted status without killing anyone. In a time of peace, Louis was seen as a killer in the ring because of the power in his fists, an athlete who was the toughest man in the universe and one who "slaughtered," "murdered," "destroyed" other men. Those were analogies, not literal interpretations of his boxing prowess.

When he was in uniform, Louis neither slaughtered, nor destroyed. An athlete once dismissed for his soft-spoken, short answers to sports writers' questions served his country by speaking loudly. Sometimes it was at large rallies where he uttered his famous comment about being "on God's side." Sometimes it was in front of gatherings of troops. World War II was far more than a few-year intermission in Louis' boxing career, however. Much around him had changed or was changing.

Most significant was the loss of trainer and mentor Jack Blackburn. The man who polished Louis' style, who guided him from his first minutes as a professional to the heavyweight title and beyond, was not in the champ's corner for his charity bout with Abe Simon in March of 1942. Assistant trainer Mannie Seamon took over because Blackburn was in fading health.

Blackburn was hospitalized in Chicago, suffering from pneumonia, and Louis visited him before returning to Fort Dix in New Jersey. Almost as soon as he got back, however, Louis received a telegram from friend Freddie Guinyard. The message was brief: "Chappie's Dead." Blackburn had recovered sufficiently to be released, but soon after going home he suffered a heart attack and passed away on April 24, less than a month after Louis' bout with Simon. When Louis received the news of Blackburn's death he broke down crying.[1]

The funeral took place in Chicago, and after the Army granted him two weeks' leave, Louis served as a pallbearer, as expected (others included Cab Calloway, Bill "Bojangles" Robinson, John Roxborough and Julian Black) as an estimated 10,000 people turned out to pay their respects. Although Black-burn was a prominent man in the boxing world, it is likely that much of the outpouring was a tribute to his connection with Louis and that many came primarily to catch a glimpse of the champ. "Chappie was buried at Lincoln Cemetery, and when the dirt went down on that coffin, I knew my life would never be the same again," Louis said.[2]

Throughout the 1940s, Louis and Marva had their share of disagreements and near-break-ups. It eventually came to light that Louis had a number of affairs while he was in uniform and some rumors even broke into gossip columns suggesting he had his next wife lined up as soon as his divorce was final. Ultimately, divorce proceedings did come. On March 28, 1945, Marva filed for a legal resolution of their difficult relationship on grounds of desertion. Louis did not fight the divorce.

"Joe thinks I ought to be happy because I've got all of the material things any woman could want," Marva said at the time. "But it's no fun being alone all the time."[3]

Actually, prevailing opinion, especially in the black community, was that Marva should have been happy being the wife of the most famous black man in the world. During the war, daughter Jacqueline was born (she was named after Jack Blackburn). Whatever press commentary there was about Joe and Marva splitting up, it favored Louis' perspective, not Marva's. Much to every-one's surprise, however, after Louis was discharged from the Army, and with a full-court press in the way of gifts and attention, Louis and Marva got re-married in July of 1946. Clearly, Marva must have believed that Louis had changed his ways, that he was going to be more of a stay-at-home husband, and certainly that he was not going to continue as a philanderer. She was wrong on every expectation. Louis did not change at all.

However, during Louis-Marva II, the couple had another child. Son Joe Louis Barrow, Jr., was born in 1947. Also during this tumultuous period, his managerial team dissolved. Roxborough had been arrested in Michigan and was sent to prison for his involvement in numbers running. To avoid tarnishing Louis' reputation, Roxborough backed away from his pupil.

Then Black did the same, perhaps because he just didn't want to be the main front man with Blackburn and Roxborough out of the picture, though it's not completely clear just how much Louis wanted him to fulfill that role, either. Black's 10-year contract as co-manager of Louis was up and Louis did not want to pay him a 25-percent rate to stay on, especially since he owed $81,000 in back taxes at the time. The problem only grew and every thousand bucks Louis could save served to his advantage. Seamon stepped up as full-time trainer, but Louis actually gave Marva a 25 percent interest in his career as manager and hired Marshall Miles, an old friend, for a 10 percent interest.

None of the trio that had guided Louis to the title and done its best to protect and safeguard his public image was involved in Louis' career anymore. If this all seemed unsettling to Louis, he had moved on from his World War II service with a more favorable public face than ever and he could ruminate that at the least he had things better than his old nemesis Max Schmeling.

In the 1930s, when Schmeling haunted Louis as the only boxer to defeat him, he was viewed as much as a representative of Germany's hateful Nazi policies as he was seen as a professional athlete. Now, in the 1940s, Louis was viewed as an outspoken proponent of the American way of life to such a degree that his fame among non-boxing fans was as high as it was among fight fans.

During the war, Louis was employed by the United States as a propagandizing morale figure because of his popularity. During the war, Schmeling, who had once dined with and taken tea with dictator Adolf Hitler, was thrust into uniform and sent to the front lines with a paratroop unit. Losing to Louis in their rematch had diminished whatever clout Schmeling possessed and he was on the outs with the German government to the point where someone who didn't like him was able to get him posted someplace he might be killed.

By the time the United States entered the war, Schmeling was 36, hardly a prime age for a foot soldier. Schmeling was not anxious for any military service, but was conscripted — he thought — to provide physical fitness training to recruits. Once on site he was impressed into the training program, promptly hurt a knee and was in a clinic for six weeks. Schmeling said he was never given any actual combat training, just thrown in with a group, taken to Greece and mixed in with a team of paratroopers. When he jumped out of the plane he re-injured the knee.

As he limped along, Schmeling said he was given charge of a British prisoner. The man recognized him and said he was a friend of English boxer Tommy Farr. Then Schmeling said he got dysentery. He was miserable, but not wounded. Yet somehow word leaked to the West that Schmeling had been killed. All of this took place before the U.S. entered the war. When the publicity surfaced that Schmeling was dead, the German government trotted him out in order to prove that Western reporting was irresponsible. Instead,

Schmeling caused a sensation with his responses to American reporters, first saying he hoped there would be no war with the U.S. and that contrary to reports he had seen no British atrocities, something the Germans were claiming. The Nazi government, which had arranged the press conference, was infuriated and Schmeling was put on trial by the military for speaking his mind.

Schmeling said he was suddenly discharged in 1943 after three and a half years in uniform and after spending only two days at the front. In the United States, Schmeling was seen not only as a representative of a defeated power, but as someone whose own image had been tarnished. He had seemed too cozy with the losing side, even if he had not engaged in any Nazi-inspired crimes, and was never a member of the party. Although Schmeling and Louis would never meet in the ring for a rubber match, their paths were fated to cross again, but much later in life.

Louis' last fight dated to early 1942 against Abe Simon and he carried a 53–1 lifetime record into the post-war phase of his career. On November 11, 1944, while still in the Army, Louis engaged in a fight against Johnny Davis at the Memorial Auditorium in Buffalo. Historians have sometimes debated what to make of this appearance. The fight was only scheduled for four rounds, so it certainly seems like it was an exhibition. However, some record-keeping sources count it on Louis' record as a victory after he stopped Davis (who had only a 3–3 mark) in the first round. Apparently, the only reason this fight is discussed as being anything beyond an exhibition is because the New York State Athletic Commission called it a title defense. It seems absurd on the face of it because title fights were scheduled for 15 rounds and only beginners in their first fights, or those participating in exhibitions, get involved in four-rounders. It is at best an oddity with a victory declared for Louis. If Louis had lost, the bout might have screwed up the boxing world for a time.

After Louis left the Army his first order of real fisticuff business was the very long-awaited rematch with Billy Conn. They signed to meet on June 19, 1946. Five years had passed since the thrilling, surprising, and entertaining first meeting between the two men. Five years that seemed like an eternity had gone by on the calendar and no one could truly predict how rust might affect either combatant. There was little question, though, that this was the right fight for Louis and the right fight for boxing to put itself back on the map of the American sporting scene after the war-time hiatus.

Like Louis, Conn went into the Army when hostilities broke out, and he also was paid $21 a month as a private instead of taking home a six-figure payday from a rematch. He also was enlisted to fight exhibitions and entertain soldiers as a respite from combat and he and Louis saw each other in London during the war. But when he was a civilian once again there was no doubt that Conn had his eye on Louis. The rematch was announced for Yankee Stadium in June, six months after the public unveiling of the idea. Plenty of time for a buildup for promoter Mike Jacobs and plenty of time for the two principals to round into form for their big test. Ringside seats were $100.

Conn's preliminary training camp was set up in Hot Springs, Arkansas, supposedly at the order of mobster Owney Madden, who apparently wanted the entertainment where he was hanging out. "Those three years in the Army didn't help my ring condition any," Conn said, dismissing his mid–1940s exhibitions.[4]

Both men had work to do to regain their pre-war form. There was nothing like putting Conn in front of Louis to focus his attention (though he did slip into the bad habit of playing golf too often again during training). "I knew I had to shape up for the fight with Conn," Louis said. "Conn was as hungry as I was and in our last fight he could have been the champion. Those exhibition bouts in the Army were just fun and games. I needed some heavy training. As far as I was concerned, I hadn't fought in 46 months."[5]

Conn was 28 and Louis was 32. Flat, muscled bellies were harder to come by, but both men looked pretty fit at the weigh-in. Conn weighed in 182 (he had come down considerably from the start of training) and Louis weighed 207. There was still a 25-pound disparity.

At one point when Conn and Louis ran into one another after the first fight, Conn said, "I had your ass beat. I could have won the title, been the champion six months, then I'd let you win it back." Louis, as he always seemed to manage, came up with a pithy reply that summarized the situation perfectly, and in this case also stung. "How were you gonna keep the title for six months when you couldn't keep it for 12 rounds?"[6]

Conn certainly aimed to keep the heavyweight crown longer than that this time. But Louis had already held onto it for nine years and had grown quite attached to it. Conn would need his fists, his stamina, and perhaps a crowbar to pry the heavyweight title belt from around Louis' waist. He had 15 three-minute rounds to make his case. One thing all should have kept in mind is that Louis always, always, performed better against a foe the second time.

The crowd was 45,266 and the gate produced just shy of $2 million for the long-talked-about rematch. For the first fight Conn was lighter on his feet and quicker with his jab. He out-boxed Louis and that was his strategy for the second fight, too, as made sense. Everyone knew that he couldn't slug with the Brown Bomber, no one better than Conn himself, who carried around the memory of his demise in the first bout in 1941 like a 10-ton weight on his shoulders.

For the first seven rounds Conn periodically attempted to stick and move (his game), but he wasn't as fast as he had been, the war years sapping more of his speed than it did of Louis' agility. Louis' style was to stalk, and he did, but Conn did not make the fight's pace as he had the first time and what he offered was largely ineffective. The same punches that penetrated Louis' defenses five years earlier did not make it past his gloves this time. There was little that Conn could accomplish, only trying to dish out more of the same and hope it took some kind of a toll (though there was no evidence it would), or that he would land the lucky punch that all boxers' dream of to finish off a foe.

The one-shot deal, though, came from the other side. In the eighth round Louis was able to briefly pin Conn in a neutral corner. He slammed him with a body punch that brought a grimace. Conn was able to escape the trap in the corner, but Louis' left opened a cut over Conn's left eye. The next time Louis landed a left, Conn was off balance and open to a follow-up smash. The Louis right did its job, cracking Conn on the chin and dropping him to the canvas. Conn never did get the license plate of that truck. The counting by referee Eddie Josephs stopped at 2 minutes, 18 seconds of the eighth.

Conn did not rise at 10, either. Once Josephs signaled the end, the challenger had to be dragged to his corner by his helpers. For all of the hype, which had percolated on a back burner for five years, the fight was far from the classic of the first one. Age and inactivity had dimmed Conn's skills. Louis was still Louis, not as purely athletically talented as he had been, but after a remarkable 22 title defenses, he was still the king.

It took quite a bit of hard work for Louis to trim down and step into the ring in first-rate shape. Only he and trainer Seamon knew the extent to which his elbows pained him because he had once again indulged in too much golf. "It was a long grind from the sulphur baths and steam baths at West Baden to the eighth round of the Conn bout at the Yankee Stadium, but the payoff wallops were good to see," Seamon said.[7]

Now that he had worked out sufficiently to regain heavyweight championship form, Louis wanted to return to his pre-war pace and fight often. As much as anything else he needed the money. Always lurking in the background (and pretty close to the foreground) for Louis, coloring every decision he made, were the demands of the Internal Revenue Service for back taxes. Louis' years of generosity, years of being a big spender, and years without making investments or stashing savings caught up to him.

Being slow to pay off was a problem growing in magnitude for Louis, too. He couldn't seem to get ahead, even with six-figure purses. He couldn't eradicate the debt, rein in his spending sufficiently, and so interest kept mounting. The only way Louis knew how to make a living was through the power in his fists. He had to keep using them to make a buck.

Unfortunately for Louis there were no other big-time challengers on the horizon immediately after World War II. The lingering take-care-of-business rematch with Conn demonstrated that there was no need of, or demand for, a third bout. So Louis signed on to meet Tami Mauriello, also at Yankee Stadium, on September 18, 1946.

Although there were no contenders with the type of drawing power of Conn, Mike Jacobs could always promote using Louis' brand name. He was not only popular as a fighter and had the nation's goodwill because of his actions during World War II, he was an American institution. Even though Louis was still the heavyweight champ, those who thought about it had to realize he couldn't continue forever in that role. Age was creeping up on the Brown Bomber.

Mauriello was of Italian extraction from the Bronx and he held the nickname of "Meatball." How flattering this was supposed to be was unknown. Since there were really no other heavyweights floating around in the ranks that Louis had not yet defeated he actually requested Mauriello as his next opponent. This was a good news–bad news opportunity for Mauriello. The good news was that he had the chance to win the heavyweight title. The bad news was that he had to go through Joe Louis to get it. Odds-makers gave him no better than an 8–1 chance to succeed, which improved on the opening odds of 12–1.

Mauriello, who weighed 198½ pounds compared to Louis' 211½, told the world that he was confident and that not only would he raid his savings account for a bet, but that his family members were going to bet on him, too. "I've just got to beat Louis," Mauriello said. "All of my relatives and friends are betting on me. They'll be ruined if I don't win."[8]

It was unknown if newspaper sleuths checked the bankruptcy court after the fight to check up on those close to Mauriello's financial fortunes, but Louis, as pledged, wiped out the contender in less than one round, 2 minutes, 9 seconds into the event. The victory marked his 23rd defense of the heavyweight title. There were 38,494 ticket-buying witnesses, and if any of them were late to their seats they missed the entire championship show.

Louis received $103,000 for the fight, but even before new manager Marshall Miles could grab a piece of it and bank it, the champ asked Jacobs to fork over the cash and he invested $43,000 in the Rheum Boogie Café in Chicago. It was part of Louis' plan of trying to find other ways to make money outside of the ring, though he did so often without expert advice and paid for it.

Also more about fund-raising than boxing was Louis' tour of South America to fight exhibitions, although he wasn't a huge hit. In addition, the champ opened the Joe Louis Restaurant and Bar on 125th Street in Harlem. Other expenditures went into the launching of Joe Louis Punch, a soft drink, a vocational school in Chicago and an insurance company. Many came under the umbrella of Joe Louis Enterprises. He was certainly trying to boost his financial fortunes to pay off the IRS. The problem was that sooner or later all of them, even the Harlem restaurant, which did well at first, failed.

Upon sober reflection it was clear to Louis that these investments were not going to maintain him in the style of luxury living to which he had grown accustomed. Nor were they going to bail him out of his money troubles with the government. There were no indications in either the Conn bout and certainly not in the Mauriello fight that Louis was fading. He seemed perfectly capable of relying on his fists to continue his reign as the heavyweight champ indefinitely. At the least he believed he could keep taking on and eliminating challengers for the money.

26

End Days of a
Brilliant Career

After his powerful fists disposed of Billy Conn and Tami Mauriello, there was little indication that Joe Louis wouldn't be able to handle Jersey Joe Walcott with the same ease. Everyone agreed that Jersey Joe was a nice man who'd had some bad luck in the fight game, but he still seemed like just another one of the many heavyweights for Louis to swat aside as he extended his reign. Jersey Joe was known more as a boxer than a puncher, but had run across enough opponents who solved his style that no one in the boxing game believed he was invincible.

Walcott, who was born Arnold Cream, was as hungry as the next man for a shot at the heavyweight crown. Like so many other boxers he had chosen the profession as a way out of poverty. Born in 1914 in Pennsauken, New Jersey, Walcott, one of 12 children, was about the same age as Louis. At times when he was young his family did not have enough food so meals were skipped. Nothing came easy to Walcott. He quit school to work when he was 15 after his father died.

When Walcott began fighting, it was decided that "Arnold Cream" didn't sound like a rough-and-tumble boxer, so Walcott took the name of a prior welterweight champion. His early influential trainer was Jack Blackburn, the same man who mentored Louis later as he rose to heavyweight champ.

Married, and trying to raise a family, Walcott could not devote his attention 100 percent to the ring. He had to work outside jobs, too, sometimes on an ice and coal truck. He was also struck by typhoid fever and the illness sidelined him from the sport for a while. As in his youth, Walcott was once again living on the edge, struggling financially. He had success in the ring in New Jersey and gained some respect, but earned no big paydays.

Walcott eventually lost contact with Blackburn, who had been hired to take care of Louis, but in 1936, two years after the two men last met, Blackburn searched him out and offered him a job as a Louis sparring partner. Louis was preparing for his first bout with Max Schmeling and the pay was $25 a round, with at least one round guaranteed each day he was in camp in Lakewood, New Jersey. It promised to be more satisfying work for Walcott than delivering ice or coal.

To some extent, what happens in training camp stays in training camp. But sometimes the other extreme takes hold — too much gossip emerging from the secrecy, where the truth may be a casualty. Walcott was not long for Louis' camp. He claimed he knocked Louis down in sparring and was fired after the first day. Louis adherents say he knocked Walcott down and he quit. A biography of Walcott says that he told a grandson that he knocked Louis down two days running and then was fired.[1]

More than 10 years passed before Louis and Walcott signed to fight for real. Louis was the most active heavyweight champion in history. Typically, he fought every few months. But after he chilled out the division with his domination of Conn and Mauriello he departed from his predictable schedule. Louis took the title on the road, fighting exhibitions everywhere from Hawaii to Mexico, throughout Central and South America. His normal fee was $10,000 per appearance and he cleared more than $150,000 from his road show. It was a solid chunk of change, but not enough for Louis' needs. Not only did he travel with a large entourage, footing the bill, but the ever-present IRS was after his purse money whenever he cashed a check.

Any payday that registered in the thousands of dollars was a blessing for Walcott, who said he worked "at every filthy job from cleaning cesspools on up to earn a living. And I never did a wrong thing."[2] Meaning he stayed on the right side of the law despite occasions when he was desperate.

It later came out that when Louis was probed by a doctor leading up to the fight there was, for the first time, suspicion voiced that he had lost some of his reflex speed. Such a diagnosis might lead a boxer to consider retiring, sooner rather than later. Whether Louis dismissed this opinion or not, he did not believe he was in any position to give up boxing. Years into his successful career, and reign as title-holder, he needed money as urgently as when he began in the sport.

Originally, Louis planned to fight Walcott over 10 rounds in a non-title fight on November 14, but unable to find anyone else who deserved a title shot, this bout was upgraded.

Louis weighed in at 211 pounds to Walcott's 194½. Whether it was embarrassment or some other reason, Louis had been uncomfortable with his weight in the days leading up to the bout — felt it was going to be too high — so he fasted and dried out, two counterproductive moves for stamina. Trainer Mannie Seamon was very unhappy with his charge when he learned what he had done.

When he stepped into the ring at Madison Square Garden, Louis, who had two inches in height over the challenger, appeared to be finely tuned, his stomach hard. Bookmakers made Louis an 8–1 favorite and the general view was that Louis would stop Walcott quicker, perhaps in five rounds. That's how Louis saw the action unfolding, expressing his desire to "get things over with quick."[3]

The referee assigned to the bout was the estimable Arthur Donovan, who ended up being the third man in the ring 20 times in Louis bouts. Donovan, enshrined in the International Boxing Hall of Fame, was the son of a prominent early boxer named Mike Donovan and the father of football Hall of Famer Arthur Donovan, Jr., a defensive tackle with the Baltimore Colts. Walcott's side protested the appointment of Donovan as ref, delicately seeking to work around the issue of whether a man whose job it was to be impartial could be prejudiced in favor of Louis out of familiarity.

"It is not that I question Donovan's honesty or ability," said Walcott manager Joe Webster. "Rather, it is because I feel, and I suspect that most of the boxing fans share the feeling, that Donovan has worked in too many of Louis' bouts and a change would be welcome."[4]

The New York State Athletic Commission, under chairman Eddie Eagan, did make a change, subbing another famed referee, Ruby Goldstein, in for Donovan. What Goldstein and the other 18,000-plus witnesses in the Garden saw that night shocked them. Joe Louis, idol of millions, looked as if had suddenly aged 10 years. Jersey Joe Walcott, the underdog in the view of millions, seemed to dominate the fight. There was little question he set the pace.

From the opening bell Walcott was the superior aggressor. He boxed and moved. He punched and connected. Walcott's style flummoxed Louis. Before the first round ended Walcott dropped Louis to the floor with a well-timed right-hand blow to the head. Louis was up at the count of two, seemingly determined to prove that Walcott's success was a fluke.

Louis seemed tangled in his own limbs as he frustratingly couldn't unwind and clip Walcott with his heavy artillery. He scored, but not consistently. Then in the fourth round Walcott scored a second knockdown. The Garden was buzzing, astonished at the manner in which Walcott seemed in command. By the fifth round Louis was also dripping blood from his nose.

As the rounds played out, Louis' exchanges grew sharper, and Walcott employed a strategy of staying outside more. Walcott frequently backed up, but after a while Louis refused to come to him and waited for the challenger to move back in. Their exchanges evened out and Louis belted Walcott's body. Walcott pummeled Louis' face, causing swelling.

When the bell ended after 15 rounds Louis appeared dispirited, in no way resembling the recently overwhelming champion. He attempted to climb out of the ring before the decision was announced, but his seconds grabbed him, informing him he would be disqualified if he did so. One eye shut, cheeks swollen, Louis looked beaten. However, when the officials' scores were read he prevailed. Two judges voted for Louis, 8-6-1 and 9–6, while Goldstein backed Walcott, 7-6-2 on his scorecard.

Goldstein raised Louis' hand and proclaimed that he was still heavyweight champion of the world, but the New York fans, usually so kind to Louis, booed the split decision. Almost immediately, Webster protested again, this time the result, requesting that the commission conduct a review a few days hence.

When the fight ended, the boxers embraced in the ring. Louis said, "I'm sorry," to Walcott and some took that to mean he was apologizing for the bad decision, Walcott among them. Louis said later he was apologizing for his own bad performance. "I won," Louis said, "but I was disgusted with myself. It was a bad fight. I always said I wasn't the man I was before."[5] Walcott believed he was the winner of the fight and said so. "I thought I had won nine rounds," he said in his dressing room at the Garden.[6]

A couple of days after the Friday night fight, the commission upheld the verdict, but ordered a rematch that Louis had already agreed to for June of 1948, this time at Yankee Stadium in anticipation of a $1 million gate because of Walcott's new-found stature.

Public opinion was on Walcott's side after the disputed result. While it was to be expected that Walcott and his manager, Webster, said he had won on points, less expected was a poll of 40 ringside sports writers who favored Walcott by a 24–16 margin.

Louis' 24th defense of the title was not as convincing as most of his others.

Louis did some hard thinking and announced that his next title fight was going to be his last. He admitted he made a mistake in dropping four pounds in two days prior to the Walcott bout. Louis also said he injured his right hand in the fifth round and thought it was broken, although it turned out to be merely badly bruised. He considered the Walcott fight a bad day and less than proof that he was slipping. Yet he did think that age 34 the next summer he would be ready to bid boxing farewell.

"After that the next fight I have will be in a bar room," Louis joked. "I've had enough. I've been around a long time."[7]

He had. Louis had owned the heavyweight title since June 22, 1937. No one had come close to that record. Neither had anyone come close to his 24 defenses. One more and then he would leave the sport that had carried him from being an unknown poor boy in Alabama and then Detroit and transformed him into a famous and admired American whose name was known in every household. Given his track record Louis had every reason to believe that a second match-up with Walcott would unfold the way so many of his other second meetings with boxers went. When it came to adapting and adjusting, and learning from first impressions, Louis was definitely the king.

For Louis, it was a matter of pride. He wanted to beat Walcott decisively. Walcott genuinely thought he had won the first encounter and relished a second chance at the crown.

However, the second bout did not turn out terribly pleasing for fans. Louis wanted to make Walcott come to him and Walcott knew that was Louis' strategy, so he kept his distance. Action was hard to come by for the first nine rounds. Things were so stagnant that in the 10th round referee Frank Fullam urged both men to fight. Louis took him up on the idea and in the 11th he saw his opening. He blasted Walcott with one right and three lefts and put him on the canvas. Walcott was counted out at 2 minutes, 56 seconds of the round. Joe Louis by knockout in his final fight! It was poetic.

There were no boos when Louis' hand was raised in victory this time. "The cheers were for me and I loved every minute of it," he said.[8]

On the night of June 25, 1948, Louis had no intention of fighting again. He was sincere about this. The win was sweet and an appropriate punctuation mark to his great career, although members of the press did not all give him a warm sendoff.

"Moths fluttered frantically about the ring under the great lights, caroming crazily off the head and shoulders of both Joe Louis and Jersey Joe Walcott," wrote *New York Times* columnist Arthur Daley. "For 10 dreary rounds the moths did about as much damage to the contestants as the fighters did to each other. If this were not the worst fight ever staged, it came mighty close to it, a grotesque parody of the Manly Art of Modified Murder. The challenger wouldn't fight. The champion couldn't."[9]

When he actually voluntarily relinquished the title, Louis had held the heavyweight championship for a still-record 12 years.

Although Louis owed big money to the IRS — the actual dollar amount seemed to be a shifting target — he felt by parlaying his name into success in other businesses he could still live the high life he enjoyed and pay off his debt. That was his ambition on the night he knocked out Jersey Joe in their second fight. Louis was walking away from life as heavyweight champ and hopefully walking into a new life as an entrepreneur.

For starters, Louis was put on the payroll of the Twentieth Century Sporting Club for $25,000 a year — he considered it to be a pension of sorts. Then, with the aid of his old friend and attorney Truman Gibson, Louis made a deal with another boxing promotional entity — the newly formed International Boxing Club — to arrange a heavyweight elimination tournament to choose his successor as heavyweight champ since the title was now vacant with his retirement.

These activities would keep Louis in the sport where he was famous and would provide an income. But the dollars coming in were insignificant compared to his debt. He could never catch up with the IRS. An audit showed he owed more money than previously believed, that he had been victimized by bad advice, and the government agency informed Louis that he owed more than $500,000. The only way Louis could ever hope to satisfy the government was to make more money and the only profession he knew that could provide him with six-figure paydays was boxing.

Louis had surrendered the heavyweight crown, the most lucrative title in boxing. But he still had his unenviable record to stand on and his name and reputation. He knew all too well that what he no longer had was the speed and sharpness of his youth. Most boxers are somewhat delusional (and Louis was no exception), but he had a more accurate sense of self than most. He may not have admitted it publicly (though he sometimes did), but when Louis did not fight well he recognized it. He knew that he should stay retired, but also felt cornered. He had little choice — his best way to raise money was to fight.

Before the end of 1949, in November, Louis returned to the ring against Johnny Shkor. Then in September of 1950, Louis made a true comeback. The fighter who emerged as the new heavyweight champ following Louis was Ezzard Charles, aka "The Cincinnati Cobra." Regarded more as a slick-boxing light-heavyweight, Charles fought as a heavyweight at under 190 pounds. Charles gained the heavyweight crown by besting Walcott in a 15-round fight.

Charles was a small man compared to Louis. He didn't have the ex-champ's punching power, and to some he was judged as a caretaker of the title rather than the genuine article. When Louis announced he was coming out of retirement, Charles welcomed the challenge in order to add legitimacy to his crown. As a young black fighter, Charles considered Louis to be his idol and role model. That did not matter now. This was business.

Many believed that Louis could emerge from two years of inactivity and win back the crown. His personality, his record, his history, had such a hold on boxing fans that they failed to see what he had recognized on his own, that there had been a serious deterioration in his skills. Still, maybe he had enough left in the tank to pull this sucker off.

For much of his reign, Louis weighed between 198 pounds and 202. In his post-war defenses his weight began inching up, though it pretty much stayed under 210. For Charles, however, he weighed in at 218 pounds. This was a sign that Louis had had trouble shedding weight in training. It was bound to slow him down a little bit, and he was slowing down anyway.

Charles was younger, faster, and more accurate with his punches. Louis didn't seem to ever hurt him and he ran Louis to exhaustion, winning the vast majority of the 15 rounds. Some even said he didn't pursue a sure knockout in the 15th, with Louis ready to go, because Charles respected him too much. While Louis ended the bout on his feet he was wobbly and his face was cut up. Charles retained the heavyweight title.

More than ever Louis fans urged him to retire. He thought that way, too, but he still faced the same problem. The IRS kept knocking on the door and Louis didn't have the ready cash to shut them out. Instead of immediately trying to rebuild his reputation for another shot at the title, Louis mostly retreated from New York and took on opponents that were not as highly thought of as a Charles or Walcott.

To stay trim, to add to his ever-shaky bank account, and to refurbish his reputation, Louis fought and beat Cesar Brion, Freddie Beshore, Omelio Agramonte, Andy Walker, Agramonte again, Lee Savold (the British heavyweight champ), Brion again and Jimmy Bivins. He ran off eight straight victories and his record stood at 66–2.

Meanwhile, demonstrating just how extraordinary it was that Louis had held control of the heavyweight title for so long, the belt was changing hands rapidly. Charles had won the title from Walcott and defended against him. He then made two more defenses and lost the title to Walcott. Walcott was 37 years and 168 days old when he won the crown, the oldest man in history to do so until George Foreman came along in 1994. Walcott and Charles continued their wars and Walcott made a successful title defense against the Cincinnati foe.

While all of this was going on Louis, blitzing everyone in the next tier of opponents, needed a win over someone important in the division to gain another crack at the crown. The up-and-comer everyone was talking about was a slugger out of Brockton, Massachusetts, named Rocky Marciano.

Marciano was not a stylish boxer, but he possessed incredible knockout power. He battered his foes to the ground and stepped right over them as he climbed the ladder. When he was growing up and became a follower of boxing, the man he most admired and appreciated was Joe Louis. It didn't matter that Marciano was white, either. Louis was the best there was and he wanted to be the best, too.

On October 26, 1951, Marciano, the young Italian Stallion, met the veteran Joe Louis, the Brown Bomber, in a scheduled 10-rounder at Madison Square Garden. It was a $300,000 check for Louis. The winner just might get a shot at the title. Marciano was an in-his-prime 28. Louis was 37, well past his prime. For Louis, it was like the *Titanic* hitting the iceberg in the middle of the night. He was a long time picking up the pieces. Bleeding and fatigued, Louis was stopped in the eighth round.

It was apparent that his career was finished. Marciano, who cried because of the beating he handed to his hero, would soon be champ and became the only heavyweight title-holder to retire undefeated. Louis was 66–3 and there was no pretense about him being just one fight away from regaining the crown.

Not only did Marciano shed tears, he made his way to Louis' dressing room to say, "I'm sorry, Joe." Sugar Ray Robinson was there with his friend and he cried, as well. Not Louis. "What's the use of crying?" he said. "The better man won. That's all."[10]

At one point during Louis' rise to the heavyweight championship, and during the period when he became more and more popular by knocking out all challengers, including so-called enemies of the state like Primo Carnera and Max Schmeling, sports writers had begun offering the backhand racist compliment on Joe's behavior: "He's a credit to his race."

It was not as if people did not recognize Louis' blackness anymore, but he was much more than just some African American from the ghetto who came off the street and happened to be the best fighter in the country. He had represented the United States with dignity and class during the frenzied days leading up to the Schmeling fight, with a demeanor that at all times stressed taking the high road, and then with his brilliantly simple comment that enhanced the view of him as a patriot at the outbreak of World War II.

That phrase, "a credit to his race," was bandied about for a while, until it was uttered in front of the wrong man. Jimmy Cannon, a famed New York sports columnist for the *Post*, *Journal-American* and syndicated by King Features, was Louis' closest friend in the press corps. They enjoyed one another's company and Cannon was one of the first big-time sports writers to write supportive columns about black athletes. When someone said of Louis, "He's a credit to his race," Cannon responded, "Yes, Louis is a credit to his race, the human race."[11]

27

Real Life Tougher
Than Boxing

The fighting did not end for Joe Louis when he hung up his boxing gloves. The Internal Revenue Service proved to be a tougher foe than any of the others, Max Schmeling, Jersey Joe Walcott, or Rocky Marciano. The IRS was trained to go 15 rounds, 20 if it had to, and as interest penalties kept mounting up Louis felt besieged and at times unable to cope.

Any time he made any money, the IRS pounced. It wiped out savings accounts set aside for his children. It jumped on any earnings from boxing promotion. Worse, Louis' other investments fizzled. He couldn't possibly keep up with payments. During the course of his long professional boxing career, it was estimated that Louis made around $5 million. Once, later in life, a friend asked Louis if he didn't wish he had come along in later decades when boxers made much more than that for a single title defense. Louis shrugged and said it wouldn't have mattered how much money he made, he would have spent it all anyway.

"In my time I made $5 million, wound up broke, and owe the government $1 million in taxes," Louis said. "If I was fighting today, I'd earn $10 million, would still wind up broke, and would owe the government $2 million in taxes."[1] It was a telling lament, if lament is the proper word. Louis didn't have many regrets.

There is little doubt that most of the rest of Louis' life was defined by his struggles with the IRS. It colored public perception of him. Some shook their heads and wondered how he could be broke. Others, Louis fans, wondered how the government could so persecute a man who did so much for his country — including raising millions of dollars for the effort during World War II. Alfred Sieminsky, a Democratic representative from New Jersey, introduced a bill in Congress that would have required the IRS to forgive Louis' debt. It did not pass. But the IRS did make a payment plan deal with Louis that would allow him a set amount to live on. Before that Louis had said out loud to friends, "You don't think they'd put me in jail, do you?"[2] The tension emanating from the IRS sometimes seemed unbearable to him, understandable since the debt mushroomed to $1.3 million.

Although he sought out other activities and money-making opportunities, the early 1950s were not kind to Louis. He was mentally at loose ends, depressed by the IRS situation, and trying to find out what a middle-aged Joe wanted to do now that he was finished fighting.

Promoter Mike Jacobs died, one of the men who had guided Louis' career. Louis' mother, Lillie, died. The IRS kept on his tail. Louis' oldest brother Lonnie died in 1960.

While Marva Trotter was seemingly the love of Louis' life, he never lacked for female companionship. He bedded waitresses and hat-check girls, models and actresses. Occasionally he became serious about one of them, but occasionally he became involved with the wrong type of girl. In a startling turn, Louis, who had never even smoked cigarettes as a young man (he adopted that habit later, too), got hooked on heroin through an ill-advised, tempestuous relationship with a woman. Louis referred to this woman as Annie, but the FBI called her a parasite. Agents informed Louis that Annie was running drugs for the mob and was using Louis and his good name to shield her business. He dumped her and worked to get clean of the drug addiction. Oh, and Louis, who throughout his boxing career drank only soda, began drinking alcohol in retirement, too.

Louis married Rose Morgan, a Harlem beauty shop owner, in late 1955, his second wife. Morgan worked mightily to manage Louis' finances, though short of banning his name from control of all bank accounts there was little she could do to curb his spending inclinations. Partially because he did not travel as much as he previously did, Louis became a television game-show lover. Without telling him, Morgan entered the couple as contestants on *High Finance*, and Joe on *Masquerade Party*. While Louis enjoyed appearing on television, when he and his spouse teamed up for $60,000 in winnings on *High Finance* the IRS was waiting with hand out. The Louis' kept half of it because it belonged to Morgan. Just because he married again didn't make Louis monogamous. He roamed at will and the couple split up after a year and a half together.

In 1959, Louis married for the third time, to a California attorney named Martha Malone who in her own way seemed to be as tough as Louis, mentally, at least. Malone cared for two girls whose father had been a client but passed away. When Louis' philandering produced another offspring, she arranged to adopt the child.

By the early 1960s, the heavyweight championship had passed from the retired Marciano through some others to Sonny Liston, a feared puncher with almost no schooling who had been in and out of prisons. However, when Louis and his wife moved to Denver, Colorado, Liston moved in with them. Louis and Liston became friends. There were many disturbing rumors and stories about Liston during the height of Louis' friendship with the title-holder who would face an untimely end before he turned 40. Sometime in the years he was friends with Liston, the Brown Bomber became addicted to cocaine.

The unsavory aspects of Louis' life were mostly kept out of the public eye. There was no tabloid journalism to rival the supermarket papers' hysteria of future decades, nor was there as much competition among regular newsmen to report dirt. In between activities, Louis dabbled in a night-club act that at best was so-so, and then to make a buck he became a professional wrestler.

Louis was not in any way ashamed of his attempts to earn a living after retiring from boxing, even if some of his fans thought it unseemly that he would indulge in the fake world of wrestling. Naturally, Louis, in keeping with his persona, played the part of a good-guy wrestler who had to put up with certain indignities from villains, but he was always going to prevail. In addition, the money was good. Louis signed a contract for $100,000 to wrestle on tour. He was unable to fulfill it, not because of any public outcry or his own doubts, but because he got injured only a couple of matches into his new career.

At one match in Washington, D.C., Jersey Joe Walcott, also in need of money, was the referee. That match ended with Louis "hurling" his opponent, Cowboy Rocky, out of the ring. It was a charade, of course. Louis pulled his punches or Cowboy Rocky would have become rocky road.

One peculiarity of Louis' retirement years, or perhaps a development that most would have considered extraordinarily unlikely, was a friendship that blossomed with Max Schmeling, his arch-foe from the 1930s. Schmeling survived the war, too old to return top-level boxing, his country in ruins. His U.S. connections from his prime boxing days saved him, though. James Farley, once chairman of the New York State Athletic Commission, had taken over operations of Coca-Cola. He made Schmeling a key figure in the company's post-war efforts in devastated Germany and Schmeling became a millionaire.

In 1954, Schmeling returned to America for the first time in years. One thing he did was visit the grave of his old manager, Joe Jacobs, in New York. Then he traveled to Milwaukee for an event. Unannounced, he then drove to Chicago, where at the time Louis maintained his home. Schmeling wanted to make peace with Louis, to let him know he never hated him and never said many of the things ascribed to him in the press, especially the Nazi press. Almost as soon as he launched into his apology speech, Louis interrupted him and said, "Forget all that stuff!" The men ended up talking for hours and in the ensuing years crossed paths several more times.[3]

Stories leaked out that Schmeling, at great risk, had actually helped Jewish families elude the Nazis before and during the war, and there were other suggestions that he quietly gave Louis money when he needed it.

These were strange times for Joe Louis. For his entire adult life he had been either the heavyweight champion of the world or a celebrity, or both. He liked being that Joe Louis. He didn't want to go back to work on the assembly line at Ford as he had as a teenager, he wanted to own a Ford dealership where he could greet the customers. (That never happened.) For most of his life, either through his co-managers and trainers, or his wives, somebody was always there to take care of Joe Louis when he was home or preparing for some big event in his life. It could be said even the Army played a role in taking care of Louis, since it housed him, fed him, and drew up his itinerary during World War II.

Above all, he didn't want to be an average Joe, a nine-to-five Joe. He was the famous Joe Louis and he wanted to remain Joe Louis, even without the heavyweight title. In his mind he had earned the right to be treated like one of the most famous Americans, which he was, whether he had the funds to live high or not.

For decades, Joe Louis had always picked up the tab. He provided for his mother and siblings, wives and children, managers and trainers, friends and strangers. Although there is no real proof that he consciously thought this way, Louis was probably trying to find someone to provide for him now in a manner that allowed him to still be Joe Louis. To his good fortune, he found such a benefactor.

Louis was king of the heavyweights long before boxing and Las Vegas joined forces to become one of the world's great fight meccas, the showcase for the biggest and best bouts, whether they were heavyweight matches or fights at other weights. The oasis in the Mojave Desert was home to high rollers who were the types of risk-takers and big spenders that always commandeered the ringside seats at big fights. Back in Louis' day they were the $100 ticket-holders.

In a less homogenized America, when there weren't gambling boats on every shore or casinos on Indian reservations, Vegas was sin city, the place to go to for the slots, blackjack, and legal poker. It was the adult Disneyland. If you were in show business, it was also the place to be seen. Playing Vegas meant something and Frank Sinatra, Sammy Davis, Jr., Jerry Lewis, Dean

Martin, Nat "King" Cole, and Judy Garland appeared at palatial hotels on the Strip, sometimes adjacent to bare-breasted showgirls with long legs and foot-tall feathery hats.

New York was called the city that never sleeps, but Las Vegas was usurping the title. You could get anything you wanted, and you were likely to see anybody who was famous, at any hour of the day or night, in the loud casinos that had no windows in order to disguise the time of day, or if you were crazy enough to walk outside, in the 110-degree day-time heat.

When he was fighting Louis was no regular in Vegas. When he was finished, when he was bored, he loved the action in the bright-lights town. Ash Resnick, an old Army friend who said he met Louis in 1942 and stayed in contact, ran the Thunderbird Hotel. When Louis came to town he stayed there and Resnick provided a few thousand dollars in house money to gamble. (Certainly Louis couldn't afford to take risks like that out of his own pocket.) Louis was not a serious gambler and always lost the money back to the casino. Resnick acted out of the goodness of his heart, but it soon became apparent that Louis, just sitting at a table, was an attraction. It was good for the Thunderbird and good for business. People crowded around and played when Louis was there.

Soon enough Resnick's acumen earned him a better job elsewhere. He took over the casino operation at Caesars Palace and this time when Louis followed he made him an employee. No business investment, no professional wrestling, no boxing promotion deal could match Louis' new gig.

Correctly gauging Louis' popularity, Resnick paid Louis $50,000 a year as a greeter, beginning full-time in 1970. For this work he basically had to be visible at the casino, shake hands and sign autographs. It was like being heavyweight champ again without early-morning road work or hitting the heavy bag. He was also given house money to play at the tables, and he could play golf, his still-lingering passion, on the casino's course, whenever he felt like it.

"It feels good to walk through the casino and have people calling out, 'Hey, Champ,'" Louis said. "'Hi there, Champ, come stand next to me for luck.'"[4]

Once again there was some buzz from Louis fans who believed he was demeaning himself with such work. They didn't know the real Joe Louis if they said that. He may have been a symbol of African American achievement and an American hero, but this was perfect retirement work for the man accustomed to being fawned over by millions. He was out in public and the public greeted him every day as much as he greeted the public. With their warm welcomes, they let him know he was not forgotten. That mattered.

"My dad liked the limelight," his son, Joe, Jr., said. "If there was anything that he missed after he retired, it was being at center stage."[5]

In the late 1960s, after Louis began making appearances in Vegas, and as he was transitioning to a full-time Nevada resident, the former champ began displaying signs of mental deterioration that alarmed his closest family members. He showed signs of paranoia, claiming that people were after him. He unscrewed light-bulbs in lamps in hotel rooms searching for surveillance gear. He stuffed air vents in those rooms so he couldn't be poisoned. He built in-room forts to provide "security" before he went to sleep.

Eventually, through trickery, though sad about the need for it, on a visit to Colorado, Louis was taken for observation to the Colorado Veterans Administration psychiatric ward. Joe, Jr., conspired with his step-mother, Martha, and signed the commitment papers. After a couple of months Louis was able to return to Las Vegas (sooner than his family wanted him to), taking medication that helped him maintain his grip on reality better than the in-and-out bouts of coherence he had been facing. For the most part he was back in business.

The fight business had come to him in Las Vegas and that meant that Louis was in on the action. His friend Sonny Liston lost the heavyweight belt to Muhammad Ali, who had changed his name from Cassius Clay and aligned with the Black Muslim movement. Unlike Louis, he was boastful and loud and became a polarizing figure. Louis frowned at Ali's actions, funny as many of them were, and did not give him full credit for his boxing skills, naming several heavyweights of the past he felt could best Ali. When Ali exercised his right as a conscientious objector rather than go in the Army, it offended Louis. Louis had signed up quickly and worked hard for the American cause during World War II. Louis did not see any difference between what historians labeled "the good war" and the Vietnam War, which was the most vociferously opposed war in American history.

There was eventually a certain rapprochement between the two men, though they represented different eras in African American fights for rights and in their chosen sport. Both became beloved and respected. Whenever all-time rankings are made of boxing figures, it is concluded that either Louis or Ali is the best heavyweight ever. Naturally enough, Louis believed he would have won if they fought in their primes, and naturally enough Ali believed that he would have won. There is no true answer to the riddle of who was best.

In 1977, Louis' health began to fail. By then, John Roxborough, the man who had started the Louis legend with his keen eyesight and ability to imagine the future, was two years gone. Louis needed the best medical help and he got it. Frank Sinatra, for whom Louis once did a favor, footed the cost of Louis' medical needs. Dr. Michael E. DeBakey, the world-famous heart surgeon and innovator of breakthroughs that advanced heart surgery techniques, operated on Louis. While the operation was deemed a success, a short while later Louis suffered a stroke.

This was the most damaging blow. Louis could no longer perform as a greeter at Caesars. He got around in a wheelchair and his speech was slowed. If there was a big fight in town that brought the worldwide press and the luminaries of the boxing world out, Louis sometimes appeared at the combatants' training sessions. His arrival was met with excitement. In those days he fancied wearing cowboy hats with brims that were nearly as wide as his grin.

Throughout the years, Louis and Jesse Owens shared a special friendship and understanding. Before Jackie Robinson, they were the two most famous black men in America at a time when black men only got their names in the papers if they committed major crimes. They were loved by millions and admired for their achievements, but had difficulty parlaying their celebrity into lucrative work after their athletic days ended. Yes, Louis was criticized for engaging in professional wrestling, but Owens raced horses to make money. On March 31, 1980, Owens passed away. When Louis got the news he couldn't stop shaking.

Louis wasn't talking so much in those days and his frailty was evident. But he was revered as an elder statesman and enthusiastically welcomed to fight camps. Louis' last public appearance — fittingly — was at a heavyweight title fight in Las Vegas. He sat ringside in his wheelchair on April 11, 1981, to watch Larry Holmes and Trevor Berbick mix it up. Holmes, another of the best heavyweights of all time, won a unanimous decision.

The next morning Louis suffered a heart attack at home while walking to the bathroom and was pronounced dead after being rushed to Desert Springs Hospital. He was 66 years old.

Jimmy Cannon, the New York sports writer who was Louis' best friend among the many writers who followed his career, could be eloquent and poignant, when writing about his favorite fighter. "He was a great champion and I'm glad he was champion in my time," Cannon said. "He was mean at his work, but he was able to leave it in the ring. The cruelty was there, all right. The poverty of his boyhood formed him, as it does all fighters. But he was never resentful and he always did the best he could. His best was wonderful. Louis was a boy's dream of a fighter. There was joy and innocence in his skills and this gave him what the others lacked. Joe was a fighter. It is the finest compliment I can give him."[6]

A statue of Joe Louis decorates a huge lobby hall in Detroit's Cobo Hall in the downtown section of the city where his family moved after his earlier years in Alabama (photograph by the author).

The city of Detroit remains proud of Joe Louis, who spent his junior high school and teen years in the city while becoming a national amateur boxing champion before turning professional. As a way of honoring him Detroit displays a gigantic fist sculpture in the middle of its busy downtown (photograph by the author).

It seemed strange to some, but before his funeral, Louis' body lay in state in the Caesars Palace Sports Pavilion. Normally such a setting when a great man passes away is either a place of worship or a large government facility. For Louis, this made sense, and his third wife, Martha, made the call. Many of the happiest days of the final stretch of his life took place at Caesars, the pavilion was the site of many major boxing championship bouts, and Las Vegas was Louis' home at the end of his life.

Joe Louis Barrow, Jr., said, "I probably would not have done it differently. My father once told me, 'Your whole life is your funeral.'"[7] It was a much-less publicized way saying of Louis', but was worthy of deep thought.

Some 3,000 people attended a service for Louis in Las Vegas, and the Rev. Jesse Jackson offered a eulogy for a memorable man. "Joe was a second-class citizen by birth and a first-class man by effort," Jackson said. "The human race was enhanced and rewarded because of Joe. Joe made a nation proud of him and ashamed of itself."[8]

At the time of Louis' death, Jersey Joe Walcott was the New Jersey State Athletic Commissioner. He was sitting ringside at an Atlantic City fight when someone whispered the news that Louis had died that morning. Walcott started crying and kept trying to dry his eyes with a handkerchief. After the fight, the announcement of Louis' death was made at Bally's Park Place Casino Hotel and fight fans joined Walcott in standing for a moment of silence.

"I lost a great friend," said Walcott, 67 at the time. "He was one of the great Americans and one of the great champions. He was a great inspiration in so many ways to so many people. We'll all miss him. May his soul rest in peace."[9] At the same venue, Slim Robinson, a trainer who had been a fighter, talked of Louis' influence. "I think he meant a lot to all black people," Robinson said.[10]

Although he was an Army veteran, Joe Louis did not qualify for burial in Arlington National Cemetery in Virginia. But President Ronald Reagan granted an exception. Louis' funeral service was conducted at the Fort Meyer Memorial Chapel at the cemetery with 800 people in attendance. Tributes were so widespread it was difficult to catalogue them all. Frank Sinatra, such a good friend to Louis in his final years, said, "It is nice to know that the man who never rested on canvas now rests on clouds."[11]

At Arlington Cemetery, son Joe Louis Barrow, Jr., spoke, saying that Louis' final resting place was appropriate. "You're a patriot," he said. "You provided guidance and faith at a time when our country was down and people needed a lift. It's fitting that you will be with many other great Americans."[12]

Louis was the son of an Alabama sharecropper, who was not educated as a youth, but learned to handle the greatest of fame through experience as he became one of the best-known and admired sports figures in American history. Unlike his predecessors, he was a fighting champion, defending the heavyweight crown as often during his reign as all heavyweight champs did combined between 1913 and 1937.

On the biggest of stages, when the stakes were highest and he had to win, Louis won. He became a symbol of success for African Americans and a hero for all Americans during World War II. At all times he retained his dignity. At no time did he belittle others. His life was defined by class and he left lasting impressions on those who saw him fight and those whom he met. He put on no artifice and he was generous to those who crossed his path. His record of 25 title defenses seems unbreakable. He handled his few losses without excuse and he coped with life's setbacks in ways that made others sympathize with him. Louis was determined to enjoy his life, and for the most part he accomplished that, as well.

In the years following Joe Louis' death, he was honored in many ways. At Pompton Lakes, New Jersey, where Louis trained often for his New York fights, a monument was raised at Joe Louis Memorial Park.

In Detroit, where Louis grew up after leaving Alabama as a youth and began his professional boxing career, a gigantic sculpture of Louis' fist reposes over a mid-town traffic island. Nearby, in the lobby of Cobo Hall, stands a huge statue of Louis in fighting pose. The National Hockey League Detroit Red Wings play their home games in Joe Louis Arena, christened in 1979.

In 1992, the United States government announced the creation of a 29-cent postage stamp with Louis' image on it for 1993 release. The announcement at the International Boxing Hall of Fame — where Louis is enshrined — featured past and future heavyweight champion George Foreman. Foreman said that during his years out of the sport when he was a preacher based in Houston he visited Louis in Las Vegas and together they read from the Bible.

Sometime later, Joe, Jr., was talking to Ali, and the boxer who always bragged, calling himself "The Greatest," turned the tables and said, "Joe, your father was the greatest, truly the greatest."[13]

Millions of Americans thought so.

Chapter Notes

Chapter 1

1. Gerald Astor, *"...And a Credit to His Race": The Hard Life and Times of Joseph Louis Barrow, aka Joe Louis* (New York: E.P. Dutton, 1974).
2. Ibid.
3. Ibid.
4. Joe Louis, Edna Rust, and Art Rust, Jr., *Joe Louis: My Life* (New York: Harcourt Brace Jovanovich, 1978).
5. Randy Roberts, *Joe Louis* (New Haven, CT: Yale University Press, 2010).
6. Chris Mead, *Joe Louis: Black Champion in White America* (Mineola, NY: Dover, 1985/2010).
7. Ibid.

Chapter 2

1. Bill Libby, *Joe Louis: The Brown Bomber* (New York: Lothrop, Lee and Shepard, 1980).
2. Ibid.
3. Margery Miller, *Joe Louis: American* (New York: A.A. Wyn, 1945).
4. Libby.
5. Astor.
6. Louis, Rust, and Rust.
7. Astor.
8. Louis, Rust and Rust.
9. Ibid.
10. Miller.
11. A.O. Edmonds, *Joe Louis* (Grand Rapids, MI: William B. Eerdmans, 1973).
12. Richard Bak, *Joe Louis: The Great Black Hope* (Dallas, TX: Da Capo Press, 1998).
13. Bak.

Chapter 3

1. Louis, Rust, and Rust.
2. Ibid.
3. Ibid.
4. Libby.
5. Louis, Rust and Rust.
6. Bak.
7. Nat Fleischer, *The Louis Legend* (New York: The Ring, Inc., 1956).
8. Louis, Rust and Rust.
9. Ibid.

Chapter 4

1. Miller.
2. Gene Kessler, *Joe Louis: The Brown Bomber* (Racine, WI: Whitman, 1936).
3. Mead.
4. Bak.
5. Louis, Rust, and Rust.
6. Ibid.
7. Ibid.
8. Bak.
9. Fleischer, *The Louis Legend*.
10. Ibid.
11. Dave Anderson, *In the Corner: Great Trainers Talk About Their Art* (New York: William Morrow, 1991).
12. Ibid.
13. Lew Freedman, "Longtime Cornerman has Seen the Great Ones," *Anchorage Daily News*, October 25, 1985.

Chapter 5

1. Astor.
2. Ibid.

3. Ibid.
4. Louis, Rust, and Rust.
5. Ibid.

Chapter 6

1. Geoffrey C. Ward, *Unforgivable Blackness: The Rise and Fall of Jack Johnson* (New York: Alfred A. Knopf, 2004).
2. Ibid.
3. Ibid.
4. Ibid.
5. Ibid.
6. Louis, Rust, and Rust.
7. Astor.
8. Bak.

Chapter 7

1. Bak.
2. Astor.
3. Libby.
4. Ibid.
5. Bak.
6. Louis, Rust, and Rust.
7. Libby.
8. Louis, Rust, and Rust.
9. Ibid.
10. Fleischer.
11. Louis, Rust and Rust.
12. Ibid.
13. Miller.

Chapter 8

1. Fleischer, *The Louis Legend.*
2. Astor.
3. Louis, Rust, and Rust.
4. Bak.
5. Jack London, *Sporting Blood: Selections From Jack London's Greatest Sports Writing* (Novato, California, Presidio Press, 1981).

Chapter 9

1. Frederic Mullally, *Primo: The Story of "Man Mountain" Carnera* (London: Robson Books, 1991).
2. Astor.
3. Mullally.
4. Mead.
5. Astor.
6. Libby.
7. Miller.
8. Fleischer.

9. Libby.
10. Bak.
11. Roberts.
12. Louis, Rust, and Rust.
13. Ibid.

Chapter 10

1. Roberts.
2. Ibid.
3. Louis, Rust, and Rust.
4. "Detroit Ace, 'Killer Type,' On His Way Toward Peak," Associated Press, September 25, 1935.
5. Bak.
6. Grantland Rice, "Beating From Louis Ends Baer's Career," "The Sportlight" syndicated column, September 25, 1935.
7. Ibid.
8. Roberts.
9. Louis, Rust and Rust.
10. Associated Press, September 25, 1935.
11. United Press, September 25, 1935.

Chapter 11

1. Louis, Rust, and Rust.
2. Ibid.
3. Ibid.
4. Bak.
5. Ibid.
6. Roberts.
7. Ibid.
8. Ibid.
9. Astor.
10. James Gavin, *Stormy Weather: The Life of Lena Horne* (New York: Atria Books, 2009).
11. Louis, Rust and Rust.
12. Ibid.
13. Ibid.
14. Ibid.
15. Gavin.

Chapter 12

1. Mead.
2. Libby.
3. Louis, Rust, and Rust.
4. Ibid.
5. Ibid.
6. Ibid.
7. "Uzcudun Is 22nd Victim Of Bomber's K.O. Punches," United Press, December 14, 1935.

Chapter 13

1. Max Schmeling, *Max Schmeling: An Autobiography* (Chicago: Bonus Books, English translation, 1998).
2. Ibid.
3. Ibid.
4. Ibid.
5. Patrick Myler, *Ring of Hate* (New York: Arcade, 2005).
6. Myler.
7. Schmeling.
8. Ibid.
9. Ibid.
10. Ibid.
11. David Margolick, *Beyond Glory: Joe Louis vs. Max Schmeling and a World on the Brink* (New York: Alfred A. Knopf, 2005).

Chapter 14

1. Schmeling.
2. Ibid.
3. Ibid.
4. Myler.
5. Margolick.
6. Ibid.

Chapter 15

1. Louis, Rust, and Rust.
2. Ibid.
3. Ibid.
4. Libby.
5. Louis, Rust and Rust.
6. Libby.
7. Louis, Rust and Rust.
8. Libby.
9. Ibid.
10. Grantland Rice, syndicated column, June 20, 1936.
11. Ibid.
12. Ibid.
13. Joe Williams, "Sports Roundup," *New York World-Telegram*, June 20, 1936.
14. Schmeling.
15. Ibid.
16. Bak.
17. Mead.

Chapter 16

1. Louis, Rust, and Rust.
2. Mead.
3. Fleischer, *The Louis Legend*.
4. United Press, August 19, 1936.

5. Fleischer, *The Louis Legend*.
7. United Press, September 23, 1936.
8. Grantland Rice, syndicated column, September 23, 1936.
9. Bak.

Chapter 17

1. Jeremy Schaap, *Cinderella Man* (New York: Houghton Mifflin, 2005).
2. Ibid.
3. Ibid.
4. Ibid.
5. Mead.
6. Schaap.
7. Libby.
8. Louis, Rust, and Rust.
9. Fleischer, *The Louis Legend*.
10. No byline, unattributed publication, archives of International Boxing Hall of Fame, Canastota, New York.
11. Richard M'Cann, "Champion Knockout Winner Over Contender in 'Secret,'" NEA Service, April 1, 1937.
12. Louis, Rust and Rust.
13. Libby.
14. Schaap.
15. Libby.
16. Ibid.

Chapter 18

1. Mead.
2. "Joe Louis Regains Ring Prestige," United Press, February 24, 1938.
3. Ibid.
4. Bob Considine, "K.O. Victor Over Mann, Louis Plans Another Title 'Tune-Up,'" *Buffalo News*, February 24, 1938.
5. Associated Press, April 2, 1938.
6. Chester Youell, "Champion Wins as He Pleases Before 10,468," International News Service, April 2, 1938.
7. Louis, Rust, and Rust.

Chapter 19

1. Bak.
2. Louis, Rust, Art Rust.
3. Schmeling.
4. Ibid.
5. Ibid.
6. Louis, Rust, and Rust.
7. Ibid.
8. Roberts.

9. Margolick.
10. Libby.
11. Margolick.
12. Louis, Rust and Rust.
13. Ibid.
14. Myler.
15. Ibid.
16. Jerry Izenberg, "At Large, Radio Days," *Newark Star-Ledger*, no date, International Boxing Hall of Fame archives.
17. Myler.
18. "June 22, 1938, Vindication for Louis," United Press, *Bergen Record*, June 22, 1973.
19. Myler.
20. Roberts.
21. Emmett Berg, "Fight of the Century," *Humanities*, July-August 2004.
22. Ibid.
23. Nat Fleischer, "Max Fouled? Bunk!" *The Ring*, September 1938.
24. Daniel M. Daniel, "Schmeling's Squawk Makes Kidney Famous," *The Ring*, September 1938.

Chapter 20

1. HBO Sports Film, *Joe Louis*, Big Fights, Inc., 1989.
2. Ibid.
3. Ibid.
4. Ibid.
5. Astor.
6. Ibid.
7. Ibid.
8. Gilbert Odd, "Why Louis Took Pity On His Best Friend," *British Boxing News*, no date, International Boxing Hall of Fame archives.
9. Ibid.
10. Lester Scott, "Knocked Down Thrice, John Henry Lewis Loses in One Round," *New York World-Telegram*, January 26, 1939.
11. Ibid.
12. Libby.
13. Donald McRae, "Heroes Without a Country" (New York: HarperCollins, 2002).

Chapter 21

1. Tony Galento, "I Will Mash Joe Louis," *Liberty*, June 24, 1939.
2. Ibid.
3. Ibid.
4. Joseph Moninger, *Two Ton: One Fight, One Night, Tony Galento vs. Joe Louis* (Hanover, NH: Steerforth Press, 2006).
5. Ibid.

6. Ibid.
7. Libby.
8. "Negro Stops Tony Galento in 4th Round of Wild Bout," United Press, June 28, 1939.
9. Bak.
10. Ibid.
11. Louis, Rust, and Rust.
12. "Champion Has Revenge on New Yorker," Associated Press, September 21, 1939.
13. Bob Considine, article with headline eliminated, International Boxing Hall of Fame archives, Hearst Newspapers, February 10, 1940.
14. Sid Feder, "Iowan Throws Only One Blow in Weak Effort," Associated Press, March 29, 1940.
15. Arturo Godoy, "How I Mean to Beat Joe Louis," *Liberty*, June 15, 1940.
16. "Louis Stops McCoy After Five Rounds in Boston Ring," Associated Press, December 17, 1940.
17. John Lardner, "Louis' 'Hardest Punch' K.O's Burman — Joe Fights Clever, Planned Battle," *Buffalo Evening News*, February 1, 1941.
18. Caswell Adams, "Musto Will Be Bomber's Next Victim in April," newspaper name missing, International Boxing Hall of Fame archives, March 22, 1941.
19. Dick Heller, "Louis Held On to His Title in D.C.," *Washington Times*, April 1, 2002.
20. Ibid.
21. Andy Piascik, *Gridiron Gauntlet* (Boulder, Colo.: Taylor Trade, 2009).
22. Ibid.
23. Bak.

Chapter 22

1. Andrew O'Toole, *Sweet William: The Life of Billy Conn* (Urbana: University of Illinois Press, 2008).
2. Ibid.
3. Ibid.
4. Ibid.
5. Louis, Rust, Rust.
6. Mead.
7. Bak.
8. Louis, Rust and Rust.
9. Libby.
10. Bak.
11. Ibid.
12. Louis, Rust and Rust.
13. Ibid.
14. Nat Fleischer, "Cockiness Costly," *The Ring*, September 1941.
15. O'Toole.
16. Libby.

Chapter 23

1. O'Toole.
2. Ibid.
3. Roberts.
4. Libby.
5. Roberts.
6. Ibid.
7. Wilfred Smith, "In Baer's Favor: He's Not Afraid," *Chicago Tribune*, January 6, 1942.
8. Nat Fleisher, "Louis, Back at Peak, Gives Savage Display," *The Ring*, March 1942.
9. Libby.
10. Ibid.
11. Carl Byoir, "Joe Louis Named the War," *Collier's*, May 16, 1942.
12. Roberts.
13. Ibid.
14. Astor.
15. Joe Louis Barrow, Jr., and Barbara Munder, *Joe Louis: 50 Years an American Hero* (New York: McGraw-Hill, 1988).
16. Fleischer, *The Louis Legend*.
17. Ibid.

Chapter 24

1. Louis, Rust, and Rus.
2. Ibid.
3. Mead.
4. Jonathan Eig, *Opening Day: The Story of Jackie Robinson's First Season* (New York: Simon and Schuster, 2007).
5. Ibid.
6. Ibid.
7. Roberts.
8. Louis, Rust and Rust.
9. Mead.
10. Bak.
11. Roberts.

Chapter 25

1. Bak.
2. Louis, Rust, Rust.
3. Bak.
4. O'Toole.
5. Louis, Rust, and Rust.
6. Bak.
7. Ibid.
8. "'My Relatives Betting On Me,' Says Mauriello," United Press, September 16, 1946.

Chapter 26

1. James Curl, *Jersey Joe Walcott: A Boxing Biography* (Jefferson, NC: McFarland, 2012).
2. Bak.
3. Dana Mozley, "'Will Finish Him Quick,' Says Louis of Walcott," *New York Daily News*, December 1, 1947.
4. James P. Dawson, "Protest is Issued on Fight Referee," *New York Times*, December 4, 1947.
5. "18,194 Cheer Joe Walcott After Fight," Associated Press, December 6, 1947.
6. Jack Cuddy, "Louis' Disputed Ring Victory Over Walcott to be Probed," United Press, December 6, 1947.
7. "Louis to Fight in June, Then He'll Retire," Associated Press, December 12, 1947.
8. Louis, Rust, Rust.
9. Arthur Daley, "Sports of the Times: The Kid's Last Fight," *New York Times*, June 26, 1948.
10. Mead.
11. Larry Schwartz, "'Brown Bomber' Was a Hero to All," ESPN.com, ESPN Sports Century, September 20, 2000.

Chapter 27

1. Roberts.
2. Bak.
3. Schmeling.
4. Louis, Rust, and Rust.
5. Joe Louis Barrow, Jr., and Barbara Munder, *Joe Louis: 50 Years An American Hero* (New York: McGraw-Hill, 1988).
6. Jimmy Cannon, "The Joe Louis I Remember," in W.C. Heinz and Nathan Ward, eds., *The Book of Boxing* (Kingston, NY: Sports Illustrated Classics, 1999).
7. Barrow and Munder.
8. "The Champ Gets a Last Ovation," United Press International, April 18, 1981.
9. Lewis Freedman, "Friends of Louis Feel Loss Deeply," *Philadelphia Inquirer*, April 12, 1981.
10. Ibid.
11. Barrow and Munder.
12. "'Brown Bomber' Laid to Rest," United Press International, April 22, 1981.
13. Barrow and Munder.

Bibliography

Books

Anderson, Dave. *In The Corner: Great Trainers Talk About Their Art*. New York: William Morrow, 1991.

Astor, Gerald. *"...And a Credit to His Race": The Hard Life and Times of Joseph Louis Barrow, aka Joe Louis*. New York: E.P. Dutton, 1974.

Bak, Richard. *Joe Louis: The Great Black Hope*. Dallas, TX: Da Capo Press, 1998.

Barrow, Joe Louis, Jr., and Barbara Munder. *Joe Louis: 50 Years an American Hero*. New York: McGraw-Hill, 1988.

Cannon, Jimmy. "The Joe Louis I Remember," in W.C. Heinz and Nathan Ward, eds. *The Book of Boxing*. Kingston, NY: Sports Illustrated Classics, 1999.

Curl, James. *Jersey Joe Walcott: A Boxing Biography*. Jefferson, NC: McFarland, 2012.

Edmonds, A.O. *Joe Louis*. Grand Rapids, MI: William B. Eerdmans, 1973.

Eig, Jonathan. *Opening Day: The Story of Jackie Robinson's First Season*. New York: Simon and Schuster, 2007.

Fleischer, Nat. *The Louis Legend*. New York: The Ring, 1956.

Gavin, James. *Stormy Weather: The Life of Lena Horne*. New York: Atria Books, 2009.

Kessler, Gene. *Joe Louis: The Brown Bomber*. Racine, WI: Whitman, 1936.

Libby, Bill. *Joe Louis: The Brown Bomber*. New York: Lothrop, Lee and Shepard, 1980.

London, Jack. *Sporting Blood: Selections From Jack London's Greatest Sports Writing*. Novato, CA: Presidio Press, 1981.

Louis, Joe, Edna Rust, and Art Rust, Jr. *Joe Louis: My Life*. New York: Harcourt Brace Jovanovich, 1978.

Margolick, David. *Beyond Glory: Joe Louis vs. Max Schmeling and a World on the Brink*. New York: Alfred A. Knopf, 2005.

McRae, Donald. *Heroes Without a Country*. New York: HarperCollins, 2002.

Mead, Chris. *Joe Louis: Black Champion in White America*. Mineola, NY: Dover, 1985/2010.

Miller, Margery. *Joe Louis: American*. New York: A.A. Wyn, 1945.

Moninger, Joseph. *Two Ton: One Fight, One Night, Tony Galento vs. Joe Louis*. Hanover, NH: Steerforth Press, 2006.

Mullally, Frederic. *Primo: The Story of "Man Mountain" Carnera*. London: Robson Books, 1991.

Myler, Patrick. *Ring of Hate*. New York: Arcade, 2005.

O'Toole, Andrew. *Sweet William: The Life of Billy Conn*. Urbana: University of Illinois Press, 2008.

Piascik, Andy. *Gridiron Gauntlet*. Boulder, CO: Taylor Trade, 2009.

Roberts, Randy. *Joe Louis*. New Haven, CT: Yale University Press, 2010.

Schaap, Jeremy. *Cinderella Man*. New York: Houghton Mifflin, 2005.

Schmeling, Max. *Max Schmeling: An Autobiography*. Chicago: Bonus Books, English translation, 1998.

Ward, Geoffrey C. *Unforgivable Blackness: The Rise and Fall of Jack Johnson*. New York: Alfred A. Knopf, 2004.

Magazines

British Boxing News
Collier's
Humanities
Liberty
The Ring

Newspapers

Anchorage Daily News
Buffalo Evening News
Chicago Tribune
New York Daily News
New York Times
New York World-Telegram
Newark Star-Ledger
Philadelphia Inquirer
Washington Times

News Services

Associated Press
Hearst Newspapers
International News Service
NEA News Service
United Press
United Press International

Television

ESPN
HBO

Index

Adirondack Mountains 152
Agramonte, Omelio 217
Alabama 2, 6, 12, 13, 14, 16, 18, 19, 20, 21, 22,
  24, 28, 32, 53, 73, 86, 87, 132, 144, 165,
  194, 195, 215, 228, 229
Alaska 195
Alaska Gold Rush 60, 65
Ali, Muhammad 43, 46, 48, 106, 158, 189,
  224, 229
Amateur Athletic Union 166
Amos and Andy 72
Angelou, Maya 160
Anti-Nazi League 155
Apostoli, Fred 180
Arcadia Gardens 54, 55
Arlington National Cemetery 228
Armstrong, Henry 153, 154
Army Emergency Relief Fund 192
Associated Press 173
Astor, Gerald 162
Atlanta Journal 124
Atlantic City, New Jersey 69, 88, 153, 228
Atlantic Ocean 115, 131, 146, 150
Australia 45, 65

Bacon's Arena 51
The Bad and the Beautiful 91
Baer, Buddy 80, 175, 176, 189, 190, 192
Baer, Max 71, 74, 77, 78, 79, 80, 81, 82, 83,
  84, 85, 96, 97, 100, 101, 109, 116, 127, 129,
  131, 137, 175, 189, 190, 191
Baer, Max, Jr. 80
Bak, Richard 30
Bakersfield, California 45
Balboa, Rocky 118
Baldwin, James 200
Bally's Park Place Casino 228
Balogh, Harry 74
Baltimore 45, 175
Baltimore Afro-American 202
Baltimore Colts 213
Barcelona 70

Barrow, Alvanius 14
Barrow, DeLeon 14, 25
Barrow, Emmerall 14
Barrow, Eulalia 14
Barrow, Jacqueline 92, 204
Barrow, James 14
Barrow, Joe Louis, Jr. 92, 195, 204, 224, 228
Barrow, Lillie 13, 15, 16, 17, 18, 19, 21, 25, 30,
  31, 56, 98, 121, 220
Barrow, Lonnie 14, 220
Barrow, Munroe 13, 14, 15, 16, 144
Barrow, Susie 14
Barrow, Vunice 14, 119
Barry, Don 59
Bavaria 114
Beacon, New York 180
Belgium 104
Bell, Eddie 176, 177
Bennett, Biff 64
Berbick, Trevor 225
Berlin 104, 114, 115, 132, 156, 166
Beshore, Freddie 217
Bettina, Melio 180
Beverly Hillbillies 80
Binghamton, New York 106
Birkie, Hans 57
Birmingham, Alabama 20
Bivins, Jimmy 217
Black, Julian 5, 10, 11, 12, 36, 37, 39, 40, 42,
  47, 49, 50, 56, 59, 61, 62, 63, 75, 77, 82,
  97, 98, 100, 101, 109, 117, 120, 127, 130, 143,
  145, 162, 176, 182, 190, 204, 205
Black Tuesday 25
Blackburn, Jack 5, 10, 11, 12, 36, 37, 39, 40,
  41, 42, 49, 50, 51, 52, 55, 56, 59, 61, 62,
  64, 73, 75, 77, 83, 88, 97, 100, 109, 117, 119,
  120, 121, 124, 125, 126, 127, 138, 140, 142,
  153, 154, 155, 162, 176, 184, 185, 190, 191,
  203, 204, 211
Borchuk, Alex 53
Boston 33, 45, 69
Boston Garden 60, 175

Bottoms, Bill 40, 182
Bow, Clara 106
Boxing News 137
Braddock, James J. 77, 80, 81, 118, 123, 124, 127, 128, 131, 132, 133, 134, 135, 136, 137, 138, 139, 140, 141, 143, 144, 145, 155, 179
Bremen 158
Brescia, Jorge 130
Brewster Recreation Center 9, 26, 28, 29, 30
Bridgeport, Connecticut 45
Brimstein, Whitey 100, 172
Brion, Cesar 217
Broadway 61
Brockton, Massachusetts 217
Bronson Trade School 24
Brooklyn Dodgers 194, 198, 200
Brooks, Charley 45
Brooks, Pat 16, 17, 19, 21, 32, 33, 144
Brooks, Pat, Jr. 17, 18, 124
Brown, Bingo 54
Brown, Natie 59, 62, 63, 134
Brown Bomber Softball Team 100, 145
Brundage, Avery 114, 115
Brussels 104
Buffalo 130
Buffalo Memorial Auditorium 206
Bunche, Ralph 75
Burman, Red 175
Burns, Ken 49
Burns, Tommy 43, 45, 46, 65
Byoir, Carl 192

Caesars Palace 1, 223, 225, 228
California 71, 117, 164, 188
California Boxing Commission 79
Call of the Wild 65
Calloway, Cab 74, 99, 204
Camilli, Dolph 79
Camp Upton 191
Campbell, Frankie 78, 79
Cannon, Jimmy 154, 218, 225
Canzoneri, Tony 118
Carnera, Primo 63, 64, 66, 67, 68, 69, 70, 71, 72, 73, 74, 75, 76, 77, 79, 80, 96, 100, 101, 116, 129, 148, 152, 218
Carpentier, Georges 103, 104
Carter, Earl 157
Carter, Jimmy 157, 158
Carver, George Washington 200
Cavanaugh, Billy 174
Chambers County 13
Charles, Ezzard 216, 217
Chelsea, Massachusetts 45
Cherokee Indians 13
Chicago 3, 5, 10, 11, 20, 33, 39, 45, 51, 53, 54, 55, 56, 59, 64, 69, 74, 96, 106, 125, 138, 139, 143, 176, 178, 204, 209, 210, 221
Chicago Bears 11, 69

Chicago Cubs 58
Chicago Defender 64, 201
Chicago Stadium 55, 101, 148
Chicago White Sox 135
Chile 172
Cincinnati 92
Cinderella Man 79, 127, 136
Cleveland 20, 69, 74, 107, 130, 166, 167
Cobo Hall 229
Coca-Cola 221
Cole, Nat "King" 223
Colma, California 45
Colorado Veterans Administration 224
Comiskey Park 96, 135, 140, 144
Coney Island 61, 169
Conn, Billy 178, 179, 180, 181, 182, 183, 184, 185, 186, 187, 188, 189, 202, 206, 207, 208, 209, 210, 211, 212
Conn, Maggie 182
Conn, Mary Louise 179, 187
Conn, William 179
Considine, Bob 148
Corbett, "Gentleman" Jim 46
Cornwall, England 45
Corum, Bill 137
Cosby, Bill 160, 161
Cotton Club 71, 74, 92
Crawford Grill 163

Daley, Arthur 215
Daniel, Daniel M. 159
Darrow, Clarence 24
Davis, Johnny 206
Davis, Sammy, Jr. 222
Davis, Willie 53
Dayton, Ohio 64
DeBakey, Dr. Michael E. 225
Dempsey, Jack 24, 25, 37, 38, 60, 68, 82, 83, 85, 96, 98, 103, 104, 106, 138, 145
Denver 69, 221
Desert Springs Hospital 225
Detroit 3, 5, 7, 9, 12, 20, 21, 22, 24, 28, 30, 31, 34, 39, 45, 50, 52, 53, 54, 56, 57, 59, 62, 73, 87, 100, 172, 175, 176, 178, 179, 192, 194, 195, 215, 229
Detroit Golden Gloves 26, 34
Detroit Naval Armory 31, 53, 54
Detroit Red Wings 57, 229
Detroit Tigers 24, 100
Detroit Urban League 194
Dickson, Jeff 69
Dieckhoff, Hans 158
Dietrich, Marlene 104
Donovan, Arthur 76, 122, 148, 155, 156, 157, 171, 173, 176, 213
Donovan, Arthur, Jr. 213
Donovan, Mike 213
Dorazio, Gus 175

Douglass, Frederick 200
DuBois, W.E.B. 72
Dudas, Steve 109
Duffield Elementary School 22, 23

Eagan, Eddie 213
Eagle Bend, Minnesota 148
Ecklund, Emil 51
Ellington, Duke 74, 75, 99, 138
Ellis, Atler 33
Emeryville, California 69
Ethiopia 67, 72, 73, 74, 116, 152
Ettore, Al 130
Evans, Stanley 9, 34
Everett, Buck 53

Fairbanks, Douglas 106
Farley, James 221
Farnsworth, Bill 61
Farr, Tommy 145, 146, 147, 149, 164, 172, 205
Federal Bureau of Investigation 220
Fetchit, Steppin 72
Fitzsimmons, Bob 45, 46
Fleischer, Nat 25, 33, 34, 55, 59, 62, 75, 118, 129, 138, 158, 185, 190, 196
Fletcher, Dusty 98
Foord, Ben 109
Foreman, George 217, 229
Ford, Henry 3, 17
Fort Dix 203
Fort Hood 199
Fort Meyer Memorial Chapel 228
Fort Riley 194, 198, 199
France 69
Franklin, Bennie 24, 87
Frayne, Ed 61
Frazier, Joe 34
Frog Club 62, 663
Fullam, Frank 215
Futch, Eddie 34, 35

Gable, Clark 91
Galento, Tony 167, 168, 169, 170, 171, 172, 173, 175
Gallico, Paul 84, 192, 193
Galveston, Texas 43, 44, 45
Gans, Joe 11
Garland, Judy 223
Garmisch-Partenkirchen 90, 114
Genoa, Italy 70
Georgia 107
Germany 91, 104, 109, 111, 112, 113, 114, 115, 116, 120, 123, 125, 128, 132, 133, 150, 153, 157, 158, 186, 193, 197, 205, 206
Gibson, Truman 89, 193, 194, 195, 198, 199, 200, 216
Gloucester, Massachusetts 45

Godoy, Arturo 172, 173, 174
Goebbels, Joseph 113, 150
Goering, Herman 113
Goldstein, Ruby 213, 214
Gould, Joe 131, 133, 134, 136, 137, 139, 140, 150
Grange, Red 24
Great Britain 145, 206
Great Depression 25, 32, 50, 70, 91, 131, 135, 136
Great Migration 3, 20
Great White Hope 49
Greb, Harry 11
Greece 205
Greenlee, Gus 163
Gregory, Dick 160
Griffin, Corn 136, 137
Griffith Stadium 175
Guinyard, Freddie 23, 53, 88, 121, 203

Hagler, Marvelous Marvin 2
Hamas, Steve 109
Harlem 71, 74, 76, 81, 85, 88, 92, 124, 155, 158, 162, 176, 200, 201, 210, 220
Harlem Opera House 98
Harvard University 72
Havana, Cuba 47
Hawaii 212
Hearst, Millicent 61
Hearst, William Randolph 61
Heifetz, Jascha 25
Helmuth, Arno 155, 156, 157
Henie, Sonja 90, 91, 118
Hennessy, Sam 172
Herman, Kid 78
Hillsboro, Mississippi 34
Hindenberg 124
Hippodrome 61, 120
Hitler, Adolf 67, 80, 91, 111, 112, 113, 114, 115, 116, 120, 125, 131, 132, 150, 151, 152, 153, 155, 156, 165, 193, 205
Hollywood 2, 71, 79, 80, 90, 91, 94, 106, 117, 118, 162
Holmes, Larry 2, 225
Holyfield, Evander 106
Horne, Lena 74, 91, 92, 93, 94, 95, 124
Horne, Teddy 92
Hot Springs, Arkansas 207
Hotel Theresa 162
Houston 229
Howard University 119
Hungary 105
Hunkerfoot, Charles 13
Huston, Walter 80

Internal Revenue Service 190, 208, 210, 216, 217, 219, 220
International Boxing Club 216

International Boxing Hall of Fame 49, 213, 229
International News Service 76
International Olympic Committee 114
Israel 120
Italy 67, 68, 70, 72, 74, 116, 197

Jackson, Rev. Jesse, Jr. 228
Jacksonville, Florida 69
Jacobs, Joe 105, 109, 115, 132, 134, 221
Jacobs, Mike 60, 61, 62, 63, 64, 66, 68, 74, 75, 77, 81, 96, 97, 98, 100, 115, 120, 125, 128, 131, 132, 133, 134, 135, 143, 146, 147, 155, 156, 162, 163, 169, 172, 175, 182, 190, 194, 207, 209, 220
Japan 186, 188, 189, 198
Jeffries, James J. 46, 47, 65
Joe Louis Arena 57
Johnson, Jack 3, 6, 14, 36, 37, 41, 42, 43, 44, 45, 46, 47, 48, 49, 52, 61, 65, 76, 77, 86, 137, 138, 141, 144, 176
Johnston, Jimmy 60, 61, 133
Jones, Bobby 24
Jones, Buck 23
Josephs, Eddie 183, 208

Kansas 199
Kansas City 69, 134
Kansas City Monarchs 200
Keeler, O.B. 124
Kentucky Derby 72
Ketchel, Steve 130
Klein, Izzy 51
Klondike Gold Fields 60
Kracken, Jack 51, 52, 53
Kranz, Jack 53
Krieger, Solly 180
Ku Klux Klan 19, 20, 72

Lacy, Sam 202
Lafayette, Alabama 13
Lake Geneva, Wisconsin 138, 140
Lake Placid, New York 90
Lakewood, New Jersey 117, 212
Lancaster, Pennsylvania 45
Langford, Sam 11, 38
Las Vegas 1, 162, 222, 223, 224, 225, 229
Lasky, Art 137
Lazer, Roy 64
Lehman, Herbert 156
Leonard, Sugar Ray 2
Levinsky, King 96, 97
Lewis, Jerry 222
Lewis, John Henry 137, 162, 163, 164, 168
Lewis, Nate 149
Liberty (magazine) 169
Liebling, A.J. 45, 168
Lillehammer, Norway 51

Lincoln Cemetery, Illinois 204
Liston, Sonny 221, 224
Little Rock, Arkansas 47
London 69, 70, 206
London, Jack 65
Long Island 106, 138, 191
Long Island City, New York 80, 127, 136, 153
Los Angeles 45, 69, 117, 164
Loughran, Tommy 71, 96, 106, 118
Loy, Myrna 80

Machon, Max 123, 157
Macon, Eddie 176
Madden, Owney 70, 71, 75, 207
Madison Square Garden 1, 60, 61, 62, 79, 100, 133, 148, 162, 172, 173, 175, 180, 191, 213, 214, 218
Madison Square Garden Bowl 106, 108, 138
Malcolm X 177
Malone, Martha 220, 224, 228
Maloney, Jim 69, 70
Mann, Nathan 147, 148, 149
Mann Act 47
Marciano, Rocky 217, 218, 219, 221
Marek, Max 33
Marigold Gardens Outdoor Arena 53
Markson, Harry 62
Martin, Dean 222
Massera, Charley 55
Maston, Rev. J.H. 99
Mauriello, Tami 209, 211, 212
Maynard, Ken 23
McCoy, Al 175, 181
McKinney, Thurston 9, 26, 30, 31, 33
McTigue, Mike 106
Mead, Chris 30
Meen, Reggie 70
Mein Kampf 111
Memphis, Tennessee 45
Meredith, Burgess 118
Mexico 212
Miami 71
Michigan State Athletic Commission 54
Miler, John 30, 31, 32
Miles, Marshall 205, 209
Miley, Jack 182, 183
Miller, Davey 149
Miller, Margery 29
Millinocket, Maine 45
Milwaukee 221
Minnesota 101
Missouri 104
Mix, Tom 23
Mobile, Alabama 20
Monte, Joe 105
Monteith, Scotty 65
Moody, George 34, 35
Morgan, Rose 220

Morrison Hotel 143
Mount Sinai, Alabama 17
Mount Vernon, Alabama 15
Munich 111
Mussolini, Benito 67, 70, 71
Musto, Tony 175

Naples 196
National Association for the Advancement of
   Colored People 194, 200
National Boxing Association 107
National Golden Gloves 33
National Hockey League 57
Nazis 80, 111, 113, 114, 115, 120, 132, 133, 151,
   152, 153, 154, 157, 158, 189, 205, 206, 222
Negro Leagues (baseball) 72, 97, 163, 200
Neusel, Walter 109
Nevada 60, 224
New Haven, Connecticut 147
New Jersey 73, 92, 105, 119, 136, 167, 168,
   203, 211, 219
New Orleans 7, 47
New York 45, 62, 70, 71, 72, 73, 74, 77, 88,
   98, 103, 105, 109, 112, 115, 120, 125, 130,
   136, 151, 152, 153, 155, 156, 158, 178, 180,
   187, 192, 214, 217, 221, 223
New York Daily News 117, 190
New York Milk Fund 61
New York Post 218
New York Rangers 60
New York State Athletic Commission 107,
   132, 133, 206, 213, 221
New York Times 215
New York Yankees 24
Newark, New Jersey 69
Newspaper Enterprise Association 139
Nichols, Joe Louis 13
Nordhein-Westfalen, Germany 103
North Carolina 177
North Dakota 101
Norway 91
Nostradamus 183
Notre Dame 33
Nova, Lou 188, 189
Nova Scotia 38

Oakland, California 45
Oates, William C. 20
O'Brien, "Philadelphia" Jack 11
O'Dowd, Jack 54
Ohio State University 132, 166
Oklahoma 56
Olympia Stadium 57, 59
Omaha, Nebraska 69
On the Waterfront 170
Ondra, Anny 104, 114, 124, 125
Orange, New Jersey 170
Oslo, Norway 91

Owens, Jesse 2, 72, 97, 132, 165, 166, 167,
   191, 225

Pacheco, Ferdie 158
Paige, Satchel 72, 99
Parker, Dan 144
Pastor, Bob 72, 133, 172, 181
Paychek, Johnny 173
Pearl Harbor 188, 198
Pennsauken, New Jersey 211
Pep, Willie 62
Perroni, Patsy 57
Peyton Place 91
Philadelphia 24, 45, 55, 69, 130, 175, 177
Pickford, Mary 106
Pittsburgh 20, 57, 74, 163, 179, 182, 183
Pittsburgh Courier 64, 201
Pittsburgh Crawfords 163
Plains, Georgia 157
Plymouth, England 45
Poland 104
Polo Grounds 182, 188
Polyclinic Hospital 158
Pompton Lakes, New Jersey 48, 72, 73, 88,
   153, 170, 229
Poreda, Stanley 54, 55
Portland, Maine 45
Portland, Oregon 69
The Poseidon Adventure 84
The Postman Always Rings Twice 91
Powell, Adam Clayton, Jr. 75
Powers, Jimmy 190
The Prize Fighter and the Lady 80
Pueblo, Colorado 47

Queens, New York 70

Radford, Susan 13
Ramage, Lee 55, 57, 58, 59, 65
Rangel, Charles 160
Ray, Johnny 181, 184, 185, 188
Reading, Pennsylvania 45
Reagan, Ronald 228
Recreation Park 78
Reno, Nevada 46
Resnick, Ash 223
Retzlaff, Charley 101, 117
Rheum Boogie Café 209
Rice, Grantland 84, 122, 123, 130, 154
Rickard, Tex 60, 61
Rickey, Branch 200, 201, 202
The Ring (magazine) 55, 56, 75, 118, 129,
   139, 156, 158, 159, 185, 190
Rinson, Amsey 26
Risko, Johnny 105
Robeson, Paul 201
Robinson, Bill "Bojangles" 72, 99, 139, 201,
   204

Robinson, Jackie 194, 198, 199, 200, 201, 202, 225
Robinson, Slim 228
Robinson, Sugar Ray (Walker Smith, Jr.) 2, 35, 62, 194, 218
Rocky 118
Roosevelt, Franklin D. 98, 114, 152, 157, 189, 193
Roper, Jack 164
Ross, Barney 51, 153, 179
Rowe, Billy 162
Roxborough, Charles 8
Roxborough, John 5, 7, 8, 9, 10, 11, 12, 35, 36, 37, 39, 40, 41, 42, 47, 49, 50, 51, 54, 56, 59, 60, 61, 62, 63, 75, 77, 97, 98, 100, 109, 117, 120, 127, 130, 133, 143, 145, 162, 163, 176, 190, 204, 224
Runyon, Damon 61, 136
Ruth, Babe 24

St. Louis 20, 160, 176
St. Moritz, Switzerland 90
San Francisco 45, 59, 78
Savold, Lee 181, 217
Savoy Hotel 76
Schaaf, Ernie 68, 79
Schaap, Jeremy 136
Schmeling, Max 67, 70, 80, 88, 92, 101, 103, 104, 105, 107, 108, 109, 110, 111, 112, 113, 114, 115, 116, 117, 118, 119, 120, 121, 122, 123, 124, 125, 127, 128, 130, 131, 132, 133, 134, 135, 137, 138, 139, 140, 141, 142, 144, 145, 146, 148, 149, 150, 151, 152, 153, 154, 155, 156, 157, 158, 159, 160, 162, 164, 176, 179, 190, 193, 205, 206, 212, 218, 219, 221, 222
Schwader, Vada 23, 25
Seamon, Mannie 153, 203, 205, 208, 213
Searcy Hospital for the Negro Insane 15
Selassie, Hailie 72
Sharkey, Jack (Joseph Paul Cukoschay) 68, 70, 96 106, 107, 108, 128, 129, 130, 142
Shkor, Johnny 216
Shreveport, Louisiana 47
Sieminsky, Alfred 219
Simms, Eddie 130
Simon, Abe 175, 192, 193, 202, 203, 206
Sinatra, Frank 222, 225, 228
Slayton, George 9
Smith, Gunboat 11
Smith, Jimmy 187, 188
Somaliland 67
Spain 100, 109
The Spirit of Youth 117
Spring Hill, Michigan 162
Stamford, Connecticut 139
Stanley Hotel 88
Staten Island Ferry 155
Stockton, California 176

Stribling, Young 69, 106, 107, 108
Sullivan, Ed 117
Sullivan, John L. 37
Summer Olympics 114, 132, 165, 166
Swanson, Gloria 106
Sweet, Dr. Ossian 24
Sydney, Australia 43
Sykes, Art 54

Texas 199
Third Reich 112, 150
Thomas, Harry 148, 149
Thomas, Henry 109
Thomas, Otis 32, 33
Thomas, Tommy 140, 141
Thunderbird Hotel 223
Tilden, Big Bill 24
Time (magazine) 91
Topeka, Kansas 45
Toronto 33
Trafton, George 11, 69
Trafton's Gym 11
Trotter, Marva 55, 56, 81, 82, 83, 87, 88, 89, 91, 92, 93, 94, 117, 118, 119, 121, 124, 127, 130, 153, 161, 162, 170, 195, 204, 205, 220
Trotter, Novella 82
Trotter, Rev. Walter 81
Tunney, Gene 24, 25, 68, 98, 109
Turner, Lana 90, 91, 94, 95
Twentieth Century Sporting Club 61, 216
Tyson, Mike 106

Udell, Larry 53
Unforgivable Blackness 49
United Press 100, 129, 130, 148, 171
United Service Organizations (USO) 94
United States 104, 105, 111, 115, 132, 133, 135, 138, 146, 150, 152, 153, 157, 160, 179, 186, 188, 189, 191, 192, 193, 195, 205, 206, 208, 221
U.S. Navy Relief Society 190, 191, 192, 198
United States Negro Horse Show 89
United States Olympic Committee 114, 115
University of California–Los Angeles 198, 200
University of Chicago 56, 88
Urban League 8
Uzcudun, Paulino 69, 100, 101, 105, 109, 110, 120

Versailles, Kentucky 11
Victor, Colorado 45
Vietnam War 48, 189, 224
Virginia 228

Wagner, Richard 157
Walcott, Jersey Joe 211, 212, 213, 214, 215, 217, 219, 221, 228